Shadows

IN THE SAND

Shadows
IN THE SAND

A Koevoet Tracker's Story of an Insurgency War

Sisingi Kamongo
and Leon Bezuidenhout

Published in 2011 by 30° South Publishers (Pty) Ltd.
16 Ivy Road, Pinetown 3610
South Africa
www.30degreessouth.co.za
info@30degreessouth.co.za

Copyright © Leon Bezuidenhout, 2011
Front cover photo © Herman Grobler
Back cover photo © Kallie Calitz
Design and origination by 30° South Publishers (Pty) Ltd.

Printed and bound by Pinetown Printers, Durban

ISBN 978-0-620474-79-5

Dedicated as a monument to those in the Namibian bush war without any memorial
—the 128 black Namibian Koevoet policemen who died in action or from wounds

*

Kuyofa abuntu rusale izibongo, yizona eziyosala emanxiweni
'People will die and their praises remain;
it is these that will be left to mourn for them in their deserted homes'
—From the praises of Dingane, Zulu king

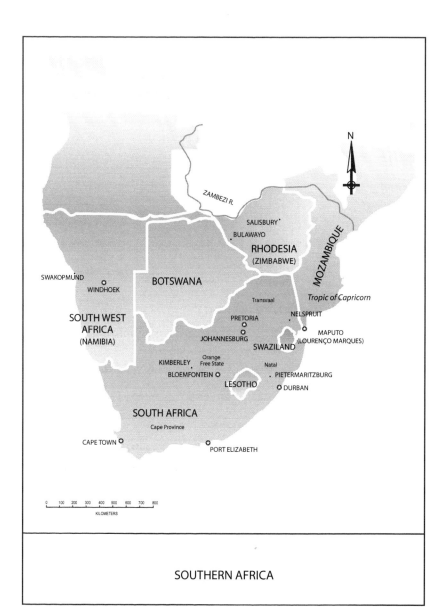

ZAMBEZI R.

SALISBURY

BULAWAYO

RHODESIA
(ZIMBABWE)

MOZAMBIQUE

SWAKOPMUND
WINDHOEK

BOTSWANA

Tropic of Capricorn

SOUTH WEST
AFRICA
(NAMIBIA)

Transvaal

NELSPRUIT

PRETORIA
JOHANNESBURG

MAPUTO
(LOURENÇO MARQUES)

SWAZILAND

KIMBERLEY
BLOEMFONTEIN

Orange
Free State

Natal

PIETERMARITZBURG

LESOTHO

DURBAN

SOUTH AFRICA
Cape Province

CAPE TOWN

PORT ELIZABETH

0 100 200 300 400 500 600 700 800
KILOMETERS

SOUTHERN AFRICA

Contents

Acknowledgements

The co-author, Leon Bezuidenhout, is grateful to the following:

Francois du Toit, who introduced me to the people at Vingerkraal as well as to the incomparable Sisingi 'Shorty' Kamongo. For sharing a few of his stories. He has many more.

Herman Grobler, the start of everything. A man who taught me a lot about physical and moral courage. A more humble man you will not find, a braver man, never.

Kallie Calitz, a brave man, for his photographs and input.

Willie Roux, for his photos and advice.

Marinda Conradie, for the English translation of the Herman Grobler story, her advice and suggesting the title for this book.

Rustus Mbundu, for his contribution about his involvement at the battle of Opepela.

Sakkie Kaikamas, Casspir driver who shared a story or two.

Attie Hattingh, for his photographs and advice.

Jacques Myburgh for allowing us to use his account of 3 April 1989.

Annetjie Bezuidenhout, my wife, who had to share my time writing this book.

Ilse van Staden, for the maps.

Preller 'Prop' Geldenhuys, for assistance with the structure and English translation.

Leopold Scholtz, historian, author and journalist, for his foreword and critical perspective.

Alec Wainwright, for his critical reading and advice.

Theo de Jager, for helping solve the 'bull' riddle.

Geraldine Paulsen, for the initial English translation.

Hendrik Engelbrecht; I would have loved to have met him, but he died while I was tracing him. I should have tried harder.

My wheelchair-bound friend, Sisingi 'Shorty' Kamongo, an exceptional and talented human being, a man among men.

Foreword

During the past years, a host of personal reminiscences have been published by people who fought in the Border War—some in book form, others on the Internet. At the highest level former minister of defence, General Magnus Malan, put pen to paper, as did the chief of the defence force in the latter half of the 1980s, General Jannie Geldenhuys. The others are troops, all of them from the South African army, people who tell of the endless patrols, the flies, the heat, the boredom, or of the fear, blood and guts of conventional cross-border operations in Angola.

The stories of some SWAPO members have also been recorded. However, there are two important lacunae in this literature. Firstly, there is one unit on the South African side from which not a single member has told his story: the South African Police's special counter-insurgency unit, known as Koevoet. The writer Peter Stiff has, it is true, written a book about Koevoet, based on interviews with ex-members, but that is that. Secondly, not a single black member of the then security forces has dared to present his story to the world.

In this book, Sisingi Kamongo, nicknamed 'Shorty', fills these two lacunae. Kamongo, who hails from the Kavango, was a black member of Koevoet who fought in the '80s in Ovamboland and the Kavango against SWAPO insurgents. For the first time, the public may now view the war through the eyes of a black man on the South African side.

Kamongo has indeed a story to tell—and what a story. His remarkable memory is proven by the statistics of the various fights he describes and from the verbatim quotes of radio conversations. More importantly, he explains why he fought on the side of the South African 'racists', and against SWAPO, which was, after all, recognized by the United Nations as the 'only legitimate representative of the Namibian people'.

Kamongo does not spare his readers. He tells of the contacts, the sweat, blood and guts. Without him spelling it out expressly, his story illustrates the blunting effect on feelings which every war has. He relates very honestly the human-rights violations which he and fellow members committed against SWAPO prisoners. But he also makes clear that the political propaganda against Koevoet was highly exaggerated, that it was a very disciplined unit, that those guilty were strictly, and sometimes summarily, punished. He places this propaganda in the context of war, of the crimes SWAPO itself continually committed and the bitterness this created with him and his comrades. (As a matter of fact—and Kamongo does not go into it—but SWAPO's crimes against its own supporters in exile have been excellently documented.)

Kamongo does not hide his bitterness against the then South African government. Though he and his fellow black members of Koevoet often put their lives on the line (he himself was thrice wounded severely), they were paid a small salary of just R280 a month together with 'head money' for insurgents killed or captured. And when SWAPO took over, they had to flee for their lives to South Africa, with no help from the South African government, without recognition, with nothing. Today they live in poverty, Kamongo in a wheelchair because of his wounds.

To what extent is Kamongo's story simply a question of self-justification? This is a legitimate question. Memoirs like those of Generals Malan and Geldenhuys—and others—always contain an element of that. There can be no doubt that Kamongo tries to justify his actions, and undoubtedly some people will not be convinced by it. So be it.

But this does not detract from the fact that his is a dramatic story, which is told factually and soberly, without too much commentary. After reading this book, everyone is entitled to think what he wants about Kamongo and his case. But what nobody can deny is that Kamongo's story is worth telling, even less so that he has done it well. I am glad that I made Sisingi Kamongo's acquaintance by reading the manuscript. It was an enriching experience.

Leopold Scholtz
Brussels
March 2011

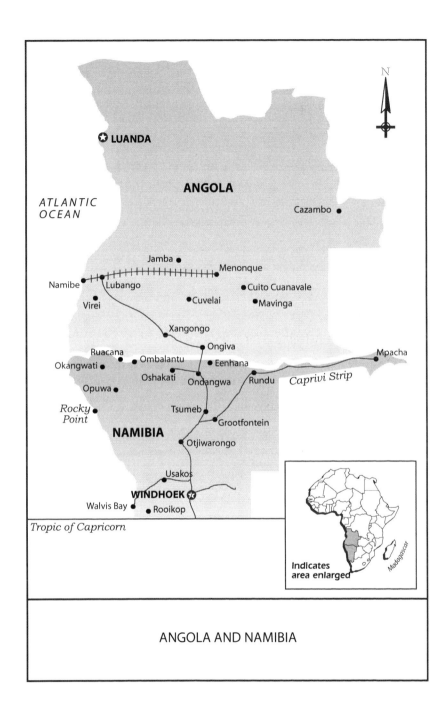

N

LUANDA

ANGOLA

ATLANTIC
OCEAN

Cazambo •

Jamba •
Menonque
Namibe • Lubango • Cuito Cuanavale
Virei • Cuvelai • Mavinga

Xangongo •
Ongiva •
Ruacana Mpacha •
Okangwati • • Ombalantu • Eenhana
Oshakati • Ondangwa Rundu Caprivi Strip
Opuwa •

Rocky Tsumeb •
Point Grootfontein
NAMIBIA Otjiwarongo •

Usakos •
WINDHOEK
Walvis Bay • • Rooikop

Tropic of Capricorn

Madagascar

Indicates
area enlarged

ANGOLA AND NAMIBIA

13

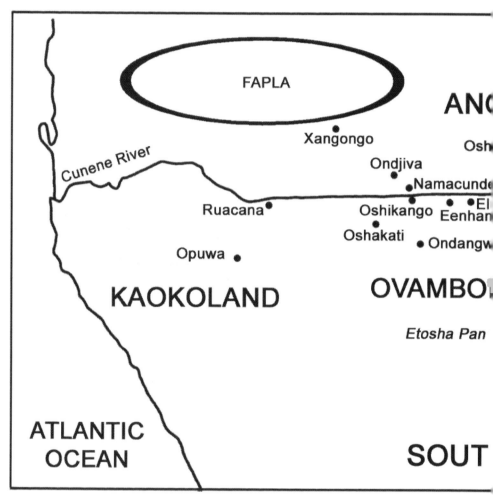

FAPLA

AN(

Xangongo

Osh

Ondjiva

Cunene River

Namacund(

Ruacana

Oshikango

•El

Oshakati

Eenhan

Opuwa

• Ondangw

KAOKOLAND

OVAMBO

Etosha Pan

ATLANTIC
OCEAN

SOUT

Ilse van Staaden

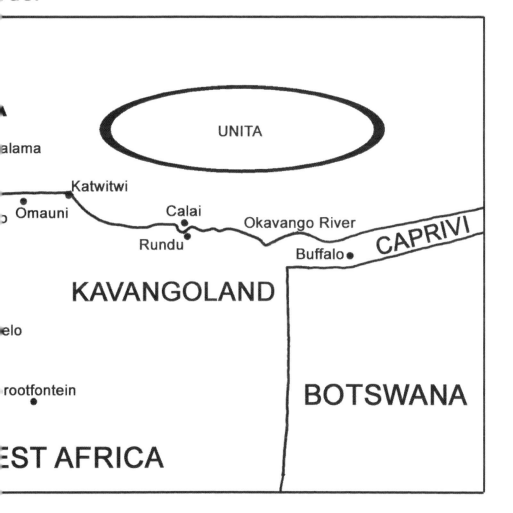

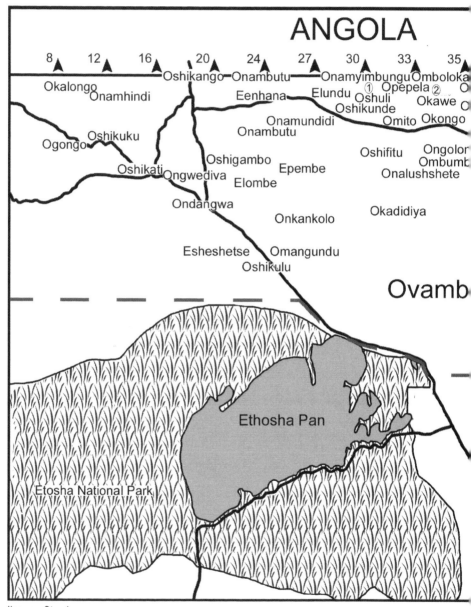

Ilse van Staaden

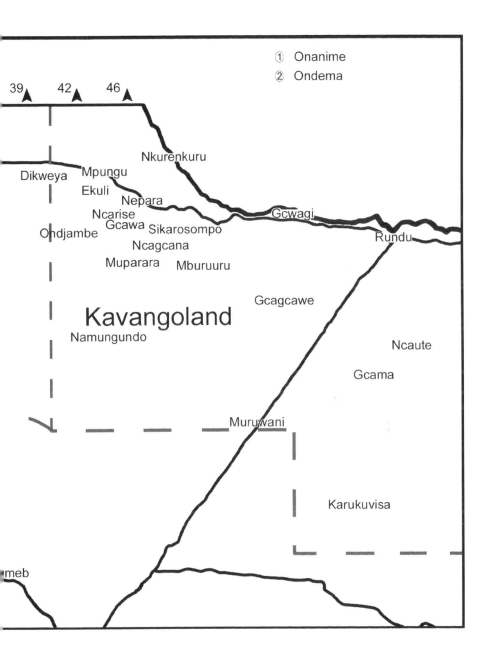

① Onanime
② Ondema

39 42 46

Nkurenkuru

Dikweya Mpungu
Ekuli
Nepara
Ncarise
Gcawa Sikarosompo
Ohdjambe
Ncagcana
Muparara Mburuuru

Gcwagi
Rundu

Gcagcawe

Kavangoland

Namungundo

Ncaute

Gcama

Muruwani

Karukuvisa

meb

Introduction

by Leon Bezuidenhout

Shadows in the Sand is the story of Special Sergeant Sisingi 'Shorty' Kamongo, a Koevoet tracker in the Namibian insurgency bush war. The appendices include accounts from Koevoet combat team leaders, Francois du Toit and Herman Grobler; the story of a (previously) inexperienced SADF Ratel gunner, Jacques Myburgh, who gives his account of a day spent in action with Koevoet in April 1989, is also included.

Cold war, hot war

Namibia, previously South West Africa, eventually obtained its independence in 1990. Had it not been for world macro-politics, it probably would have happened sooner. South Africa had wanted to rid herself of South West Africa for a long time but her fear of communism and the reality of communism in Africa caused the delay. When South Africa sent troops over the Angolan border in 1975 to prevent the communist MPLA from taking power, Cuba in reaction—with support from the communist bloc—sent 20,000 troops to the country. The number of Cubans in Angola would later rise to more than 50,000. The door to Namibian independence only opened after communism fell in Europe and the Cubans announced their willingness to go home.

Over the next two decades of the Cold War, the South West Africa People's Organization (SWAPO) was supported by the USSR, the communist Eastern Bloc (particulary East Germany), Cuba and a host of pro-communist African and Asian countries (all from the so-called Non-Aligned Movement), not to mention many other liberal groups and governments such as the Scandinavians.

The bush war in Namibia and southern Angola took place against this background. It was in essence a hidden element of the Cold War, which eventually developed into a drawn-out insurgency war, spanning 23 years.

The collapse of communism in the USSR also spelled the end of many governments and movements with Marxist/Leninist ideologies. SWAPO also had to change; they had to quickly reposition themselves; communist systems were not attractive any more. The removal of hard-line communism from the SWAPO mindset and the possible withdrawal of the Cubans allowed the South Africans an opportunity to talk peace. The result was a democratic constitution in Namibia.

The impact of South Africa's administration of Namibia, as well as the South African forces who served in Namibia, can never be denied; they ensured that Namibia did not become another war-torn African country. Contrary to many other countries in southern Africa, there are no signs today of the war that took place there: no buildings damaged by war, no landmines making the countryside unsafe and, ironically enough, a working infrastructure which is better than the current one in South Africa.

For this turn of events the South African Police and South African Defence Force must be credited. During the last years of the war, the anti-communist banner was carried by the Namibians themselves. Units such as 101 Battalion of the South West African Territorial Force (SWATF) and Koevoet of the police consisted mainly of Namibians. By the end of the war, 70 per cent of all the security-force members were non-white and non-South African. With Namibians to the fore, SWAPO was fought to a standstill and was so battered that the eventual peace agreement was negotiated between South Africa and Cuba, and to a lesser extent Angola. SWAPO was not included in the peace agreement at all, although the UN recognized SWAPO as the 'only legitimate representative of the Namibian people'.

It must have been very difficult for the Namibians to decide which side to support during the war. In most cases they were not given a choice: SWAPO simply kidnapped their recruits from the schools. Conversely, it is also true that many SWAPO insurgents left Namibia and joined PLAN, with valid political reasons. In a similar vein, poverty was a motive to join the army and the police—just like in many other places in the world; many policemen joined Koevoet for a better future.

Much has been said about the so-called violent and reckless behaviour of Koevoet. As a result, the unit has been much maligned. It is a fact that some incidents did take place, but these were blown completely out of proportion considering the size of the unit. If there were a few bad apples, was the whole orchard rotten?

The problem with this war was the one-sidedness of information. People with anti-apartheid views and, in other instances, people with pro-communist and liberal views, unfortunately never made the distinction between South Africa and her allies, often deliberately and mischievously so. The South African approach did not help either; their secretiveness and unwillingness to trust journalists in the operational area prevented the 'other' side of the story from being told.

This book is by no means an attempt to voice support for Koevoet or glorify the war. It merely tells the story of an outstandingly brave, talented individual who was involved with Koevoet. This is simply his story. He is highly critical of the South Africans' handling of the war and, more so, the handling of the black policemen during and after the war.

On the ground, in the bush, a Koevoet prisoner was summarily shot by SWAPO. If you were a member of SWAPO and were caught by Koevoet, the chances were that you would still be alive a year later. SWAPO prisoners were treated humanely and kept in prison. However, not one captured or abducted Koevoet member lived to tell his tale.

In nearly every SWAPO camp that was liberated by the South African army, cases of torture were reported. Prisoners were kept in holes in the ground. Hundreds were murdered, not because of proven facts but because of suspicion. Unfortunately, some SWAPO members brought this conduct with them after independence and the National Society for Human Rights found in 2008 that SWAPO had been responsible for a number of mass graves of Koevoet members *after* independence. These atrocities took place between 1999 and 2002, but this is also part of history now.

A fresh breeze of reconciliation is blowing over Namibia.

The Anglo-Boer War was fought more than 100 years ago and a measure of bitterness continues to this day. Two cases are worth mentioning, both of which concern guerrilla incidents. In one, a Boer commandant named Gideon Scheepers was executed, in a cruel travesty of justice, for 'war crimes' in the Cape Colony, The same deeds—arson, destroying infrastructure, killing enemy sympathizers—were in fact official policy of the British occupation forces in the Transvaal and the Orange Free State. The second case concerns the execution of an Australian officer serving in a counter-insurgency unit in the Transvaal. Lieutenant Henry 'Breaker' Morant was executed after he'd shot Boer prisoners and a German missionary, supposedly out of hand. As a result, the British army lost its authority to court-martial Australian soldiers during the First World War.

The lessons learned from these examples are blunt: an insurgency or guerrilla war is merciless and bitter, sometimes with more emotion than blood. There are times when the boundaries of war are blurred or even disappear completely. This is not easily forgotten, on either side of the struggle. We can only hope that the bush war in Namibia will eventually be remembered as a period when both sides fought for reasons they considered honourable—a period when the keepers of the law did what they felt was right. Their legacy is a peaceful country with an intact infrastructure. Hopefully the scars among the Namibian people themselves will also heal.

This book has been compiled from the stories of Sisingi 'Shorty' Kamongo. It was first written in Kavango Afrikaans and then translated into standard Afrikaans and eventually into English. It consists of a number of incidents put into chronological order.

It is the first, and thus far only, account by a non-white member of the South African security forces during the bush war. Sisingi Kamongo has the most wonderful memory; he would give me handwritten pieces of paper with his stories, each ending with an inventory of captured weapons and equipment: 'We fought against five insurgents in this contact. We found three AKs with six full magazines, one RPG with five rockets and one SKS with five pencil grenades.' When reading the proofs, he would also say: 'This day we took three AKs with six full magazines, one RPG with five rockets, one SKS with five pencil grenades, after this contact.' I have left out most of this type of detail to prevent the book from becoming a tedious inventory. I mention this only to highlight how, nearly 25 years later, he remembers everything and can provide precise details of the contacts he took part in.

His account is supplemented by two incidents that happened to a Casspir driver, Sakkie Kaikamas.

Appendix I is dedicated to a few incidents that happened to Sergeant Francois du Toit, recounted from his time spent with Koevoet and later. He was the most successful Koevoet team leader during his service with the unit.

The story of Sergeant Herman Grobler is told in Appendix II. His one action is probably the most heroic ever to come out of the Namibian bush war, something for which he never received any recognition (like many other Koevoet policemen). It is not included as an afterthought; indeed, his story is another that warrants a complete work. It is nevertheless important to write a concise history of his involvement; the world needs to know about this brave man. He also gives his views how the black members were ill treated after the war.

Appendix III is the story of a 19-year-old SADF Ratel gunner who went from a raw soldier to fighting some of the fiercest battles of the war. He tells of his experience working with Koevoet trackers.

Police as militarists

The militarization of police in South Africa has its origins with the Dutch in the 17th century when soldiers were utilized as policemen. By the 1880s, the republic had its own police, the Zuid-Afrikaansche Republiek Politie (ZARP). The ZARP's hour of glory came on 28 August 1900 at the battle of Berg-en-Dal during the Anglo-Boer War. Their last stand against a superior force gained even the respect of the British.

With the advent of the First World War the police sent mounted units to fight in the then German West Africa (Namibia). They were also used to quell the 1914 Boer rebellion. Major Trew and his policemen forced the rebels of Jopie Fourie to surrender near Hammanskraal. Trew's men were mostly attached to General Louis Botha's personal bodyguard.

During the Second World War an attempt was made to recruit a division of policemen to fight in North Africa. This was not achieved and eventually only two battalions were formed. To complete the brigade the Transvaal Scottish offered their 3rd Battalion. The fighting policemen of the 6th Brigade (the Police Brigade) unfortunately had to surrender with General Klopper at Tobruk.

When the bush war began in South West Africa the South African government decided to contain the war with policemen rather than soldiers. The initial involvement of the police was linked to a few factors, one of which was an obvious political decision to portray the war as a low-intensity insurgency affair. Another was the powerful influence of former policeman General Hendrik van den Berg in the government of John Vorster, the South African prime minister of the time. The first skirmish took place in 1966 when a few men from the soon-to-be-established South African Defence Force (SADF) Special Forces and the police destroyed a SWAPO base at Omgulumgashe. The police shouldered the security burden until 1973 when the SADF took over control of the war on the 'international side', i.e. across the Zambian and Angolan borders, with the police maintaining control within South West Africa.

The police in Rhodesia and South West Africa

The police were also deployed in Rhodesia (Zimbabwe) from 1968 to 1975, as a result of the same political considerations as in South West Africa, but this time contesting ANC guerrillas infiltrating from their bases in Zambia. The South African Police (SAP) would eventually be withdrawn but remained involved in a non-official capacity until 1980. Apart from the military successes, their most famous 'battle' was the 'Battle of Bulawayo' when they were 'withdrawn' in 1975; two trucks loaded with policemen encountered some of their men in front of a Bulawayo hotel in a fight with a group from the Rhodesian Light Infantry. The two groups then 'greeted' each other. The police claimed to have won the battle.

Meanwhile, the war in the north of South West Africa was heating up and the police had to jump to counter these developments. With the knowledge obtained by a few of them who had fought in Rhodesia, it was decided to establish a reaction unit to stop the enemy, SWAPO, inside the country.

In cooperation with the Council for Scientific and Industrial Research (CSIR), the police decided to build a vehicle that was mine-proof and that could withstand small-arms fire without injury to the passengers. So was the Casspir born. A number of local trackers were recruited and the end result was a unit consisting of about 2,500 men. The unit that would be known colloquially as Koevoet ('crowbar'), or Operation K, developed unique, highly successful tactics designed mainly around the Casspir's mobility and firepower.

In time, Koevoet would be vilified by the world as 'murderers' and 'violence-prone', a unit that would burn, plunder, destroy, rape and torture unrestrainedly—unfounded information disseminated by propagandists. Koevoet was subjected to this type of propaganda more so than any other military or police unit of its time. Newspaper journalists, often nothing more than liberal or pro-communist mouthpieces, spread their stories of Koevoet 'murders' across the world. The local police read about these so-called murders in the papers and investigated, only to find that there was no substance to the allegations; they were works of fiction trumped up to discredit the security forces. Take for example the destruction of a kraal that took place many months before, done by 'soldiers' in armoured vehicles. Everybody drove Casspirs and Buffels—32 Battalion, 101, Koevoet—and they all wore camouflaged clothing. So who was it? Blame the most successful unit: Koevoet. But it could have been anybody.

It must also be remembered that there was financial gain to be made from allegations against the security forces. If a kraal was damaged by fire or a crop by a vehicle, a claim could be made against the government. Again, the easiest option was to blame Koevoet. Herman Grobler was a detective in Ovamboland before he asked to be transferred to Koevoet. In a number of interviews he made it very clear that he did in fact investigate a number of serious allegations against his later unit and he did help prosecute a number of Koevoet members. But he also helped successfully prosecute a white paratrooper who killed an officer, as did he prosecute other policemen and soldiers who broke the law. That there were cases against Koevoet members is indisputable, but as an old member of the unit later said: "There were two groups among us: those who fought with rules and those who fought without rules. But we, the ones with the rules, far outnumbered those without. They were by far the minority and what some of them did could never be seen as the norm."

However, in essence, it was a highly motivated, extremely disciplined unit of ordinary white policemen from South Africa who led black Ovambo, Kavango and Himba policemen from the north of Namibia. Together they would arguably become one of the most successful—if not the most effective—counter-insurgency forces of the Cold War era.

This era cannot boast many success stories of outright victory against communist insurgents. Those of the British in Borneo, Malaya and Kenya are probably the most notable. But the British had one advantage—they could kill the insurgency at the roots. Unhindered, they could suppress the insurgents in their home bases, i.e. before the act of insurgency could take place, the insurgents were destroyed, a luxury the South Africans seldom had. SWAPO was protected by the Angolans and the Cubans, the ANC by the Angolans, Tanzanians, Zambians and latterly the Zimbabweans. The South African Defence Force at stages controlled southern Angola, which forced SWAPO farther north but SWAPO was always somewhere, under Cuban or Angolan protection. It must be said though that 32 Battalion was deployed in southern Angola on a virtually continuous basis and did great work to hinder, and sometimes totally destroy, the insurgents on their way south through southern Angola. Even so, the SADF and police were engaged in a passive 'defence of the border' position, a situation to which the police quickly adapted tactically. The recruitment of the local population into the counter-insurgency forces, with the requisite tactics and equipment, meant success against the insurgents unrivalled elsewhere in Africa. In hindsight, the result of the counter-insurgency operations by Koevoet and the South African Army in Namibia, will likely fall in the same bracket as the British conflicts in Malaya and Borneo. The SADF would eventually blunt the insurgency which ultimately proved unable to undermine the administrative and military powers in control at the time.

Koevoet: a short review

Koevoet—or Operation K, SWAPOLCOIN (South West African Police Counter-Insurgency)—was the counter-insurgency unit of South West Africa, established in January 1979 and officially disbanded in January 1990.

A series of meetings took place between the SADF and the police in 1978 concerning the amount of intelligence provided to the army by the police, which, according to the police, did not receive the attention it deserved. The result was that the police established their own unit to immediately act upon the information. The man in command of the unit was Colonel Hans Dreyer who exploited the experience gained by the SAP in Rhodesia. Project Koevoet would fast develop into a unit with its own trackers and reaction units.

The police quickly realized that they were not equipped for the new task. They enlarged the unit by appointing trackers from the communities in the tribal areas along the border of Angola—Himbas from Kaokoland; Kwanyama, Kwambi and Ndonga from Ovamboland; and Kwangali and Shambyu from Kavangoland. These were all people of the veld—every one of them exceptional trackers.

In time, the South African Police and the CSIR would develop the armoured ambush- and mine-resistant troop carrier, the Casspir. This came about as a result of the large number of landmine incidents. The vehicle could also withstand small-arms fire. The Nambian/South West African-designed and -manufactured Wolf would also later be used. In conjunction with the South African Air Force's Alouette helicopters (armed with 20mm cannons), the unit fast developed into a formidable fighting force.

Koevoet would officially take part in more than 1,600 contacts, or firefights. More than 3,200 PLAN fighters were killed or captured; 161 policemen lost their lives, with more than 950 being wounded during the course of the war.

Koevoet predominantly consisted of fighter teams of about 45 men—four Casspirs, each containing ten men, a support vehicle and an operational medic. Initially, each of the four fighting vehicles had a white commander. This arrangement later fell away and in many cases the commanders were black Namibians.

The team was usually under the command of a sergeant or warrant officer, but some teams had a junior officer in command. Eventually there would be 42 combat teams: 30 in Ovamboland at Oshakati (callsign Zulu), another eight at Ongwediva (Zulu 1), eight in the Kavango at Rundu (Zulu 4) and another four at Opuwo in Kaokoland (Zulu 5). There was a relay station at Eenhana in eastern Ovamboland (Zulu 2).

The name Koevoet was changed to the South West African Police Counter-Insurgency Unit (SWAPOLCOIN) in 1985. Throughout its existence, Koevoet would constantly be exposed to unfounded malicious propaganda and the defamation continues to this day. Much brouhaha was made of the fact that money was paid per head. It is true that head money was paid—not only for dead insurgents but also for captured ones. Payments were also made for captured weapons, landmines, etc. Civilians could also claim the money—anybody could—with the army managing the money, not the police.

The fact that dead SWAPO members were strapped to the front fenders and wheel arches of the Casspirs also drew much comment. The plain fact was that there was nowhere for the bodies inside the vehicles. To carry a bloody body inside a troop-carrying vehicle in the African sun was also a health hazard. Many lies did the rounds claiming that live insurgents were tied to the fenders for bush clearing. This was never proved and is simply untrue.

When the United Nations took over control in 1989, they initiated and investigated the more serious complaints. Of these 41 were totally unfounded, 18 could not be substantiated and 25 warranted further investigation. Three of the 25 were passed on for possible prosecution. In virtually all cases the complaints were against off-duty members of the unit in a civilian capacity.

The SWAPOLCOIN units were eventually demobilized in October 1989. A meeting took place on 8 October in Oshakati. Nine hundred members were given their discharge certificates. Nearly 1,700 members were eventually honourably discharged on 30 October 1989. Initially, the plan was to resettle the nearly 2,500 members in South Africa; this was never done. From late 1989 to 1990 about 600 former members and their families realized it was unsafe to stay in Namibia. They fled either to Angola or South Africa. The ones in South Africa were re-instated in the police as 'auxiliary policemen'.

Unfortunately, the ruling National Party, as well as some senior policemen, betrayed these former fighters shortly thereafter, forcing the former Koevoet members to break all contact with the police. This was a deed of utter betrayal perpetrated against people who had sacrificed their all, even their country.

Shortly after this, some members bought the farm Vingerkraal, under acrimonious circumstances, near Warmbaths (now Bela-Bela), where most of them still live. Most former Koevoet men work in the security industry in South Africa; some of them are also in places such as Iraq, Afghanistan and Sierra Leone. The last of the white Koevoet members came home on 12 January 1990, their Casspirs already on the train to South Africa. All white members were transferred to police stations across the country. One of the final ten policemen to return was sent to the most densely populated place in South Africa: Hillbrow, Johannesburg—the 'concrete jungle'. He resigned on the Monday after his arrival.

The manner in which the government treated the black members of Koevoet would soon be the cause of the resignation of many white members. The refusal of Police Headquarters in Pretoria to do anything about the situation resulted in further resignations.

Lost brothers: the start, January 2010

Francois and I, Leon, are waiting in the parking lot at the Shoprite supermarket in Warmbaths on a Thursday morning. We are there to meet 'One-Four'. He was Francois's Koevoet driver, and he is late. After a few minutes, an early-model white Toyota Corolla drives into the parking area. There are five men in the car. Four of the occupants get out and greet Sergeant 'Toitjie' with warm handshakes and embraces: clearly men who have walked a long road together—good friends glad to see each other.

After Warmbaths we travel in convoy west toward Thabazimbi, then 35 kilometres later, onto a dirt road. With the onset of the rainy season the road is washed away and full of potholes. There are high game fences on both sides of the road. After ten kilometres we arrive at a boomed gate manned by two smart, alert guards. We are required to fill in our particulars and are then permitted to proceed. Two hundred metres farther on is a new school building. From there a small track turns left, with galvanized-iron huts standing everywhere—bright iron, like the storerooms in Ovamboland. Here and there small patches of maize and *mahango* (pearl millet) are evident. We drive another 200 metres on the nearly impassable track to one of the houses.

A few middle-aged men welcome us. Once again, Francois is greeted like a long-lost friend. The passengers of 'One-Four' get out. The boot is opened and a wheelchair is taken out and unfolded on the wet ground. The fifth occupant is helped into the wheelchair. He wheels himself to us and introduces himself in perfect Afrikaans as Shorty.

The number of men around us has now grown to about thirty-five or so. Francois and I retreat to my vehicle about ten metres away from the group of men under the two red-bush willowtrees where animated discussions are taking place. A list is completed by those present and after about 30 minutes of 'pre-meeting' negotiations and talks, Francois and I are invited to take part in the meeting proper. This is how the Ovambos conduct meetings, Francois whispers to me. Most of them stand and Francois and I are given two green plastic chairs on the edge of the circle. I am uncomfortable because I am sitting while the others have to stand, but Francois and I are the guests.

We start off with a prayer. With my eyes closed and the Ovambo praying in their strange language, I am suddenly swept away to a place 20 years earlier—in another country, with the same people, a time when the hot Namibian sun shone on one of the most feared counter-insurgency units of the modern era—Koevoet, Ops K. We could just as well have been back in some Ovambo kraal far away in northern Namibia, but we were not.

This was Vingerkraal, 'farm of sorrow', the farm 'purchased' by former Koevoet members because the SAP had thrown them out like soiled linen and left them to fend for themselves. The place of galvanized-iron huts, away from everything, 15 kilometres from the nearest tarred road, hidden away, like a big embarrassment.

The prayer ends. Francois is given the opportunity to speak. He asks permission to pray as well. He prays in Afrikaans, but it is different from the prayers of 20 years ago when we were warding off communism. It is short and powerful and asks only for a blessing for these children of Africa.

Francois continues and explains the reason for our visit. We are here to write a book. We can see the suffering. We want to make a difference. All the previous books have been written by white men about white men. Where do you fit into history? We want to tell the world about the role you played.

In a community where unemployment is rife I expect a lot of drunken people. But apart from the chairman who had taken one for his nerves, everyone is sober. They drink in every word. Then the discussion starts.

"You *shirumbu* left us here."

"Where is the money owed to us by Fouché?"

"When we saw you the last time, you were the paymaster!"

"You abused us."

Francois whispers to me, "This is bad, very bad."

These people are bitter. Twenty years of rage aimed at the white man. Francois has to bear the brunt of it. I sit and watch. This is not a good time to ask people for help or to ask them to open their hearts.

But Sergeant 'Toitjie' of Zulu Quebec did not work with these people for six years in vain. He knows them, he knows their pain, he saw it coming. He and a few other non-commissioned officers tried to help. He took a police vehicle at Rooiberg without permission and drove 190 kilometres to Pretoria to go and see the Commissioner of Police. The commissioner was not in town, but the senior staff officer, a brigadier, was. He offered the warrant officer the rank of major to keep quiet. He relates all this to the Ovambos and also says he was not the paymaster. It was somebody else. Some at the meeting concur. It was a Portuguese sergeant, Sergeant Tony da Costa, not Sergeant Toitjie. Francois explains that Tony da Costa was also not guilty; he could only pay out what he received.

Then I am asked to speak. In front of me in the sand lie two five-cent pieces. Someone must have dropped them; maybe it was a sign of the 50 silver pieces symbolic of treachery.

"I am not here to make you any promises. I don't know you. I only know two Koevoet people and they are both white. All I ask is that you trust me." Then there is chaos. I am not finished, but everyone has something to say. They speak in Ovambo and I don't understand it, but the aggression and fire in their voices is unmistakable. The word 'trust' does not go down well. The chairman tries to intervene, but to no avail.

After some minutes order is restored.

Shorty, the man in the wheelchair, starts talking. Once more the conversation is in Ovambo. The aggression does not abate A younger man has also joined in at the back of the crowd. He has a beer in one hand, he also says something in Ovambo. We will not get any help here; we must go and look somewhere else, I think to myself.

Then the conversation reverts to Afrikaans. "Fine, I cannot change your past, but we can try and make a difference to your future. I work with people who want to work. If you do not want to, take your name off the list."

One man takes the list. He is definitely going to remove his name. The chairman adjourns the meeting. They will let us know what they have decided. They will have a meeting on Saturday.

Francois and I get up and walk to my vehicle. Two of the Ovambos walk with us. One of them is still working in Iraq. "Don't worry, sir; it will work," he says. The other agrees.

Shorty asks if we can drop him off at Radium on our way back and we agree to. We load his wheelchair into the back of the car and put him in the front seat. We say our goodbyes and leave.

On the way back Shorty explains the whole debate. He told the men that the past is over. Life goes on. If the *shirumbu* did not treat you right, this is another time, other people. Let us work together. The young beer drinker had agreed with him, but not everyone had.

Francois says we will get their permission. This is just their way; the Ovambo have a way of furious debate. The rage and disappointment has to be vented; it has festered in their isolation.

Shorty tells us how he lived through five POMZ mine incidents. Three times he got up and brushed the dust off but once a piece of shrapnel lodged in his back. Fifteen years later he would lose the use of his legs. The legacy of that day. He would not be able to walk any more after that.

We arrive at a neat little RDP (Reconstruction and Development Project) house in the Mashakane township. The dirt roads are muddy. Next to the house is another Vingerkraal-type galvanized-iron hut. Shorty, his uncle and his aunt live in these two little houses. His uncle, Daniel Kambungo, was in 32 Battalion. He works in Johannesburg. Shorty gets a disability pension of

R1,000 per month from the South African government. It was too difficult on the farm so he moved away because of the limited possibilities and the inconvenience for a person in a wheelchair. His second wife left him because of the wheelchair and she and their children went to Venda.

We get out and unload Shorty and his wheelchair. This man impresses me immensely. He gives me a blue-lined school exercise book: his story, handwritten in Kavango Afrikaans. He knew beforehand what we wanted to discuss and started to write down his story prior to the meeting. I feel this man has every reason in the world to be bitter, but he isn't. He stands up for his people and his community—even though he cannot walk.

We say goodbye and get back into the vehicle. I reverse and when I get to the gate, Francois says, "Stop, I want to pray for him." We get out again. Francois asks Shorty if he may pray for him. He puts his hand on Shorty's head and with his left hand clasps Shorty's left hand. Francois prays for a miracle, for a cure. When he says amen, the man in the wheelchair turns around without saying a word and rolls to the front door of the galvanized-iron *mukuku*. I know their eyes are wet, but so are mine.

It is only when we are on the tarred road a kilometre away that Francois and I are able to talk again.

Billy Joel sang, "We never knew what friends we had, until we came to Leningrad." I felt the same after we left Shorty.

The project would go ahead, even if we only did it for this brave man.

The start: through the eyes of a man from the Kavango

Koevoet originated as home guards for the tribal offices because the local communities governed themselves through the tribal chiefs in the apartheid era. The tribal chiefs sat at these offices. The tribal messengers, and later the special police, guarded the chiefs.

When the war started the chiefs were intimidated, assaulted and often murdered. The Special Police unit was established to help guard the chiefs. Because of the politics, the country was uneasy at that time. SWAPO started kidnapping children from schools, performing deeds of sabotage, planting landmines and blowing up telephone and electric lines. Some of the chiefs' kraals were also attacked with mortars, RPG-7s and small arms. The Special Police were trained for these eventualities. The tribal messengers were not armed, but the special policemen were. By 1979 some of the Special Police volunteered for the new Koevoet unit.

The police and security forces fighting terrorism in South West Africa consisted of many different units. The Special Task Force fought terrorism inside SWA and specialized in counter-terrorism. The Koevoet unit operated on the northern border. They could follow terrorists and retrieve kidnapped children—even over the border. Internal safety was the responsibility of the South African Police and the SWA Police, while Koevoet protected the border to the north. Then there were also the Security Branch, the SADF and later the SWA Territorial Force and the SWASPES (special forces).

Koevoet patrolled the border and tried to intercept PLAN fighters. Policemen always tried to apprehend their quarry, but with armed insurgents it more often than not ended in a shoot-out. We obtained a lot more information from living SWAPO members than from dead ones. Although the security forces were different, they were all there for one purpose—the protection of the civilian population.

The effect was impressive, for although there was a war in northern SWA, the area today does not have landmines, as do Angola and Mozambique.

There are no damaged buildings and the roads and infrastructure were maintained throughout the war.

Because of some politicians, there were people who hated us and still do. But the facts can never be denied: right through the war, people came to us (Koevoet) for help, people and families of those who had been murdered, kidnapped by SWAPO, assaulted by SWAPO and whose cattle had been stolen or slaughtered. We always helped. It was dangerous work because SWAPO set anti-personnel mines and ambushes which injured our people. We always tried to capture PLAN members but usually it ended in a firefight. We would take the captured PLAN prisoner to the kraal which had lodged the complaint, for identification.

"Yes, that is the man who fired the shots. He is the one who hit us," we would often hear.

Many of the PLAN members eventually turned and became Koevoet members. They were our brothers, even if it was war. No Koevoet member was ever shown any mercy by SWAPO. We were shot or bayoneted to death. Sometimes our throats were cut.

But there were also many questions. Those of us who had to protect the country also had to eat. We placed our lives on the line for very little money. The whites received 'bush pay', but we black members had to exist on a meagre salary. If we did not make a contact for a week or two in the bush, we did not get anything extra. If we were not on patrol because of ill health or other circumstances, we also got nothing. Contractually, we were treated as day labourers.

When we made contact with SWAPO we were paid 'head money': whether our contact was dead or alive, the number of rifles, landmines, mortar pipes, mortars, uniforms etc. recovered, was paid for. But all the money was divided up among the team members and sometimes among members of other teams who had helped. It was still very little. The most money I ever got was R370 ($50) when we found a B10 cannon and rounds. More often than not it was just R10 or R20 per contact. We were robbed by the police.

If I think about it today I want to cry, when I think of all the people who lost arms, legs and eyes. They were never compensated after the war. I am sitting in a wheelchair.

Is there a white member who only gets R1,000 ($130) per month?

I was never paid for three months, another three months, and later the six months I spent in hospital after I was wounded.

We will see, God knows.

The culture of tracking: from a Kavango boy to Koevoet

The Koevoet trackers came mainly from the kraals in the Kavango, Ovamboland and Kaokoveld. Some of us went to school; many never did. Some of us came from the south of Angola. The line between all the fighting factions was very thin: Unita, FAPLA, Koevoet, 101 Battalion, 32 Battalion and SWAPO.

I grew up as a temporary cattle herder at Ndonga Omuramba in Kavangoland. In the afternoon after school, with no homework to be done, we had to care for the cattle. The herd was my grandfather's pride. Just as in the rest of Africa, a man's pride is his cattle. His children and grandchildren were responsible for guarding and looking after them. By the age of eight or nine I was in the veld every day.

Together with some older boys, we started a game of trying to differentiate between the tracks of individual cattle. A herd of cattle could stray into a *mahango* field, and then we had to find out who the owner of the cattle was. We were quickly able to say whether it was ours or the neighbour's. In a herd of cattle we could very easily identify the tracks of one of our own. We learned the shape and pattern of a cow's hoof by the way it was placed and the specific impact it had on the ground, and a lot of other smaller details, like defects on the hooves and marks from injuries.

Finding a lost cow was always a challenge. But it would not only be animals: people also make tracks. We knew the difference between the tracks made by a woman and those made by a man; we could differentiate between tracks made by a large woman and a small man. We could also tell the difference between the tracks made by a proud upright man and one less so. Everything by how one walks, how your foot makes contact with the earth. The tracks of an old person and those of a young one differ. We knew the differences. It was our way of living—a culture.

It was important for the young men in our area to know this type of thing. There was no television or any other Western distraction. We spent hours in the bush where there was nothing else but tracks. It was what we were exposed to. It was the logical result of our lives.

During the 1970s and '80s, the Kavango was still a rural area. The war had just begun and Western influences in that part of Africa were limited. There were masses of game in the tribal areas of the Kavango. Guns were scarce. I and the other boys of my generation had to look after the cattle and protect them against the dangers of the land: lions, leopards and wild dogs; elephants were a threat to our crops. Our senses were so well developed that we could literally smell danger.

A big danger in the hot African sun was the Black mamba. We could smell if there was a snake in the area. We were so at one with the environment that we could see things others could not. If we told somebody in a Western city they would find it hard to believe us. We could hear the sounds made by the wild dogs from far away. We were attuned to smells and sounds. Using these same senses later in a war situation was therefore easy.

I was the second of six children and we were brought up as Kavangos. My parents moved to Namibia from Bie in Angola when they themselves were children. My grandparents were from the Mbungu tribe in southern Angola, and we were related to Jonas Savimbi. My grandfather worked on the mines of the Transvaal in South Africa. There were recruiting centres for the mines in northern Namibia. This way I ended up with my grandfather, who had by then retired.

It was a difficult time with six children in the house. There was no money and schooling was not as important as it is today. By the age of 18, I had completed Standard 7 (Grade 9) and was finished with school. The younger children also had to go to school. I had to find my way in the world.

We were never politically inclined and when the police started recruiting special constables the decision to join up was simple. Apartheid and those kinds of things were not factors in the Kavango bush. Other people were willing to make war because of it but it was not a factor in our lives. A paying job was better than politics, which we did not understand in any case.

So I became a member of the South African Police. Later I would hear the term 'apartheid police'. For me, it was never anything other than police. I was to start off unaware that Pretoria, which was 3,000 kilometres away, followed a strange policy that made me a lesser person.

What I did know was that these people were strict. They called it discipline, and as an 18-year-old boy I learned the lesson very quickly. Respect for everyone—white and black and superiors. Rifle drills, shooting, be neat and clean. You can call these guys whatever you want, but they were proud; proud of who they were and proud of what they were doing. No half measures. They did everything to the fullest extent and when you were training, you worked hard. Everything was done thoroughly. When I completed my basic training after three months, I was a better person—one with respect.

Koevoet started recruiting special constables for a new combat unit in the Kavango while we were still busy with our training. It was during 1984. Zulu-4 Sierra would be the callsign. Sergeant Hendrik Engelbrecht, who was helping us with our training, would be the commander of the new unit. As a Kavango, it was natural for me to go to Rundu where Zulu-4 Sierra would have its base.

Sergeant Hendrik Engelbrecht and I had a great relationship right from the start. After our basic training, we went into the bush for more training. Now it was combat training. We received medical, tactical, driving, heavy machine-gun, mortar and rocket training—and a huge amount of other stuff that we had to know. For the time being we were the 'Tiger' group, adopting Hendrik Engelbrecht's nickname.

We trained in the operational area so the chances that a training session could turn into a live contact were ever present. We had our first live contact experience with Zulu-4 Juliet in April 1984. After the first contact we were awarded our own shoulder patch; we decided among us that we would choose *nge* (scorpion) as our insignia.

There were not enough leaders available and I was promoted to lance-sergeant. I was barely 19 and had only been in the police for five months.

About three months later, Sergeant Hendrik Engelbrecht called me. He said he had been keeping a close eye on me over the past eight months and although I was still very young, he could see I was determined and that I had leadership qualities. He said I had already distinguished myself in the bush and that the initiative and leadership I had shown during tracking operations had not escaped him. He said he thought I had a natural affinity for what we were doing and that my knowledge and senses as a tracker were unequalled in the team. He thought I would be an asset in the future and that the SAP must invest in a future leader. He had recommended that I be promoted to full sergeant with immediate effect. All while I was in the bush! When I arrived back at Arendsnes, I was officially given the three stripes with the castle in the middle of a full sergeant in the South African Police. I was now Special Sergeant Sisingi Kamongo.

Shortly afterwards—and befitting my new rank—I was tasked with checking the supplies in the supply store. I had to see what we had and what we did not have. I counted the tins of beans—and they were short. The SAP store at Arendsnes was therefore in a crisis: someone had helped himself to SAP rations in the form of baked beans—and I had to explain the situation. When I reached the warrant officer who had given me the order to check the store, he was already busy with the war again. I told him that the beans were short.

"We have a war on here, and you are worrying about short baked beans!" he shouted. "Short, my arse!"

The warrant officer's tirade had not escaped some of the men. That is when I received a new nickname, Shorty—not because I am short, but because the tinned baked beans were short!

Now I was a 19-year-old sergeant. In police terms, this did not happen often. I was one of only a handful. I would take over command of our combat team for the first time at the age of twenty-one.

As the commander of Casspir 2, I would be in command of the tracking and in command of all forward tracking actions. My friends would call me commander. I loved the action and we would go on many more night foot patrols than did any of the other sections. Night ambushes along footpaths would become our speciality.

The leadership of a combat team has a lot to do with who is available. Usually the command of the four cars was divided among the white team leader in his Casspir and three other whites. The commanders of the cars were all white—in theory. In practice, it was an entirely different matter. Koevoet was a dynamic organization. White commanders went on leave to South Africa, or when they became ill or were wounded. Sometimes there were not enough white members to fill the leadership positions. The unit did not come to a halt because the whites were not there.

The war carried on.

Within each team there were also black leaders—sergeants and warrant officers, men with years of experience gained from many contacts. If there were not enough whites the leadership fell to the black members. In many cases, the white was the apparent leader but the decisions on the ground were made by the senior black non-commissioned officers. They knew the situation on the ground. They were experienced and understood and lived nearer to the people here than the men from the cities. I was involved in many situations where there were no white members and many more where there was only one. The white team members made communication easier but they were not indispensable. The war could go on without them. Warrant Officer Simon Nkwezi was the most respected of the black leaders, and highly regarded by all. By the end of the war, he would command a complete team consisting of black policemen, although officially the police would deny it.

First contact (Namungundo, April 1984)

It is cold and rainy in April 1984. Somewhere in the area of Namungundo, an experienced Koevoet team, Zulu-4 Juliet, is working. The commander of Zulu-4 Juliet is Sergeant Southie. They have found five tracks and inform Zulu 4. Our new team, Zulu-4 Sierra, now for the time based at Nepara in Kavangoland, is asked to assist. The tracks are about 90 minutes old and Zulu 4 sends us in support of the veterans.

We arrive at a kraal and the locals show us the tracks of the Zulu-4 Juliet Casspirs; we follow the tracks. Our team is under the command of Sergeant Hendrik 'Kwang' Engelbrecht. (Kwang was the name of honour given to him because of the respect the Kwangalis have for him.) He has just taken us through our training. Now he is the commander of the new team.

We are in Casspir number 1. With me and Sergeant Engelbrecht are four of the best young trackers—Janangura Palata, Rocco Dimbu, Blasius Kutenda and Moses Ulombe. They are all fit, energetic, sharp young men. Kutenda will be killed in action within a few months.

None of us has ever fired a shot in anger, in spite of the hours of training which have been drilled into us.

"Don't close your eyes when you pull the trigger!" Sergeant Engelbrecht would shout.

Now we could shoot and hit what we were aiming at with our eyes open! We had all heard of contacts. We had all heard of the 'terrs'; we practised hundreds of follow-up actions but now we are at the point of doing it for real.

While we are on the Zulu-4 Juliet tracks, Southie calls the gunship. It is close and the small radio's channel is changed to channel 16, the channel reserved for the air force. Each team has a large long-range radio and every car has a smaller tactical radio. The cars talk to each other over the small radio. As soon as the gunship arrives, the team leader changes the channel to 16. Then it is the tactical radio with which the teams speak to the gunship and with each other.

We are 20 minutes behind Southie when there is suddenly radio silence by all other cars except Zulu-4 Juliet, which makes contact; one of the insurgents is captured. We join them while they are cleaning up the area. We have missed the action but the enemy is far from done with.

Southie's team have captured an important insurgent, a PLAN commander by the name of Kamati. We are now part of the follow-up. For the first time I am a tracker on an enemy spoor. We chase four running tracks in a southwesterly direction. With me on the ground are the trackers from Zulu-4 Juliet. Hard, experienced men: Sergeants Paulus, Willem and Wengi and Constable Stanslaus. My heart is beating in my throat with excitement and apprehension. The older Zulu-4 Juliet trackers talk to me the whole time.

"Young man, do you see the tracks?"

"Yes, sergeant."

"Do you know whose tracks these are?"

"They are terr tracks, sergeant."

"Good, you are sharp, you must be awake; you know this is a dangerous thing we are doing. We aren't chasing cattle. The owner of those tracks wants to kill us. You must look for movement in front of you. If you stop focusing we can all get hurt. Concentrate!"

It starts raining. We lose all the tracks except for one man wearing boots. The tracks are now about 15 minutes old. Paulus gives the information to Sergeant Southie and they call the gunship again.

The cars in front cut the tracks every now and then. We climb into our cars and go to the new tracks. We rapidly catch up to where the tracks are now only a few minutes old.

We at Zulu-4 Sierra are still issued with Portuguese G3 rifles. They are heavy and clumsy but we are so pumped up that we do not even notice. The whole atmosphere is one of expectation and adrenalin.

Above us is the gunship. The pilot's name is Leon van Tonder. We will work with this man in the future in many contacts. He is a veteran of dozens of Koevoet contacts and is very experienced.

I am scanning ahead and see movement in front of me. Above me the gunship also fires at the movement. I fire a few shots like everybody else.

The pilot shouts over the radio, "Stop, stop firing!"

Southie agrees. The insurgent does not seem to have a weapon on him, and the helicopter is covering his every move. We are going to try to capture him.

The cars converge on him, but when they are a few metres from him he pulls a pistol from his belt and shoots himself through the head. Our shouts of "No! No!" do not help.

My first contact ends with a dead insurgent, but not by our rifles: a SWAPO 'own goal'.

The dead man is a very senior SWAPO commander, clad in a neat camouflage uniform. He is also a member of a SWAPO special unit. We find his RPG in the bush near him. Also a Scorpion machine pistol and a Makarov 9mm pistol, the weapon he took his life with.

More important are the documents he has on him. There is a lot of information obtained from the dead guerrilla and the one Zulu-4 Juliet captured earlier. We now know who the SWAPO leaders in the area are and at which kraals they operate. The SWAPO ringleaders in the Kavango are Hamutumwa, Kavango, Haruwadi/Danger, Janangura and Katjama. Their commander is Hakushinda Yakula, the Typhoon commander at Mpunguvlei. We take the handcuffed Kamati, and put him in the back of the car with us.

I later learn that it is usually not difficult to 'turn' a PLAN prisoner. But then there are also the hardened communists who have received training in Eastern Europe and Cuba. They are sworn and hardened 'freedom fighters'.

While riding back with us, he preaches the SWAPO doctrine: "You will see, SWAPO will rule the land. Sam Nujoma will be president of Namibia. We will drive away all the white colonialists."

Initially he says all these things while looking past the white commanders. Later he closes his eyes to make sure he does not see them. He talks of racists but he himself is guilty of the same thing.

I am just 19 and it does not bother me; I just want action.

At Nepara we find the other teams of Zulu 4. Except for the veteran Zulu-4 Juliet, none of the other teams has encountered a contact. We are the local celebrities among the new teams. When we arrive, we sit around; the other teams want to know what we saw and did. Rocco is bragging. He sits there and tells everyone that he saw the insurgents during the follow-up before the trackers of Zulu-4 Juliet saw them.

But a tracker from Juliet-4 hears him. The 'old man' walks over to him and kicks him in the ribs. He grabs him and says, "You were lucky. If you ever see an insurgent again and do nothing, I will personally shoot you."

This closes Rocco's big mouth. If the threat weren't so serious we would all have laughed. Rocco will nurse his sore ribs for a couple of days.

Our first contact has been made. We have seen the gunship in action and we were with the trackers in action. We understand the mechanics of a follow-up.

Later that afternoon, one of the Zulu-4 Juliet trackers comes to me: "What is your name?"

"Sisingi Kamongo, sergeant."

"You are young. You must be careful. Many of the men around us will not see this through."

High above us a gunship dances, playing like a young eagle. I do not understand what this man is trying to tell me. His prediction will prove correct. Much young blood will flow for a war that will later be little known and almost forgotten as a small offshoot of the Cold War and African liberation, concepts alien to me. We were caught between two sides, of which none of us understood much.

The next morning during church parade, Kwang talks to us: "You did good work. We adapted well to the circumstances. If we stick to discipline and everyone does his bit, we will have fewer casualties than others. We will be just as brave but we will do things right. You are part of a team. You don't mean much alone—that's why we try to isolate the terrs, to get them alone.

You saw what Zulu-4 Juliet did. Their habits are good. Learn their good habits. If you do these things you will stay alive."

The first contact is over, and I am impressed with the tactics and execution of the whole operation. I am proud to be part of this unit.

The elephants are on their way to water.

Nothing will stop us.

I am young and invincible.

SAAF: 1—Kudus: 0 (Gcama Karukuvisa, 1984)

We are camped at Ncaute, one of the Zulu 4 forward bases. Relatively few of our contacts take place in the Kavango. Most of SWAPO's intimidation and terrorist action takes place in Ovamboland. The macro-politics play a big role. The southeast of Angola is dominated by Unita, an ally of South Africa's. The South Africans send a lot of supplies and weapons to Savimbi through Rundu. In exchange, they keep the place free of SWAPO.

The absence of SWAPO bases across the Kavango border forces all insurgents wanting to get to Kavango to cross the border in Ovamboland and then to move east to get to Kavango. The effect is that we mostly pick up the tracks of insurgents in the drier western part of Kavango and then try to cut them off before they reach the dense bush of eastern Kavango. But if the tracks dry up we move into Ovamboland where there is always action.

Zulu 2 at Eenhana is the radio relay station on the way to Kavango. We operate there a lot. We also see much action in the Okongo area, outside Kavango. But this means that we sometimes have to move 400 kilometres from our base in Rundu to find the action.

Early one the morning, we move to Karukuvisa. I have not been with the unit for long. We obtain information that there are two PLAN members in the area. We start questioning people at the kraals. One of the seniors, Warrant Officer Clemens Kamberuka of Section 4, reports that he has found someone who has seen the insurgents at a kraal at Gcama.

He calls all the cars to the kraal. While we are still on our way, the warrant officer starts questioning an old man at the kraal where the enemy was last seen. The old man says he knows the insurgents were at a well not far from there. The team leader, Warrant Officer, later Lieutenant, Lukas Koen also arrives. Now all the cars are at the well. We are in car 3 and Sergeant Hendrik Engelbrecht is in command of the car this day.

There are many tracks at the well. The PLAN members forced the local people to walk over their tracks. But we are not the best trackers in the world for nothing. Times such as these mean that you employ all your senses and your feelings. The faintest smell means something to people who spend weeks in the bush. A human starts smelling like dust. You can smell him when he passes you, or if he was there before you. Gun oil is a giveaway: you can smell it for miles. You do not have to see the tracks. Stick to the smell and if the wind is calm you will find the tracks.

We find the tracks after a while. Two tracks going west. Hendrik Engelbrecht, Clemens Kamberuka and Lukas Koen confer. We have a plan. Hendrik asks 12 trackers to follow on foot. The Casspirs turn around and proceed in the opposite direction. It is a quiet follow-up on tracks that are four hours old. The follow-up is fast and we catch up quickly. There is a small hill in front of us and we climb it to see if we can spot them. While climbing the hill, we and the insurgents see each other simultaneously. They start running but they are too far away for us to catch them. Plans change. We call the cars. Following them on foot does not work well today. And now they know we are tracking them. The element of surprise is gone.

We call the cars and the gunships on standby are summoned. The gunships have a 25-minute reaction time. We start tracking; I am a young tracker able to run on the tracks. The gunship arrives but the pilot is new. He does not know much and he is too far ahead. At one stage, he says over the radio that he has seen movement and we can hear him firing. We follow up and find a dead kudu! The pilot's and his gunner's first kill was a kudu. We carry on following the tracks with a kudu on the back of the Blesbok.

The night overtakes us and we are forced to spend the night in a temporary base (TB). But our enemies flee ever onward. The next morning and afternoon we follow the tracks and lose them when we reach a tarred road. We have followed the tracks for more than 60 kilometres. We are tired.

The game has been played. Nobody won. It was a draw. The only other score in the follow-up was SAAF: 1—Kudus: 0. The trigger-happy gunship saw to it that we could have a break from the monotonous rat packs.

Men of war, Zulu-4 Oscar, Nepara

Koevoet teams regularly visited army bases out of necessity. There were enough supplies on the Blesbok for a week out on a patrol, but when things developed differently the supplies were usually used up more quickly than was anticipated: diesel, helicopter fuel, water, ammunition, rat packs. Sometimes circumstances developed that caused us to stay in the field longer. We often had to leave lightly wounded or ill members at the sick bay of an army base.

When we did visit the bases, TV, beer and beds were not an option. Some of the team leaders had strict rules against the use of liquor while on patrol. We would load up supplies and disappear into the bush. Most members didn't even brush their teeth for two weeks in the bush. Black and white, we were men of war, men of the bush. We lived, walked, slept, thought and talked war. Day and night. Awake during the day and awake at night. We had to guard during the night. We were always ready for a SWAPO attack.

When SWAPO attacked we had to be ready. If they fired mortars during the night or fired on us with small arms, they would be sorry early the next morning. We were specialist trackers and could easily follow any tracks. As a rule they never bothered a Koevoet team in a TB. Only the bravest and dumbest tried it. It always ended with costly consequences for the attackers.

We were young men with a lot of trust in the capabilities of our comrades. We had to see the enemy before he saw us. We fired before they fired. We had knowledge, bravery, speed and firepower on our side.

Because we, the black members of the teams, had the experience and exposure, we took new white members under our wing. These boys came from police stations in South Africa and had only completed a counter-insurgency course. That was not worth much in our area. We were specialists with specialist tactics. We had to teach them quickly. Their success would be our success and their mistakes ours. We pulled them in and taught them tactics and procedures. There was no place for politics or apartheid. Those who could not adapt were sent back. To a large extent, the black members determined the fate of a new recruit. If he was racist or arrogant, he was out. The white commanders and team leaders understood this. We had to work together as a unit and there were no exceptions. The black members were the people with the experience and if they were not happy, there was a problem. In many cases, the black members were former SWAPO who knew the thought patterns of their old comrades. That is why it was so important to make new members fit into the teams. Black ex-SWAPO and white South African Police in one team—we just had to make it work.

Out tracking abilities were legendary and we had the ability to tell the team leaders how old tracks were. Then we would chase the tracks until we caught up. Depending on the age of the tracks, we would send the front-cut cars forward about 2,000 metres to try and cut off the terrs. You could expect the insurgents to change direction, or sometimes they would do a 360-degree turn and come back on their tracks. They would try to confuse the trackers. If the cars in front did not find them, they would start looking laterally, to the left and right of the original line of the tracks.

If we found the insurgents were close by, we would call in the helicopters. The terrs would get rid of their weight and set anti-personnel and POMZ mines. The last part of a follow-up was always dangerous. Would the enemy fight back? Would they set traps? Is my hat turned inside out so the helicopter can identify me by the orange dayglo? Am I out of the way of the wheels of the Casspir if he hits a contact now? Nervous moments are endured. Sometimes it would last for hours and sometimes it would end in death and blood. Other times an anticlimax—nothing. At times, the terrain impeded us, or we encountered an experienced anti-tracking terr. Sometimes they were just lucky; a thunderstorm could save them.

A lot of sweat and tension expended, sometimes for nothing.

A PLAN leader's tyranny

Before I joined the police, I went with my friends to join the army at 202 Battalion. I eventually turned around at the gates. I did not feel like joining the army that day. I often wondered why I did not sign up and to this day I cannot explain. Most of my school friends joined the army and their intake made up most of Delta Company of 202.

In the vicinity of Mpunguvlei was an insurgent leader by the name of Kazangula. He was a fearsome and merciless man. He killed indiscriminately—civilians, army or police. He was a terrorist in the real sense of the word: he lived by creating and spreading terror.

After the young men of Delta Company had completed their training they started operating in Kavangoland. One weekend, Delta Company received a weekend pass to go home. In a treacherous act, Kazangula and some of his followers misled ten of the civilian-clothed and unarmed young men at a *cuca*. They were abducted and tortured before they were either bayoneted or had their throats slit. It was a massacre. Miraculously, one survived after he was given up for dead by the murderers.

The murder of these nine young men sent shockwaves throughout the Kavango. Many were too scared to disclose who was responsible and where the murderers were. But the insurgents became complacent and when they killed 28 cattle belonging to one headman, the game was up. Somehow one informer got hold of the gang's whereabouts and the information made its way to Hendrik Engelbrecht. In a follow-up, Kazangula and two of his gang were cornered. Before Kazangula died, he shot out the front windows and two of the tyres of one car.

But no one knew precisely who these dead insurgents were. Even the Koevoet men disagreed. Was it Kazangula or not? The dispute was eventually settled by one of the 'old men' of Koevoet, Warrant Officer 'Ou Tom' Kautondoka. He was one of the first members of Koevoet and grew up near Mpunguvlei. He knew Kazangula personally.

His question was simple: "Is one toe on the dead man's right foot deformed?"

"Yes."

"Well, that toe was damaged when a cow stepped on it while Kazangula and I were herding cattle as children."

Delta Company of 202 Battalion would have many more deaths.

The war was hard on the young men of the Kavango.

'My little brother' (Omuramba Odela, 1984)

When teams were back at the base, they rotated. You were either completely off duty and could go where you wanted, or you were on standby. Being on standby was an important component of being at base. We could go out but not unless we said where we were going, and it could not be more than ten kilometres away. If the base was attacked during the night we had to be there. If urgent reinforcements were needed during a big follow-up we were mobilized within an hour.

There were two large locations, or townships, not far from Rundu. We generally went there on rest days or when we were on standby. We usually relaxed there on a Saturday. The *cucas*—the name is derived from Cuca, the brand of Angolan beer that was sold in these shops previously—later developed into what in South Africa is known as a shebeen, or a tavern. There we drank *mahango* beer, Black Label and that old South African favourite, Lion Lager. The music of Brenda Fassie, Lucky Dube and others played on loudspeakers in the background. We did not understand the Sotho and Zulu they sang, nor the township language, but we understood the rhythm. Few of us appreciated the importance of the role these languages and music would later play in our lives. Many of us would see our children go to school and grow up with these languages. Later in South Africa, through our work, we would use these languages and many of us would have to learn to speak them.

On one particular afternoon, some of us are busy in a *cuca* when I decide to go outside. I open the door as a police vehicle pulls up in front. Two white members from the logistical unit get out and tell me to get everybody together: we are deploying. There is a big contact between PLAN and the army at Omuramba Odela. There are a few teams tracking but they need help. We have to go and assist. I go back into the *cuca* and rally the other team members. We board the vehicle and drive to Arendsnes. When we arrive, many of the other members are already there, getting ready.

We send a Casspir to the other location and it picks up the last team members. Meanwhile, we prepare the cars for deployment: ammunition, food, water, sleeping bags, medical supplies, helicopter fuel and everything we will need.

By 2100 hours everything is ready and we leave Arendsnes. Later that night we form a temporary base at Ncaute, the name the San, or Bushmen, inhabitants have given the place.

At 0400 hours the next morning, we break up the TB. Warrant Officer Lukas Koen and Sergeant Hendrik Engelbrecht are in command of Zulu-4 Sierra. Lukas Koen says that we are going to Okawe. The plan has changed. An army patrol walked into an ambush the previous afternoon. Three soldiers were killed and four were wounded. We will follow these tracks. They suspect that there are seven insurgents involved. By first light we are on our way to Okawe. I am the senior tracker in Casspir 1.

An hour or so later, we arrive at the scene. There are many tracks, army and PLAN all mixed. Luckily, the insurgents are not wearing boots. Some are wearing track shoes and some are barefoot. We count three wounded insurgents. We start following the tracks. About 1,500 metres farther on we find a POMZ. We deactivate the mine and continue.

We get to a road where there are some road workers. Some of them are SWAPO sympathizers because they have obviously tried to erase the tracks. We struggle ahead for about 15 kilometres and eventually arrive at a *cuca* shop. There is a group of people in front of the shop and I look at one of the men, but he immediately looks away when our eyes meet. This is unusual, like he wants to dismiss me. I walk straight up to him. There is blood on his foot and on his shoulder.

I question him. "Whose blood is that?"

"I carried a rabbit that I hunted," he answers.

But something is not right. I call one of the constables in my team and tell him to watch the man. I want to talk to a few more people.

I move among the people and question them while the man with the blood is out of hearing range. I find nothing but I am suspicious. I feel uncomfortable. One way or another, the man with the blood on his clothes must know something. I walk back to him.

"The people here say you are a PLAN member. I'm going to take you back to the base and interrogate you." I was aware of the stories doing the rounds of how possible SWAPO members were violently interrogated, stories in many cases spread by SWAPO themselves. The constable puts him into the Casspir.

We depart and about 500 metres farther on, the man's resolve breaks. "Anything, just not interrogation by Koevoet!" He has many answers. Yes, he found the wounded PLAN member next to the road and carried him. That is where the blood comes from. He will also show us where he has hidden him.

We turn back past the *cuca* shop and stop next to the road. There are tracks into the bush, but no person. We search further and find a warthog hole. The wounded PLAN member is hiding in it. Luckily, the hole isn't deep.

The insurgent is sitting inside the hole with a hand grenade. We don't want bloodshed; we talk to him:

"Put back the pin and come out; we will not harm you." After a few minutes, he replaces the pin and we pull him out of the hole. We give him an injection for the pain, treat his wounds and put him on a drip. He asks for water and we fetch a cold water bag from the Casspir. We give him the water. He says he has not tasted cold water in a long time. He is hungry and someone gives him a tin of food from a rat pack.

But everything comes at a price: we want information, everything he knows. We have won his trust; he has seen that we do not plan to kill him. The information comes quickly.

"Who is the commander of this patrol?"

"Hamutumwa. Danger, John Osko, Janangura and Rebecca are also there."

"How many of you ambushed the army?"

"There were fourteen of us."

"How long have you been in the area?"

"A long time; three months. We were finished with the operation and were on our way back to Lubango in Angola."

"How many of you came over the border?."

"Two hundred and fifty, but we split up into groups of five to eight. It is more difficult for the army to hunt us if we are in smaller groups. There was also a group of ten."

With the new information we now know how many insurgents we are hunting. We pick up the tracks again but it starts raining; later we lose them.

We turn back to the army base at 202 Battalion. We unload the prisoner and the army storeman gives us a few cases of beer and some meat. We depart and have a braai at Arendsnes. We are given two days off, then we come back for the next patrol. We go straight back to the 202 Battalion base.

Our prisoner looks much better and we book him out. We are not finished yet. We want to know where he left his weapon. My relationship with the man is such that the SWAPO man now calls me, the Koevoet policeman, his 'big brother'. And the big brother finds out that the whole group had a temporary base near Okawe where they stayed in a bush shelter. Near this shelter is the weapons cache. He will show us. Once more, we go to the place where the contact took place.

The 'little brother' is now very helpful. He shows us a place in the veld near the shelter and some of the constables start digging. One by one the weapons come out, including one RPG rocket launcher, ten RPG rockets, eight blocks of TNT and a lot of other equipment.

The next few months will be interesting. The mass invasion in the Kavango will keep us busy for a few months. The enemy will sabotage the eastern Kavango, plant landmines, kidnap and intimidate people.

There were many such incidents and many such small groups. By the end of the year, the unit would launch a sweep operation and we would shoot, catch or drive away most of the insurgents. SWAPO would pay dearly for their attempt to undermine the Kavango.

Once more we will have to drive very far to again see action.

Bad discipline: the murder of a Koevoet member (Muruwani, 1984)

Festus Kandundu was a PLAN terrorist who operated in the Kavango near Muruwani, about halfway between Grootfontein and Rundu. Here he became notorious among the local population. He intimidated them with violence and was well known because of his relentless retaliation against anyone who did not support SWAPO. He murdered a few locals, but his intimidation and terrorism were such that no one wanted to say anything because they were terrified of SWAPO reprisals.

In 1984 our teams operated for a time from Nepara. We would do patrols for three days and then return to Nepara. We had four teams operating from there. After a few patrols, with none of the teams managing to break through into the SWAPO ring, we investigated and questioned everywhere, but to no avail.

One day, we arrived at a kraal. Once more, the information was negative. It was ploughing season. Some of our members went into the kraal where there were people inside preparing food. Large pots of meat, *mahango* porridge and three large pots of beer were evident. We asked who all the food was for and were told it was for the people working in the fields. Kavango custom is that the community helps each other in working the lands. The owner of a particular field is then responsible for providing food for all the workers. Once the work is done, it is celebrated with a feast. We left for Nepara, completely satisfied with the explanation.

The kraal was about four kilometres from the base. Standing orders were that members on patrol, or those deployed at another base could not leave the team under any circumstance. During the evening, our driver and one of the trackers went AWOL to partake in the feast. Poor discipline: something not associated with Koevoet.

The team leaders were very strict and took no nonsense. No alcohol was allowed on a patrol; a team leader such as Sergeant du Toit of Zulu Quebec maintained discipline with a plastic pipe. Toitjie nearly killed offenders but there was no paperwork and nobody complained.

The two Koevoet members who had sneaked away made a critical mistake. In the same area, on the way to the same party, were Festus Kandundu and two of his group. The only problem was that they were at the kraal before the two policemen got there.

When the policemen arrive, Kandundu and one of the insurgents were already in a hut. The third insurgent quickly warns them. In the dark, Festus and his two followers sneak to the entrance of the kraal. One of the locals is told to call the two policemen to the entrance. Kandundu and his comrades hide in the dark. When the two come closer to the entrance, the smaller of the two policemen realizes something is wrong. He shouts to the other policeman but the bigger man is already so near to Kandundu that the insurgent fires his pistol point blank three times into the chest of the bigger policeman, which proves fatal.

The smaller man has time to fire a few rounds at the insurgents but he misses. He is trapped in the kraal. There is just one option: he must get out. He crashes into the pole fence, runs right through it and flees with the three insurgents close behind him. Luckily, the shots they fire at him miss. He escapes in the dark to Nepara.

He arrives at the base bloody and torn by branches and thorns, but otherwise he is fine. However, he is so shocked that he cannot speak. He just points in the general area of where everything happened. After a while, Warrant Officer Shifile gets the story out of him. He tells us about the murder of the other man.

We get into four cars and drive to the kraal that night. Kandundu and his men have fled. We pick up the body of our dead teammate and return to base.

The next morning, we start following up. The tracks of Kandundu and his men run south toward the dense bush near Namungundu. Here we lose the tracks. Kandundu's plan worked. He would evade us for years.

Kandundu and others like him would make it extremely dangerous for our members to go into the rural areas alone. If they found one of us or a member of the army, murder was on the agenda. The chance that you could be murdered was ever present. The enemy intimidated and terrorized. We practised mercy when we found them but they had no mercy for us. Most of us would resettle in the bigger towns of Opowu, Rundu and Oshakati. We were safe there.

Kandundu was an expert anti-tracker and a fearsome opponent. The story goes that he once attacked a Unita convoy in southern Angola—an unheard of thing. It was also rumoured that once while on a deployment, he took time out to play in a soccer game against the army! He would meet a violent death when Zulu-4 Juliet followed up on information about him. He would die in the shoot-out.

Just to muddy the waters, even after his death the army refused to pay out his 'head money' to the Koevoet team.

The experiment with the dogs (Ohameva, 1985)

We had many informers all over our area of operation. These people would supply us with information of what was happening in their area. Many a time they were people who had had a bad experience with SWAPO, or sometimes they were members of SWAPO who had become disillusioned by what it was doing: intimidation, kidnappings and landmines hurt the local population, *their* people. Many rebelled and started to work with the security forces. We were also prepared to pay for good information.

One of our informants was at Ohameva.

We are on the road to Omaheva and we sleep in the veld near Okongo. The next morning we leave for Ohameva, west of Okongo. We find our informant at a kraal and question everybody separately. In doing so, we protect the anonymity of our informant.

He tells us that five PLAN members were at a *cuca* not far from us the previous evening. They have been in the area for quite some time; they have girlfriends among the women of the area.

We follow up on this information at the *cuca* and the information is confirmed. A young man says that he heard the PLAN members talking to each other. They will most probably come to the *cuca* again tonight. He does not know what time.

I give the information to Kallie Calitz and Hendrik Engelbrecht. We decide to see if we can pick up their tracks but we have no success. There are too many people and animals in the area and the insurgents most likely have had their tracks covered by others. By 1500 hours, Kallie, Hendrik and I decide on a different strategy. We will remove the cars and set up an ambush on one of the main footpaths leading to the *cuca*.

By 1900 hours, at last light, two of our sections leave on night patrol to set up the ambush. We take sleeping bags and flares with us. After walking for about 90 minutes, we find a place that is a bit more open than the rest of the bush in the area. We take our positions in the sparse bush next to the path.

Then the waiting begins.

The locals move along the path but they are unaware of us. They walk right through the killing zone, with us positioned behind our weapons 15 metres away. Later it gets quiet. By 0100 hours, there are suddenly five armed men on the path coming straight toward the killing zone. When the last of them is in the open, Hendrik fires the first shot. A 1,000-foot illumination flare is also fired into the air. There are coloured lines all over as the tracer rounds from our R5s fly through the air.

About 60 seconds later the order comes to cease fire. We stay in our position until first light. It is too dangerous to go and scratch around in the dark. Some of the insurgents could be wounded and still able to fight back. That will put us in danger. We leave everything alone.

By first light, it is safe enough to go and look at what happened. We don't find any bodies but there are blood and tracks. Some of the wounded and dead have been carried away. We start a follow-up immediately.

The cars are now also with us. At the Eenhana–Okongo road the insurgents take to the road. It is difficult to follow them. There are vehicle tracks but to follow tracks on such a road is dangerous. We could walk into an ambush at any time. We revert to an old tactic. A Casspir takes the left side of the road, another one the right. They provide security for the trackers. The trackers are in front looking for tracks or blood. A few kilometres farther on there is another set of Casspirs conducting the same technique.

After about five kilometres we finally locate the tracks. Sergeant Botes and his team of Zulu-4 Echo have joined us and they are busy identifying the tracks which head in a southwesterly direction. He calls Hendrik Engelbrecht and Hendrik calls Zulu 2. Zulu 2 sends the gunships.

Botes is a man with a lot of experience. He learned from Eugene de Kock, Sakkie van Zyl and Frans 'Smiley' Conradie—the originals, the men who founded the unit. When the teams in the Kavango were founded, Botes was sent in to add weight and experience. He is a true professional and a master of Koevoet tactics.

Near Opepela the insurgents had heard the gunships and the cars and jumped off the road into the bush. This is where Botes and his team pick up the tracks.

But then the high brass get involved, creating animosity between the police and army, animosity in certain circles that lingers to this day. All the teams following the tracks are given the order to stop. We are told that the air force will fly in a Puma with dogs from the army to follow the tracks.

We are angry.

The helicopter lands and the handlers and their dogs get off. A few minutes later, the dogs and their handlers start following the tracks. The handlers let the dogs go. The animals disappear into the bush. The dogs bark and are very excited.

Then it is quiet.

One dog comes back but the other is gone. Sergeant Hendrik Engelbrecht and Boats Botes are arguing with the army men. They accuse the army of messing up our tracks. Hendrik and the army lieutenant are shouting. The lieutenant is upset because one of his dogs is gone.

Hendrik is angry with the outcome. The police sergeant shouts at the army lieutenant, "You fucked up the tracks!" It nearly ends in a fist fight.

We quit the area and a few kilometres away I stumble upon a track by accident. As I am getting out of the car to answer nature's call, I suddenly realize that here at my feet is one of the lost tracks.

We follow the tracks and it ends with one dead PLAN member.

That evening, Hendrik has calmed down: "Look, the higher-ups wanted to test the dogs but the dogs failed the test. But Shorty passed the test. I don't think we will see much more of the mutts."

Three weeks later, Zulu-4 Whiskey catches an insurgent at Oluwaya. He is one of the four that got away that day at Ohameva. Then the truth is revealed. The army dog found the insurgents but they were so well hidden that when the dog approached, one of the insurgents killed it with a bayonet. Three of the five who were there had been wounded in a previous contact and they were on their way to Lubango in Angola. One of the wounded was Mohlongo, a PLAN veteran and a worthy opponent. Owing to his wounds, he would never return to Namibia as an insurgent again. He was the most clever and sly PLAN member working in the Okongo area.

An army experiment with dogs saved his life.

Early morning action (Big Ondema, 1985)

We spend the night at Okongo in a TB: our team, Zulu-4 Sierra, together with our sister team, Zulu-4 Echo. Warrant Officer Lukas Koen accompanies us on this patrol. Sergeant Hendrik Engelbrecht is the commander of our team. The commander of the other team is Sergeant Boats Botes.

At 0500 hours both teams move out of the TB and head due north. We move nearly parallel to each other but a few kilometres apart. At about 0630 hours Zulu-4 Echo calls us over the radio. Sergeant Botes says that he has come across the tracks of two 'Victor Yankee'—*vyand* in Afrikaans: the enemy. He explains that the tracks were made at about 2300 hours the previous night. We should move in his direction, find his tracks and follow him. He is near the school at a place called Ondema.

Over the radio Botes says, "Zulu 4, Zulu-4 Echo."

"Send Zulu-4 Echo."

"Zulu 4, confirm two Victor Yankee tracks, seven hours old. Gunship standing by, channel 16, white phosphorus."

"Zulu 4, I'll set it up."

Now the coordination with the air force begins. There are no helicopters at Okongo but there are with Zulu 2 at Eenhana farther west in Ovamboland. The gunship could move to Okongo and be on standby from there, which would mean that it would be fuelled up and bombed up, waiting for the call at Okongo, closer to the action.

We easily find the tracks of Zulu-4 Echo and it does not take long to catch up with them; they are standing outside a kraal. The VY slept in the kraal the previous night and must still have been there only minutes beforehand.

Mossie, Kallie Calitz and I take our cars round the kraal and start looking for the tracks on the other side. We find them almost immediately. A few metres farther on, we find backpacks, dropped—like people who are fleeing. Not hidden but desperately thrown away.

Kallie relays the information to Sergeant Botes, who talks to Zulu 4 again.

Zulu 4 sends in the gunship. Reaction time is 15 minutes. We wait a while to give the helicopter time to catch up. If the gunship can do the job it will be less dangerous for us. SWAPO might fire an RPG or shoot at us and then we could lose people or suffer wounded. We know the enmy is nearby and cannot get away.

In the open African bush they are in a corner.

The gunship calls for white phosphorus and we throw a grenade to guide him in. In the air the white smoke of a phosphorus grenade can be seen from afar. The gunship joins us and we start moving along the tracks.

The gunship circles but sees nothing.

Warrant Officer Koen decides to flush the fox from its hole. The three Casspirs in the middle of the line formation are ordered forward. The drivers are Warrant Officer Haule, Constable Kakunde and, from Zulu-4 Echo, Frans Mundjanga. The tactic now is one of intimidation. Put the two PLAN members under pressure. Like true Formula One drivers, the cars race through the bush, the gunners ready to bring the guns to life with one finger on the trigger. If an enemy happens to be in the path of the wheels, it would be his end.

The two SWAPOs are not inclined to give up without a fight; each fires a rifle grenade at the gunship. The cars are approaching so fast that the helicopter cannot fire back.

"Contact, contact, Zulu-4 Echo. Contact!" Botes yells over the radio.

Then there is radio silence from everybody else; until the contact is over no one speaks except those involved in the fight.

The sound of the R5s is all around, shooting through the rifle ports in the sides of the cars. From the top of the turrets the deeper thuds of the five-0s, LMGs and three-0s. Shiny bullet casings fly all about as they are ejected from rifle and gun mechanisms. Somewhere in the bush two SWAPOs die. Their sleep in the kraal was their last.

The saying goes, the early bird gets the worm. In Koevoet terms it was the same. We surprised these insurgents while they were sleeping in the kraal, and after that there was no getting away. Had they wanted to surrender they could have. They were prepared to fight and, therefore, we respected them as fighters.

By 1000 hours everything is over. The money for two heads would be shared between 80 men.

Did we kill them for the money?

R10 for each of us.

A duel (Okawe, 19 March 1985)

We leave Rundu for a patrol in Ovamboland. We leave early in the morning from the Zulu 4 Arendsnes base. By mid-afternoon, we arrive tired and hot at Nkongo, the Zulu-4 Oscar base at Okongo. We sleep outside in the veld in a TB. Early the next morning we move north and arrive later at Okawe. We pick up three tracks which are about 12 hours old; in front of us is a heavily kraaled area. I have a feeling that the PLAN members are not too far ahead. The tracks were made the previous evening and we are here early in the morning. Maybe they spent the night in the kraal.

We talk to the team leader, Sergeant Hendrik Engelbrecht, and he calls Kallie Calitz. Kallie is level-headed, a man who listens to the senior men in his car. Together with Hendrik Engelbrecht we decide on a strategy. We stop the cars and leave them. About 20 of us start walking along the tracks. A foot patrol.

After about two kilometres, we arrive at a kraal. There is an old man but he is clearly uncomfortable. He does not want to talk to us. I call Kallie aside and tell him I think my instinct is correct: SWAPO are near, very near. They slept here. We walk to the pole fencing and start looking.

Running tracks! These guys ran when we arrived. We almost caught them with their pants down. They are fleeing directly north toward the Angolan border. Sergeant Engelbrecht calls the cars behind us and when they arrive we start following the tracks. He also calls the gunships.

Zulu-4 Echo, our sister group, is in the area and Sergeant Botes and his team join us minutes later.

Zulu-4 Sierra stays on the left side of the tracks, Zulu-4 Echo on the right, while Kallie Calitz and I follow the tracks in front.

"Zulu-4 Oscar, Zulu-4 Sierra. The gunship can come, channel 16, white phos," Hendrik Engelbrecht calls over the radio.

"Zulu-4 Sierra, 4-Oscar, the gunships are on the way. Reaction time 18 minutes," comes the confirmation from Okongo.

After a few minutes' silence, the big radio comes to life again: "Zulu-4 Sierra, Golf Sierra." (Golf Sierra is code for 'gunship')

"Send, Golf Sierra."

"Zulu-4 Sierra, throw red smoke. We are a few minutes out," the helicopter answers.

We throw red smoke to lead the helicopters to our position as all the trackers on the ground reverse their hats to present the bright orange dayglow panel to the helicopters, to prevent them from shooting at us.

The gunships have just arrived when one of the cars, 4-Echo-2, comes on the radio and says they have found a number of grenades. Most of the cars move in his direction. It is clear that these three particular insurgents have decided to run, to fight another day. We find backpacks, boots, blocks of TNT and other equipment thrown away in haste, but no rifles. They definitely still have their personal weapons with them.

Then the machine gun on the gunship starts firing. "I've got one," the pilot says coolly.

We approach the spot where the gunship fired and then: "Contact!"

I am on the ground. In front of me, nearly at point-blank range next to a tree, a man is firing an SKS at me. But he misses. I return fire with my R5 but I also miss. I dive to the ground and he crawls behind the tree. Kallie is standing in the car behind the five-0.

I shout, "Shoot the tree! Shoot the tree!"

Kallie hears me and fires at the base of the tree, killing the insurgent. The other cars kill another insurgent. Three heads in one contact. One insurgent is wearing a Libyan uniform. We load the bodies onto the wheel arches of the cars and move back to Okongo.

Following tracks through the bush was usually heavy on the cars, and a lot of damage was sometimes sustained. If we could, cars were repaired in the bush, but sometimes it was not possible. Okongo had to serve as a repair base more than once.

Charge tactics (Oshana Shanalama, Angola, 1985)

We enter Angola at beacon 29 and head in a northerly direction. We move to the Onalumono area and start patrolling. It is a sweep operation and all our callsigns are changed: 'Zulu' becomes 'Mike'. We carry out the normal interrogations, look for tracks in the footpaths, look around and talk to the local population.

If someone is evasive, or there is unnecessary nervousness or strange behaviour among the local population, we can quickly tell if there is a snake in the grass.

Tracks are an important source of information. The tracks of soldiers and locals differ and we know the difference. Feet just recently in shoes make a different spoor from feet that have been bare the whole day. When an insurgent hears us, he often gets rid of the characteristic chevron-patterned boots to mislead us.

From the local population we eventually obtain information that there is a large group of insurgents moving in a southerly direction and we go and look for them. All the Kavango teams are involved. As usual we are far from home.

One of our cars, number 3, is a few hundred metres apart from the rest and they pick up three tracks. In Angola, the cars seldom work alone up front. Shortly afterwards, they pick up backpacks that have been dumped. The insurgents are very close.

Constable Piet Neethling, the car commander, calls Hendrik 'Kwang' Engelbrecht: "Mike-4 Sierra-1, Mike-4 Sierra-1, Mike-4 Sierra-3."

"Send Piet," the answer comes.

"Three tracks, *payife-payife* [recently made] running tracks; we have picked up the backpacks already."

With me in the car is Kallie Calitz. "Are you listening? Our trackers must be careful," he says.

Sergeant Kwang calls Zulu 2 and reports the three running tracks that are about 30 to 45 minutes old. They are running in a northwesterly direction. In the ops-room at Eenhana the operations officer, Major Willem Fouché, informs us the helicopters are 38 minutes away.

You cannot front-cut too far forward on tracks in Angola. It is too dangerous for a car to be alone. To obtain information, a lone car is fine but as soon as you have a positive spoor, it becomes a question of maximum support and maximum firepower. It was easy for supposedly fleeing insurgents to draw a single car into an ambush. However, a whole team with full mobility and firepower is a different kettle of fish.

We start following the tracks at about 12 o'clock. The tracks are hot. There are other teams nearby. Engelbrecht calls Mike-4 Echo and Sergeant Botes is on his way to us. Whiskey Fox (Major Willem Fouché) is also on the radio. He is sending gunships from Eenhana.

When Mike-4 Echo approaches us there is suddenly a huge explosion a few hundred metres away, exactly where the enemy is. One of Mike-4 Echo's Casspirs has detonated a landmine and black smoke is billowing up through the bush as Botes's Casspir burns. Help from Mike-4 Echo is not forthcoming for now. They have their own problems to deal with.

Hendrik decides on another plan. He will break up his team. This is a calculated risk. Two of our cars will move forward to see if they can narrow the gap.

Just this once.

Kallie 'Kalingundula' Calitz (his Kwangali nickname, meaning 'he who fixes things', e.g. fixing tracks, fixing the problem) and I are in Mike-4 Sierra-2 and with us comes car number 4, Mike-4 Sierra-4.

The landmine incident has made us more determined. SWAPO has a problem now. We shoot forward about 2,000 metres and each car puts five trackers on the ground. I am also on the ground. We form a line with the trackers next to us and right behind us, the two cars with the rest of the 20 men in support. Our movement is determined and unstoppable—like a herd of elephants on their way to water in a time of drought.

Epalalyondyamba: 'Today the thunder will catch up with them.'

I am in command of the trackers and Kallie is in command of the front team. We find the tracks and they are still running. Kallie calls the rest of the team to the front. We also start running—rifles in hand, fingers on the safety catch. The next adjustment is to 'A' for automatic. Ten brave police trackers, with two cars in support, ready for action.

The grass has been flattened so recently that the stronger blades are already standing upright. I shout at the other trackers to be careful. In front of us is a big tree. Who knows what is waiting there? Everybody is alert and ready. The first man you see you shoot. But the people who see first are not the trackers. The men with the high vantage points have the advantage. Behind the Brownings is Kallie Calitz, the driver is Job Kakunde and the other gunner is Josef Bernabe.

BOOM—BOOM—BOOM, the shots ring from Kallie's five-0. Bernabe shoots with his machine gun from next to the co-driver's seat. Right in front of me somewhere underneath the tree only metres away lie the insurgents. Kallie's and Bernabe's fire is unrelenting and deadly. Those of us on the ground begin fire-and-movement tactics and shuffle forward. The other two cars have joined us and Hendrik Kwang is also among us on the ground. The cars race through the ambush and those of us on the ground reach the dead—shot to pieces; blood, brains and intestines are everywhere. The results of a gruesome, violent, quick and painless death are evident.

The gunships are cancelled. We finish the job ourselves.

Another day in the Angolan bush.

Night work: spying at Omito, morning follow-up (Onunda, 1985)

We operated south of Ohameva but with no success. All the sources were closed. No information was coming out of anybody. Then one of our informers said he had heard that a number of insurgents were active at one of the *cucas*. But with no further information forthcoming, without a definitive clue, we were looking for the proverbial needle in the haystack. There were so many *cucas* in the Ohameva and surrounding areas that it would be almost impossible to nail anything down.

Our two groups Zulu-4 Sierra and Zulu-4 Echo are working together. Sergeants Engelbrecht and Botes call the two teams together under a big tree in the bush where we often meet. We decide to divide the teams into sections and lay night ambushes on the bigger footpaths. This way we can cover up to ten ambushes in one night. One of the ambushes might just get lucky.

First the plan has to be cleared with Z4 and with Zulu. We do not want to kill our 'brown friends', the army, or the Recces, who might be operateing in the same area. After about 30 minutes the all-clear signal comes. We can operate without fear of the army walking into us.

We split the teams into groups of seven or eight men. I take with me Josef Bernabe, our gunner, with his LMG. Alex Tjuma, Kalevhu, Asser Samuel, Abed, Hausiku and Elias are also in the party.

Before we leave, Hendrik Engelbrecht is issuing orders: "Be careful of the PBs [*plaaslike bevolking*—local population]. Make sure before you fire. We do not want to kill innocent civilians. Be awake, be alert. Your friends will be relying on you."

My section has to lay up on a big footpath south of the Chandelier Road at Omito. We drive with the other cars until our lone car turns off the Chandelier. We continue for a few hundred metres and leave the car in the bush with one of the men to guard it. We silently and slowly walk up to a bend in the track where we will stage the ambush.

We settle in for the night. It is dark and begins to rain. Our raincoats and ponchos are not always up to the African rainstorms and we spend a wet and miserable night in the bush. Waiting, but in vain.

At 0400 hours I call two of the men and we crawl up to a kraal. Inside, a an old man is sitting next to a fire. We call him and he invites us into the kraal. The fire is a nice change from the miserable, cold and wet conditions we have been exposed to for the last eight hours. I say to the man we are from SWAPO. We need to make contact with our comrades but do not know where they are.

"You must be careful. Koevoet was here yesterday. They have been around the area for the last few days," he says. "The Casspirs moved yesterday somewhere southeast of here. I suggest you leave things for a day or two and fall in behind them. They will not come back along the same way they left. I know some of your men are operating at Onunda and Oluwayi."

We are still busy talking when the sounds of Casspir engines can suddenly be heard. I hastily inform my two trackers to "run for their lives". We will "meet" later at another place. We run from the kraal and call the rest of the section back to the car. Some of the other cars are already waiting for us— these are the sounds that cut short our spying attempt.

I tell Hendrik Engelbrecht and he decides to leave at once for Onunda. The two teams proceed on separate footpaths to Onunda. The rain has stopped but the ground is soft and all new spoor is easily visible. It does not take Zulu-4 Echo long to pick up the tracks of three VY. The tracks are a mere 30 minutes old. The gunships are put on alert. We bundu-bash and find the tracks. They are *payife-payife*. The two team leaders have a quick meeting; I and two of the other Zulu-4 Sierra trackers join the four Zulu-4 Echo trackers already on the ground.

Initially, the tracks run southwestward but when the insurgents realize we are on their tail they suddenly start to anti-track. They change direction every few hundred metres and it does not take them long to loop back on the tracks.

The front cars are called back. We form an extended line and the instruction for the whole line is to race 200 metres forward, then to slow down and start hunting with flushing fire. The rushing cars might put the insurgents under pressure and hopefully they will show their hand.

The headlong charge has barely gone 100 metres when "Contact! Contact!" sounds over the radio. Botes's five-0 has killed an insurgent. We sweep through the area and soon discover a second fatality. A third insurgent makes a break for it in a northeasterly direction. Both dead insurgents are SWAPO Special Unit members, one being the commander.

We capture one AK with seven magazines, one RPG with eight rockets, backpacks, POMZ mines, a compass, groundsheets, water bottles and a Tokarev pistol. The remaining insurgent has continued his flight but the wet ground makes anti-tracking difficult.

The gunship is called in and with the second forward surge the 20mm gun of the gunship explodes into life. One of the cars is called to investigate and the third of the trio is found dead. It is not yet noon and we are allowed to TB close to Okongo.

All very tired.

A full day's work, followed by a full night in ambush, followed by a morning hunt. But my spying attempt brought us into the right area and we have three heads to count.

A Koevoet team meet up with Unita, somewhere in southern Angola. Unless their uniforms were sponsored, Unita wore a mish-mash of military clothing.
Photo Attie Hattingh

A wounded Koevoet member is carried to a waiting Puma.
Photo Attie Hattingh

Government-built cattle trough near Gcawa, southern Kavangoland, a typical Kavangoland scene.
Photo Kallie Calitz

Regrouping on the Chandelier Road after a successful contact. Sergeant Johan 'Boats' Botes is in front of a convoy consisting of Zulu-4 Echo and Zulu-4 Sierra. Sergeant Rudolf Kamanga is standing on the front Casspir and Sergeant Shorty Kamongo is to the fore on the second.
Photo Kallie Calitz

Constable Hampuru, the only ethnic Bushman, or San, in Zulu-4 Sierra. The team consisted of many ethnic groups but the Bushmen never lasted. Except one man, a brave fighter. *Photo Kallie Calitz*

The legendary Warrant Officer Willie Roux, Zulu-4 Whiskey (or was it Zulu-4 Willie?) and Bravo Company commander, at Rundu. A brave man but always reining in the younger men under his command, his leadership style saved many Koevoet lives. Roux was a loyal supporter of the black members, even long after the war ended.
Photo Kallie Calitz

The founder of combat team Zulu-4 Sierra, Sergent Hendrik Engelbrecht, in lyrical mood. Where he 'liberated' the non-police-issue helmet from is unclear. *Photo Kallie Calitz*

Inspecting a fallen insurgent. Based on the Israeli Galil, the R5, with its potent 5.56mm round, was the South Africans' personal weapon. Light and rugged, its short barrel made it easy to operate in the confined space of a Casspir. *Photo Kallie Calitz*

Retraining. Sergeant Engelbrecht keeps an eye out at the shooting range. Sergeant Shorty Kamongo is on the right. *Photo Kallie Calitz*

Fallen insurgent with RPG rocket launcher. In typical anti-tracking fashion his boots are around his neck. SWAPO insurgents had many opportunities to surrender but most of the time they fought it out to the end. Brave men.
Photo Attie Hattingh

A dead insurgent with his boots around his neck. The patterns of the boot soles have been cut away as an anti-tracking measure. However, Koevoet still tracked them with their bare feet, boots or any other footwear. *Photo Attie Hattingh*

Lunch on a Zulu-4 Sierra patrol. Piet Neethling and Chris Cloete "eating out" ... of cans. *Photo Kallie Calitz*

Front-cut south of Okongo, searching in advance of the rest of the teams. *Photo Kallie Calitz*

Front-cut cars in support of trackers, south of Okongo. *Photo Kallie Calitz*

Warrant Officer Willie Roux and two of his men at dawn. The Casspir's nose reads Z4W1. *Photo Kallie Calitz*

A convoy in eastern Kavangoland. Dense bush and thick sand made it difficult to flush out insurgents, and ideal for ambushing road-users. *Photo Attie Hattingh*

A well, a source of water ... and information. *Photo Kallie Calitz*

Zulu-4 Sierra car commanders, Cassie Carstens, Naas van Zyl and Piet Benade, having some fun. "These boys came here from police stations in South Africa and we had to teach them ... fast." *Photo Piet Benade*

The tranquil garden at Arendsnes. Outside the gates a war was raging. *Photo Piet Benade*

Display of captured weapons inside the Arendsnes operations room. *Photos Piet Benade*

Tools of the trade. Captured explosives and detonator (with plenty of spoor around). *Photo Attie Hattingh*

The store at Arendsnes. *Photo Piet Benade*

Car 4 of Zulu-4 Echo at the gates to Arendsnes base at Rundu. *Photo Piet Benade*

Trackers searching for spoor after it has been lost. SWAPO would often double-back on their own tracks to confuse their pursuers: fresh SWAPO tracks got muddled with very recent Koevoet tracks and the older SWAPO tracks. Here is a typical example of the confusion. The Casspir is facing in the opposite direction to that which the trackers are searching, indicating that spoor has been lost. *Photo Piet Benade*

Chappa Strauss posing on a bridge.
Photo Kallie Calitz

Zulu-4 Sierra founder-leader Sergeant Hendrik 'Hendry' Engelbrecht honing his LMG skills on the shooting range outside Rundu. *Photo Kallie Calitz*

Zulu-4 Sierra and Zulu-4 Echo after a contact on the Chandelier Road. *Photo Kallie Calitz*

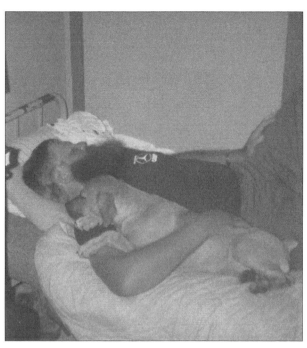

Willem and his dog having a rest at Arendsnes. The warrant officer was a strict disciplinarian who kept a tight grip on his teams, but for animals he had a soft spot. *Photo Kallie Calitz*

Below: A kraal with the flat, featureless terrain of Ovamboland in the background. *Photo Kallie Calitz*

Although Koevoet was often criticized for undermining the army's hearts-and-minds campaign, teams did much good among the locals, here seen receiving medicines from a Koevoet medic. *Photo Kallie Calitz*

A Casspir on a patrol in western Kavangoland. *Photo Kallie Calitz*

Bushmen in southern Kavangoland.
Photo Kallie Calitz

Below: Constable Johan van Heerden and Zulu-4 Sierra members on their way to possible enemy tracks. The local population was in most cases more than willing to help; here two boys assist the Koevoet men.
Photo Kallie Calitz

A weapons cache recovered at Okadidiya in December 1986. "We were quick but not quick enough; a POMZ from this cache later killed one of our men. I would stand up unscathed after the explosion."
Photo Willie Roux

Below: Firepower and mobility were two factors critical to the success of the unit. This car is fitted with twin .30-calibre Browning machine guns. *Photo Kallie Calitz*

A burned-out Casspir after it detonated a POMZ anti-personnel mine; nobody was injured but the car had to be replaced. The war was far from a one-sided affair. Most PLAN members were committed soldiers who did not run from a fight. *Photo Kallie Calitz*

Sergeant Rudolf Kamanga, an exceptional tracker and a true warrior, with members of Zulu-4 Sierra behind him. *Photo Kallie Calitz*

Enough supplies for a week: a loaded Blesbok support vehicle. *Photo Kallie Calitz*

Below: An Alouette III gunship waiting to refuel, Kavangoland, 1986. *Photo Kallie Calitz*

PLAN's own goals
(Eheke and Oshana Shanalama, southern Angola, 1985)

About two weeks after the army followed five tracks near Eheke, we are on our way from another follow-up in the same area. At one road, our car number 2 picks up five tracks. Our team gets together and starts following them. The tracks are fresh: yesterday afternoon's. We move ahead and find the place where they slept. Now we know we are about five hours behind them. But we are quick and the tracks are easy to follow. After about five kilometres, the group of insurgents breaks up and we decide to follow two of them moving in a southeasterly direction. The tracks are now only about two hours old.

For this operation Lieutenant Lukas Koen is in command at the operations room at Eenhana. He decides to send Mike-4 Hotel to us. The insurgents know we are behind them and they take off their boots and start anti-tracking. Suddenly our tracking becomes very slow. About three kilometres from us, on their way to us, the trackers of Mike-4 Hotel pick up three tracks—and the fugitives are running.

The gunship that has to come to us is taken away and sent to the more recent tracks found by Mike-4 Hotel. But Mike-4 Hotel's follow-up also comes to a standstill—helicopter and all. We continue and bit by bit piece the puzzle together. Fresh tracks! Five minutes old; the backpacks have been abandoned and they are running. We get our gunship back and about 200 metres farther on we find two PLAN insurgents in a futile ambush position where they are promptly killed.

Lieutenant Koen is always a man of action and when the gunship lands he gets out. We pull the cars up next to the Blesbok and refill the tanks from drums in the back. We have a prayer parade in the bush, someone takes a photo and the gunship with the operational commander flies back to Eenhana. We make a TB in the late afternoon, examine the cars, fix punctured tyres and go to bed early. It has been a busy day in Angola.

Early the next morning, after the usual prayers, we look for the lost Mike-4 Hotel tracks of yesterday, but with no success. We move on toward the Oshana Shanadjili area. We find two sets of tracks. We follow them in a westerly direction to a well. At the well we lose them. There are too many other tracks. After a struggle we find them again some distance away. The area is now heavily overgrown with thick bush. We find the place where they have eaten—pumpkin and milk.

We first think the fluid is water but the reaction of the flies tells another story. Once again we have disrupted a SWAPO lunch; where they abandoned their lunch there are now running tracks.

Sergeant Engelbrecht calls the gunships at Eenhana. Lieutenant Koen sends Mike-4 Echo to help. Their team only has three cars because one of their cars (Sergeant Botes's) detonated a mine two days earlier, also on their way to us. Sergeant Mossie Mostert is now in charge of 4 Echo. When Mike-4 Echo is within a few hundred metres of us, there is once again a huge explosion. Yet again, a Mike-4 Echo car has detonated a landmine on their way to us! Their only remaining vehicles are the Blesbok and two cars. Sergeant Mostert decides to make the best of a bad situation. At his damaged car he leaves one car behind with the Blesbok as protection for the wounded. Sampie Potgieter's car is sent to assist us. A recovery team is sent from Eenhana to help Mike-4 Echo back across the border. Sampie joins us.

By now, the gunship has joined us and minutes later the gunner opens up. He says it is a warning shot at a suspicious person to our front. Sampie and I charge to the front as the other cars stay on the tracks. The gunship fires around the suspicious person to let him know he is covered but he is not as yet the target—unless he tries something stupid. With the Casspirs coming closer, the insurgent grabs an RPG-7 that he has dropped in the bush and fires a rocket at the cars. He misses. The pilot is screaming into the radio not to shoot at him. The gunship peppers the area where the other RPG rockets should be and forces the insurgent to stop shooting. We are just a few metres from the insurgent and everybody shouts at him to give up. He cannot do much more. He is in a corner. But he refuses to give up. He takes a Tokarev pistol from his belt, presses the muzzle to his head and shoots himself.

Well, we did try.

Head money again, and this time we didn't have to do the shooting. At Okinawa the Japanese put the fear of death into the local population so much so that hundreds jumped from the cliffs rather than surrender to the Americans. SWAPO did the same with its members—their political commissars scared them witless about our reputation. Do anything but do not be taken alive by Koevoet.

We turn around and in the dark return to Mossie and his crippled team. A recovery team including two army Buffels has joined them. We form a TB and sleep the last few hours of darkness. The army are so militarily correct: we let them do the guard duty and we enjoy a good night's rest.

The next morning we leave Mossie and his damaged Casspir to the recovery team and press on with the operation. The wounded are also sent back with the army. The two remaining Casspirs and the Blesbok of Mike-4 Echo come with us. We will finish today. It has been a hard but successful two weeks. We carry on to Oshana Shanalama.

For old times' sake we pick up a new set of enemy tracks. They are two hours old, but are heading north and it does not take us long to reach the 'zero line'—the northernmost point at which we can operate in Angola. The tracks are now about five minutes old. They are so fresh that the insurgent has already thrown away his backpack and equipment. Hendrik asks for air support but the ops room at Zulu 2 refuses. We have to turn around.

We have an urgent meeting. We are going to break the rules. Sergeant Engelbrecht and the two Blesboks will turn around, as per instructions. The other four cars will proceed another few kilometres north and then also turn around. After about 90 minutes we get to a large open plain. We will turn around here. The next moment a burst of AK-47 fire erupts next to us. Everybody hits the deck. A trap!

"Contact! Contact!"

But nothing further happens.

Thirty metres to the left of the cars we find the insurgent. He has shot himself with three shots from his AK.

Another head, another rifle.

We turn around and find Sergeant Engelbrecht and the Blesboks at the border. We TB at Elundu and the next afternoon are back at Arendsnes. 4-Echo has had two of its cars blown up by landmines and we count two insurgents who shot themselves.

Red flags and camouflage trousers on a stick

At times, the propaganda targeted against Koevoet was very bad. So bad that we were accused of many things that we never did. We would shoot PLAN insurgents in a firefight just to hear later that we had shot innocent people. The fact that they were wearing camouflage uniforms and were carrying automatic weapons was conveniently forgotten. It was completely ignored. We had to do something to protect ourselves against the propaganda—and at the same time intimidate SWAPO sympathizers.

We never used AK-47s in the time I was with Koevoet. We wore the standard SWAPOLCOIN and SAP camouflage uniforms, and later the khaki-tan uniforms. We were clearly distinguishable from any other force—especially the insurgents.

After every contact we would fasten a red flag to a stick on the command car. We would take the insurgents' clothes and fasten them to sticks as well. The dead insurgents would be strapped to the mudguards of the cars. Then we would drive past the huts and kraals, brandishing the AKs, SKSs and RPGs above our heads on top of the Casspirs.

There could be no doubt as to who we had shot. Definitely not innocents. It would also show the SWAPO sympathizers that they too were not immune to death.

Many of the photos of fallen insurgents show them only in their underwear. Now you know why: their camouflage uniforms were blowing in the breeze, protecting our reputation.

Know your enemy! (Okongo, 1985)

Bravo Company of Zulu 4 consisted of just three teams in early 1985—Zulu-4 Echo, Zulu-4 Sierra and Zulu-4 Whiskey. Bravo Company was under Warrant Officer Willie Roux; we launched most of our patrols from the base of the Security Police 2-1 Echo at Okatope and Okongo.

One morning we leave Okongo after the usual prayer parade. The patrol moves south. We arrive at a kraal and a girl tells us that ten heavily armed insurgents passed through there the previous evening. The insurgents told her that she had to tell the security forces about them. They were not scared. She shows us the tracks on a footpath.

Hendrik Engelbrecht calls Sergeant Botes of Zulu-4 Echo for help. The gunships are placed on standby and we start following the spoor in a southeasterly direction. Sergeant Botes calls for us to stop and wait for him. He thinks it is too dangerous for a single team to advance. He feels we will probably drive right into a huge ambush. It is better to have reinforcements. He calls the security base at Okongo for backup.

Sergeant Sampie is also in this group; he is new but has a lot of combat experience. He was previously with 32 Battalion. The respected Warrant Officer Clemens, Kallie Calitz and Mossie Mostert are the commanders of the other Zulu-4 Sierra cars.

Botes is a man with wide experience. Hendrik Engelbrecht is a more-than-able warrior who loves working on foot. Between them, all these men have plenty of experience, and they are brave men. They are not going to be intimidated by SWAPO. The ten SWAPO insurgents are in for a tough time.

We start the follow-up and the ten bombshell into two groups of five. We decide to go after one group and keep our options open regarding the other five. The insurgents lose direction; as an anti-tracking technique they are walking around in circles. They go over our tracks and we go over theirs.

Sergeant Botes tells Hendrik Engelbrecht to take over control of the trackers. He will stay in command of the tactics and communication. He calls the gunships. The gunships arrive and start to search by fire. They fire bursts about 100 metres in front of us into possible ambush positions. If there is no reaction they move onto a new target, flushing SWAPO out.

The bush opens up a bit.

When we straighten the line to adjust to the more open bush, Hendrik suddenly yells, "Contact! Contact! Zulu-4 Sierra, contact!"

The gunships also spot the movement and we all simultaneously start firing at the insurgents.

The gunships are forced to stop firing. We are too close to the enemy. The cars charge through the ambush position as we on the ground run to get out of the way of the wheels. Three insurgents die and two are wounded. We retrieve the backpacks and rifles of all five.

When we interrogate the wounded, we hear that they have never heard of us! They know about the army and the police but not Koevoet. It seems there is a gap in the SWAPO training in Lubango in Angola. Maybe SWAPO deliberately does not tell their recruits about us. If they knew they were facing Koevoet, they would have run away or have shot themselves. We know both these tactics.

We leave the contact area, leave the other five for the next day and go to sleep at 2-1 Echo at Okongo.

To this day the ignorance of these two insurgents leaves me astounded. Not knowing about Koevoet! It was hard to believe and still is.

But that is the way it was.

You do not scare us

A Koevoet follow-up operation was an act of intimidation. The diesel engines of our cars would announce our intent. The sound of the engines could be heard from afar in the bush.

When we were tracking it was a noisy affair. We sang and shouted—war cries. "*Komesho-Koevoet. Komesho-Koevoet*," we would shout the whole day—Forward Koevoet, Forward Koevoet.

There were days when we were hurt by POMZs and other mines. This motivated us even more. We would shout louder and move forward. If we encountered one of our teams who had lost someone through a wound or who had tripped a landmine, we were not intimidated. Wounded Koevoet men and anti-personnel mines only made us more determined. We had a score to settle.

We indicated the tracks with a short stick in one hand; in the other hand we carried an R5 rifle. Around the waist we carried a few extra magazines and hand grenades. The rest of the firepower came from the cars. The firepower was heavily on our side.

Sometimes we were so motivated that we would leave the cars behind when they overheated in the hot African sun. By the time they caught up with us, we had already made contact and would have a dead insurgent or a prisoner.

We would sing, "You owe us no mercy, you must hear us today, we are angry, today is your last day." This song caused many an insurgent to surrender in terror. They knew we were on their heels and that they would pay.

Usually we were kept in the loop over the radio concerning the well-being of our wounded. It was part of our work. As policemen, we made the ultimate sacrifice if it was necessary. Blood never put us off; it made us more determined.

Kavango sweep operation (1985)

In 1985 there was an increase in insurgent activity in the border area. We were not allowed to operate in Angola in 1984, as a Joint Monitoring Commission (JMC) had been set up between South Africa and Angola. The JMC was established to make sure SWAPO stayed away from the border region, however, it gave SWAPO an opening: they started moving into places where they had previously been denied access. And they started making themselves heard in the Kavango again. It was time to root them out once and for all.

With 16 teams in action, we would pursue them from all corners for three weeks. The eight Kavango teams would be supported by eight teams from Oshakati. Two teams from the Kavango and two teams from Ovamboland would work together in each company. This gave us four 'companies'.

The companies would each take one of the four compass directions. In our temporary company, we were linked with Zulu November. The Zulu 4 team leader was Hendrik Engelbrecht, with Kallie Calitz and Warrant Officer Clemens Kambureka as the other senior team leaders. I was the senior tracker in car 1 with Hendrik Engelbrecht.

We move in the direction of Okawe, and it doesn't take long before Zulu November picks up three tracks. We move closer and join them. The tracks are about two hours old. The gunships are 20 minutes away, on standby at Sector 20 army headquarters at Rundu. The army also has two Buffels in the area, busy with their own sweep operation.

We have been following the tracks for about two hours, when the insurgents start running. Zulu November calls in the gunships. But the sun is going down and even with helicopter support we cannot find them. At dusk the helicopters return and we form a TB.

Early the next morning, we follow the tracks to a tarred road. You cannot look for tracks on a tarred road, so we interrogate the locals; I and another tracker question two boys. They say the insurgents headed in a westerly direction early that morning before it got light.

On the radio we hear that Zulu Golf is now following three tracks. The tracks are about ten kilometres away and about 20 to 30 minutes old. The gunships are sent in and within an hour the situation is brought to a head when a gunship and Zulu Golf are involved in a skirmish with the three insurgents. All three die. We are about four kilometres away and hear the fight.

We'd run them ragged; however, if they stayed on the tar road they would have escaped. A deadly mistake.

We go back to Arendsnes, load up with fresh water and food and leave for the Nepara area to work there. We sleep in a TB close to the army base near Musese and the next morning we drive to Yinsu. We patrol to Omungomba and later pick up four tracks left from the previous evening.

We follow the tracks in a southwesterly direction to the Silikunga area. We call in the gunships. There are now several teams involved in the operation. One of the teams cuts across the tracks toward the front, and with the help of a gunship a contact ensues within hearing distance. Of course we are disappointed that it's not us, but we're all on the same side.

Seven heads— but no money for us.

After three weeks, SWAPO is stirred and shaken. The survivors flee to safer areas and the Kavango is quiet again.

Blue on blue
(Omuramba Ekuli, western Kavangoland, 1985)

We obtain information from one of our informants that a group of six PLAN insurgents is operating in the area of Omuramba Ekuli in western Kavango. They are getting help from a local teacher who is supplying them with food and money. Hendrik Engelbrecht, Kallie Calitz, Rudolf Kamanga and I have a meeting to discuss the situation; we have to investigate the information. We decide to split up into sections and lay ambushes on the bigger footpaths.

The six insurgents are comfortable and complacent, often visiting the teacher's kraal during the day, usually around 1500 hours. We will lay an ambush at the kraal with two sections. One section will sneak up against the kraal to act as a killer group, the other will block the escape route should the first section fail to neutralize the enemy immediately.

We walk to the kraal. About three kilometres from it we form a TB, as we are early. At about 1400 hours we decide to move in. There are seven of us in the section: myself, Josef Bernabe, who is my second in command, and five other men. Two of them carry small radios. One of the five is a young Himba named Uliwa Tjimbwa. I am the only one who understands what he says and he carries one radio, so I want him near me. The Kavango and Herero languages are very different but I understand a bit of Herero. We each carry battle webbing with magazines and two water bottles. Josef Bernabe carries the LMG.

We move out, with the other section some distance away from us. We decide to wait up about 500 metres from the kraal, as we were too fast. We rest in the shade of a big tree for a while. I take out a can of fruit from my webbing and have an afternoon snack.

While we are lying up silently under the tree, unbeknown to us there are people on our tracks. While we were closing in on the kraal, a section from Zulu-4 Echo had spotted us. They had obtained the same information from their own informants and were also on their way to confront the same six insurgents—without letting us know, and unaware that we were already near the target.

Now they are moving toward us and see seven men. Victor Yankee! It must be! They have already deployed in formation and are sneaking up on us, to get as near as possible before opening fire. The young Himba and Asser Samuel are on guard when Tjimbwa sees armed men approaching. He whispers to Samuel, but Samuel does not understand him. It is only when I follow the direction in which his arm is pointed that I realize we are on the point of being attacked. We are the prey! They are wearing camouflage uniforms; when SWAPO uniforms are dirty they look no different from ours. They are about 200 metres from us when I see one of the enemy is white: Sergeant Mostert!

I tell everybody to invert their bush hats immediately so that the bright dayglow strip is visible. SWAPO do not have that kind of thing. I hold the orange side of my bush hat in their direction and slowly stand up. Mossie Mostert sees who it is and he commands his section to stop. He also gets up. The situation is defused.

It was very, very close.

We meet halfway and realize we are on the way to the same target. We work together and make ready for a night ambush on the footpath; but that night the six do not come. The next morning we go back to Zulu 4.

We first say a prayer of thanks. We very nearly shot each other one afternoon in western Kavangoland in 1985.

A Koevoet blunders, a team pays
(Dikweya Omuramba, winter 1985)

The difference between us and the insurgents regarding the local population was simple—we were held accountable. It is true that there were cases where unlawful things took place. However, we had a strict code of conduct. SWAPO could do as they pleased; the only people they were accountable to were us!

We are back at Arendsnes. We have returned from a patrol in the western Kavango, in the Dikweya Omuramba area. While we are busy unpacking everything from the cars and cleaning up after the patrol, we are called to the parade ground.

Lieutenant Lukas Koen calls out an identification number of a Casspir. It is one of ours—number 4. Next to the parade ground stands a man from one of the kraals which we have recently visited. One of the trackers of Casspir number 4 torched this man's *mahango* field. The man duly identifies the policeman.

Now we have to decide what to do. All the senior members, black and white, quickly form an impromptu disciplinary committee, with Lukas Koen as the chairman. It is decided that the whole team will have to contribute financially so *mahango* meal can be purchased as compensation for the man. Each member will pay out R75; the total comes to R3,000—a lot of money in Kavangoland, and for us especially. The money is soon collected and we send the Blesbok to buy 20 bags of *mahango* meal as well as tinned food and other stuff. The local headman accompanies us as a witness when we deliver the food to the kraal.

Our disciplinary committees were serious affairs. If you were guilty, the sjambok (a short hide whip) was the verdict. Either that or you were charged and you took your chances with the official punishment: either jail or dishonourable discharge from the unit. Few opted for the official charges.

Unfortunately, this information was never disseminated to the public. If

SWAPO screamed about a *mahango* patch that had been flattened, or kraal walls that had been damaged, or of a rape or assault commited, there were enough bleeding hearts out there only too willing to spread the communist gospel. Nobody ever really looked for the truth.

As a result, we were in a bad situation when the war was over.

Bad things happened a few times, but in all the time I was with Koevoet there was never a rape while we were on patrol. The white members were relentless about it. To slap someone about a bit was okay, but sexual violations were out.

That was one rule that was strictly enforced.

Two turned insurgents and a hard-praying Christian (1985)

It was often said that we were responsible for the large-scale slaughter of SWAPO members when we captured them.

A PLAN commander by the name of John Sam was operating at Omuramba Nongena. One day, we get information from Zulu-4 Echo that they are following three VY tracks in the area of Silikunga and the tracks are heading in the direction of Lihaha. We have to go and help; we are at Nepara. While we are on the way, the insurgents cross the dirt road and we drive along the Chandelier Road until we cut the tracks and those of Zulu-4 Echo. After a few kilometres, we reach Zulu-4 Echo.

The tracks are now running tracks, and they are moving in circles. We ask for a gunship but none is available. The air force sends a spotter plane. There are a few directions in which they could run; the most probable is directly north to Angola. In the dense bush we lose the tracks; however, they won't stay here—they have to get away.

At 202 Battalion in Rundu, an army major is in command. We don't often work with the army unless we are sure they will finish the job. However, this time, Hendrik Engelbrecht contacts nine-zero, the operations room at 202, who agrees to send two platoons to secure the area around Odela.

The insurgents have been in the area for some time and have changed their camouflage uniforms for civilian clothes We pick up the tracks again and, just as we thought, they are heading for the border. Now the army has to do their thing. We make quick progress and it does not take us long to drive into one of the army's ambushes—with the spoor running right past them!

It is impossible that they could have missed them!

After some questioning, the platoon leader says the only thing that passed them was a herd of cattle with three cattle herders. I go back to the tracks and show the sergeant—he does not believe us.

I take two of my trackers, the army sergeant and two of his troops and start following the tracks. About 200 metres from the ambush position we find a half-set POMZ. I call the cars and we start on the tracks again—but they disappear because someone has sent a herd of cattle over them. They are now well and truly gone, and our relations with the army do not improve.

Later we caught John Sam. He would tell us that it was he who escaped that day. He joined us and became a loyal and fearless fighter. He was also an important source of information. He knew a lot and was trained in the USSR and Libya. He had been a senior PLAN commander and knew intimately the operational thought patterns and modus operandi of SWAPO. We fetched his wife and children and gave him a house at Rundu. He would later become an important member of the unit. Unfortunately, he died in a POMZ incident.

John Sam did much to change perceptions about Koevoet. He would go out in the rural areas to show to the people that he had survived Koevoet. At his funeral there were many tears.

One day, Sergeant du Toit of Zulu Quebec captured an insurgent. Inside his jacket was a Bible, with several passages underlined.

Toitjie asked: "What do you as a communist know about the Bible?"

"I am a born-again Christian, sir."

"What! This is the communist way to undermine good Christians!"

"No, sir. I have accepted Christ as my saviour," says the KG (*krygsgevangene*—prisoner of war) in perfect English.

"Well, there is only one way to know for sure. You must pray for us!" du Toit says.

The insurgent kneels and prays for about ten minutes. He wants to make sure that the white Koevoet sergeant knows he knows how to pray! This insurgent also joined Koevoet. For him, as well as others, the other side turned out not to be so bad. We also prayed, something SWAPO's Soviet and German trainers did not do.

After all, we knew mercy.

Not what our captives expected.

Sorrow and tears (1986)

A war never goes smoothly: there are times of victory and times of defeat, times of success and times of compassion, times of tragedy and times of setback. The year 1986 was one of great disappointment for us, a year when it seemed that all the disasters had conspired at the same time for Zulu-4 Sierra. Death, wounds and landmines were our companions that year.

First, Sergeant Kallie Calitz's Casspir hit a POMZ. There were many wounded. Just after that, my own Casspir, number 2, also hit a landmine, then our Blesbok, which was completely destroyed. It was our support vehicle and carried all our supplies—food, extra diesel, helicopter fuel, sleeping bags and other non-first-line items. When the landmine exploded the drums of helicopter fuel on the back caught alight. The driver and the gunner were able to get out and take the machine gun off before the whole vehicle was engulfed in flames. The fire was ferocious and as a result we could not rescue anything but the machine gun. We went back to our base. We got a new Blesbok, equipped it at the stores and within an hour were back on patrol. We were the best team in the Kavango in 1986. SWAPO were waiting for us—so that they could begin.

Every team had its high and low days. The war was waiting for Zulu-4 Juliet in 1985. Wherever they went, they hit a contact. They walked into new PLAN area commanders in the Kavango more than once. They caught them every time. Then the next one came and they also captured him. SWAPO must have thought that Zulu-4 Juliet had appointments with their new area commanders.

Zulu-4 Echo would have their hour of glory in 1987 when they gave SWAPO hell.

One time, Zulu-4 Hotel was conducting a low-key, quiet follow-up. They left their vehicles behind the hot tracks and followed the PLAN members on foot. SWAPO was not aware of the follow-up. Zulu-4 Hotel was following five tracks and by the time the gunship arrived there were already five dead in the Kavango scrub. The enemy was taken totally by surprise with the silent tactics, which became a successful tactic in many subsequent operations.

For Zulu-4 Sierra 1986 would be a year of sorrow and tears. In contrast to what was being spread by the communist propaganda machine, those of us in Koevoet were mainly rural people accustomed to peace and togetherness. We were sucked into a situation of blood and violence through circumstances beyond our control. We had to make a choice where we stood. Innocent civilians were constantly being intimidated by SWAPO. As policemen, we could not stand by and let this happen. Our system was poles apart from what the Cubans and Russians were teaching SWAPO. We opposed communism and paid in blood for a conflict that had its origins in Moscow.

When our friend Constable Blasius Kutenda died in 1984, two teams attended his funeral: Zulu-4 Sierra and Zulu-4 Whiskey. It was a funeral filled with tears. His mother, his younger sister, all of us; we were angry and fed up. The war had hurt us. Kutenda's mother cried. It was tragic. She only had two children, her son and daughter. Now only the daughter was left, her only son was dead. She was very emotional and wanted to know how it could happen that a young, healthy man could leave them and come back dead. We had to calm her down and console her. We explained to her that the others who had been in the contact with him were still in hospital and that we did not know if they would make it.

That was war.

But there were a lot more dead among SWAPO than us; our work was dangerous; we were exposed to ambushes, landmines and firefights. Unfortunately, Blasius was one of those who died on our side.

I was in the same Casspir as Sergeant Naas van Zyl the day he died in 1988. Naas was a brave man and we respected each other. When a man dies who has worked alongside you every day, it is a huge blow. You cannot simply turn the page and carry on with your life. Everybody is involved. His blood was on my hands as I tried to help him. But policemen are also hard men; we hide it but our hearts weep. I cried a lot for Naas.

An army camper's knowledge of tracking (1986)

The police and the army were always at odds over where our responsibilities began and ended. When I started with Koevoet we could move to the 'zero line' inside Angola. That meant we had a free hand to hunt SWAPO deep into that country. It helped our success rate.

When we were following tracks, we could chase SWAPO for a longer distance. Then the army came and changed things. We could pursue tracks up to the border and then the army would take over. It was a huge mistake which in fact saved may SWAPO lives.

The army sent in a bunch of 'campers', part-time, or territorial, soldiers who'd completed their national service and were doing call-ups, or camps. They were simply South African civilians who'd swapped their civilian clothes for army browns. They did not have a clue about tracking or following tracks. It was a total waste of time and effort.

In one case, an army section with a Buffel picked up tracks and started following them. When we asked them how many tracks there were, they answered twelve. When we got there, there were forty. Mercifully for them, SWAPO had not set an ambush. All ten in the army section would have been annihilated.

But things changed quickly in the operational area.

Before long, we were back in Angola.

A rainy day or two in Angola (February 1986)

We cross the Jati, a strip of deforested land about 60 metres wide that serves as the border, between beacons 28 and 29 and drive into Angola. We head in the direction of Onalumono, and from there north to Oshana Shanandjili. The bush starts getting very dense and overgrown and we move north very slowly. By 1200 hours we find four tracks and we start to follow them. The insurgents know we are behind them and start anti-tracking tactics. It does not take long before they get rid of their equipment. We find backpacks hidden in the bush. A while later, we make contact and in the firefight two of them die.

It is too late to continue and we form a TB in the dense bush. The next morning, we follow the tracks of the other two. We are now in the same area where four other teams shot 37 PLAN members a while back, during another follow-up. Dangerous country.

Then it starts raining, and rain and tracking are not good partners. We lose the tracks. The next day, we arrive in the Omemba area where we find Zulu-4 Whiskey. They have information and are searching a kraal, but while they are busy inside, we find the tracks of four suspected PLAN members some distance off. It starts to rain again, but we get enough information from the leaves, grass and mud to follow the tracks.

Later that afternoon, we make contact when an RPG is fired at one of the cars. We find the weapon but the operator is gone. The rain is his salvation. It is raining so hard now that his tracks are obliterated.

It is late. We again form a TB in the rain; another wet night in the Angolan bush. Zulu-4 Echo joins us. The next morning, Zulu-4 Echo moves in the direction of yesterday's tracks. But our water ration is depleted and there are no tracks to follow owing to yesterday's rain. We turn the noses of the cars south toward Rundu. The Kavango commander, Captain—later Major—Josie Engelbrecht, who was visiting his teams in the bush, is also there. He climbs into one of our cars, and our team goes back to Arendsnes.

Sweep operation (southern Angola, 18 February 1986)

We cross the Jati at beacon 29, into Angola. North and then northwest to Eheke, the SWAPO base that was destroyed by the Recces and 32 Battalion a few years earlier—at great loss. Then farther north to Oshana Shanandjili, where we form a temporary base.

Early the next morning, we move onward and it does not take long before we find many tracks near Omemba—tracks made by boots. The amount of tracks is an indication that SWAPO are not there just for the day; they have a permanent base somewhere nearby.

Sergeant Hendrik Engelbrecht reports the find to Zulu 2 and Major Willem Fouché in the operations room at Eenhana places air support on immediate alert. Major Fouché's orders are clear: if you find them, attack. We are joined by two other teams—Zulu-4 Echo and Zulu-4 Whiskey. It is not long before we make contact. The SWAPO group is big, but their bravery lets them down. They bombshell into groups of three and five after a furious firefight. We are on their tracks the whole day but when the dark comes it is too dangerous to continue.

Tomorrow is another day. During the night there is a huge thunderstorm and all the tracks are washed away.

The next morning, we make our way to a well in the area to get water. Sergeant Mossie Mostert and his team go back to where we had the contact yesterday. He searches the area and identifies five new tracks and the tracks show they are running—fresh. He contacts the rest of us and three teams start following the tracks. Once more, I am the tracker up front. The tracks are heading south. We call in the gunships which have 28 minutes' flying time to reach us. All the trackers from all the teams are now tracking in front of the cars. I am in the lead group, with many of the other trackers and their supporters around me. Some are looking for tracks, while others scan the grass for booby traps and the bush for hidden ambushes.

Then there is a hellish explosion next to me. My side, back and lower legs burn as if I have been stung by a thousand wasps. I fall to the ground with around 14 others. One of the other trackers has activated a POMZ anti-personnel mine. A POMZ mine is sometimes set at knee or hip height and then explodes above ground, causing havoc. Legs, torsos, arms and eyes are all in danger.

It is a dark day.

One gunship is transformed into an ambulance and takes the badly wounded men away. There are five of us seriously wounded, but my wounds first have to be stabilized. They leave me there to wait for the Puma.

SWAPO is close and Sergeant Mossie Mostert sweeps ahead with typical Koevoet aggression. The other gunship provides support. I am lying near the Blesbok support vehicle and can hear the group following SWAPO, making contact as they go. In the meantime, Sergeant Hendrik Engelbrecht arrives. He is also a medic.

He gives us injections for the pain and talks softly: "Don't worry, the giant is on the way. You will all be fine."

The Puma comes to pick us up and takes us to the large air force base at Ondangwa. We are transferred to an aeroplane and flown to 1 Military Hospital in Pretoria.

I spend six months in hospital. A piece of shrapnel has gone right through my leg just below the knee. I have shrapnel in both legs and in my back. One large piece in my back has to be left there; it is too near the nerves in my spine—I could lose the use of my legs.

The time in the hospital was bad. Koevoet regulations state that you do not get paid if you are not operational.

I was not paid for six months.

The piece of shrapnel left in my back would cause problems in the future. In November 2003 my legs gave way under me. Afterwards, I was confined to a wheelchair.

No remuneration or police pension would follow.

Watermelon thieves
(Omangundu, southern Ovamboland, September 1986)

We search far and wide for PLAN. From Arendsnes, south to the boundaries of the white farms at Mankete, then farther, past Tsumeb to Namatuni, the border between Ovamboland and the Tsumeb mining area. We sleep there. It has been a long day and the Casspirs are not built for comfort. The next morning we leave, heading west for Okatope.

We lost most of our white leaders in 1986. Most of them resigned or asked to be transferred back to South Africa, or contracts had expired and they were in search of greener pastures and new challenges. Some of them had been with the unit for a long time and felt that they had used up their quota of luck. To stand behind a machine gun in the turret of a Casspir was one of the most dangerous jobs. More gunners were wounded and killed than anybody else. When we hit a contact the white members were the biggest target, because mostly they were behind the guns and cannons.

It is Kallie Calitz's last month with Koevoet.

At Okatope we question the local population thoroughly and the information we obtain drives us on to Omangundu. Here we find a set of tracks. I am on the ground and lead the tracking. It is *mahango* harvesting season and there are ripe plants everywhere. At a kraal I climb over a pole fence and find an opening between the *mahango* where people have been sitting, helping themselves to the watermelons that grow in abundance among the *mahango*. I whistle and the other trackers come to investigate my call. We start looking around and there in the watermelon patch between the *mahango* we find the tracks.

Not one, but five VY.

The follow-up winds into full swing. In front, cars 2 and 4 are front-cutting. I am following the tracks with Kallie and car 1, but my legs are dragging; I cannot keep up. Kasinda nearly drives over me with the car. Kallie sees this and takes me off the tracks. I have just been discharged from hospital in

Pretoria after the POMZ incident. Maybe my recuperation had been too slow for me to try and run up front. Kallie's judgement most probably saved me from a worse incident. The driver of a Casspir cannot see directly in front of the nose and wheels. Accidents were commonplace if you were not alert. I have seen what a man looks like who has been crushed under a Casspir. I didn't want it to happen to me. I spend the rest of the follow-up in the car.

I reluctantly climb into car number 1 with Kallie and explain the situation to him. The tracks are three days old, but clear. We have to send the front tracking cars farther ahead to go and question the local population.

He does it, and it works.

At a kraal some distance ahead they obtain information from an angry old woman. "They were here, five of them, and they were aggressive. They took my children's food and drank all the milk. They threatened me and told me that if we gave away their presence to the security forces, they would come back for us. They will come and kill me. These are bad people."

She takes the trackers to the goat kraal and shows them where the insurgents slept the previous night.

The cars tracking in front call us up. When we get to the kraal we initially cannot find the tracks. The insurgents have anti-tracked. We search 360 degrees and car number 3 finds them. All five insurgents were still together when they left the kraal. The tracks are just four hours old.

Kallie calls Zulu-1 Zero, the Koevoet support base at Ongwediva in Ovamboland, where there is also a helicopter support area.

"Zulu-1 Zero, Zulu-1 Zero, Zulu-4 Sierra."

"Send 4-Sierra" the answer comes from the radio room in Ongwediva.

"Ja, this is Zulu-4 Sierra. Five Victor Yankees moving direction whiskey. Golf Sierra can stand by, channel 16, white phos."

"Zulu-1 Zero. Golf Sierra standing by. 18 minutes' reaction time."

We follow the tracks for about an hour when we notice that the insurgents are not walking any more, but running. Our follow-up is not a secret any more.

Kallie contacts Zulu-4 Whiskey, another one of the teams operating nearby. They are on their way.

The Casspir Kallie and I are using punctures a tyre. For those of us who work with a Casspir every day, changing a tyre takes five minutes. We are always prepared for it. We carry wooden blocks on the back of the Blesbok to stop the jack from sinking into the sand; every man knows what to do. The blocks come off and are placed under the differential and then the jack (which can take 12 tonnes) is placed on the blocks. The 12 bolts are loosened and the heavy spare wheel on top of the Casspir comes down. The wheel is changed and the 12 bolts are refastened. The damaged wheel goes back on the Blesbok with the wooden blocks.

During the few minutes that it takes us to change the wheel Zulu-4 Whiskey catches up with us. We carry on, but shortly the insurgents bombshell into one, two and two. Warrant Officer Willie Roux from Zulu-4 Whiskey sends one car on the spoor of the single insurgent. We take two, and Zulu-4 Whiskey follows the other two.

About 200 metres after they had bombshelled, my driver shouts, "Contact, contact, in front! 200 metres, twelve o'clock!"

From about 200 metres, an insurgent fires an RPG-7 at us. The projectile comes fast, barely misses and detonates somewhere behind us in the bush. It is a near miss. He fires another one but mercifully the moment is too big for him. Maybe the man needs big-match temperament. Luckily, he does not have it. The second projectile also misses and flies over our heads.

Kallie sits behind the five-0 and fires with all he has at the insurgent. "I've got one!" he shouts. He sees more movement in the bush. He fires without stopping and then shouts: "I've got another one!"

Meanwhile, the gunship arrives. I throw smoke to identify our position, and the gunship also fires a burst or two into the area of the contact.

A few hundred metres from us, the sounds of another contact are also reverberating: R5s, five-0s, LMGs and AK-47s. The gunship moves off and before long the cannon and machine guns of the gunship are also heard.

A minute later and the fight between Zulu-4 Whiskey and the two insurgents is a thing of the past. Another two dead PLAN members.

One left.

The action shifts to the single car following the individual spoor. Car number 3 of Zulu-4 Whiskey is already calling us to come and help. The insurgent is very close by. We climb back in the cars and on the way to the lone car waiting in the bush, we pass a young man who looks like a cattle herder

One of the trackers asks the boy if he had seen a person with a rifle.

"No, nobody" comes the reply.

But the driver screams through the hatch "It's him. It's him!"

The insurgent has got rid of his boots and donned a tracksuit over his camouflage uniform. The trackers yank open the tracksuit top—and lo and behold!—there is the camouflage uniform. They back-track his spoor and find his rifle and equipment.

Of the watermelon thieves, four are dead and one has been captured.

SWAPO had to depend on the local population to look after them. If the harvests were plentiful, this was mostly not a problem for SWAPO. But if resources were scarce the local population was not always so generous.

Then 'requisitioned' food could mean an insurgent's life.

We withdraw from the contact area at Omangundu back to Zulu 2 at Eenhana, where we get cold beer.

As usual, we sleep in the veld that night.

Tracking and information

In all wars, intelligence and information about the enemy are of the essence. In a counter-insurgency war they are even more important. The insurgents worked under the radar and somehow the security forces had to gather information about their whereabouts and doings.

Koevoet gathered information in various ways.

From captured insurgents: in many cases we were instructed to bring back a live insurgent. It was not always so clear cut. How do you capture an armed man willing to fight to the death? But a captured high-ranking insurgent always had good information.

From dead insurgents: many insurgents carried documents with useful information.

Information from the local population: many of the local population had grievances against SWAPO. They gave information freely. SWAPO's behaviour toward the peasants sometimes made it very easy for us.

Informers: Koevoet as a unit, as well as individual members, had extensive networks of informers. We would go to the kraal of an informer. He would say that he had attended a soccer game over the weekend—maybe 100 kilometres away. There he heard someone mention that there were insurgents active in a specific area. That was all he knew. We would then take this vague information and try to follow up on it. Often, it would be the start of something big.

How did we obtain the information? Often it came voluntarily. A captured insurgent might realize the futility of resistance and freely offer information, as would an aggrieved tribesman. But there were times when we did overstep the boundaries. Sometimes an insurgent was stubborn and uncooperative. We were fighting a war and had little patience with a captured insurgent who murdered or intimidated. In some cases, a small electric dynamo was used—like the ones in the old telephones. But this was the exception. We would rather beat it out of him and would take a spade from the back of the Blesbok.

Not many brave men can stand firm when beaten on the buttocks with a spade. After the third or fourth blow the insurgent usually realized we had the whole day to continue and that he might as well cooperate. But nobody ever died because of this type of interrogation or even ended up in hospital.

There was much negative propaganda that we threw insurgents out of helicopters. Why would we? Helicopters were scarce and expensive. If we wanted to kill someone we would have shot him instead. But only once was a captured insurgent shot by our team. And the result came as a shock: the white policeman who did it was transferred when everyone asked for his removal from the team. He was threatened with death if he ever did it again and was immediately sent back to Ovamboland.

But our real source of information came from tracking. Tracks were always good indicators of what was happening. It was always a game of hide-and-seek between us and the insurgents.

Every person on earth has his own unique way of stepping on the ground. A young, strong soldier walks differently from an old man. A young man's feet hit the ground from high; an old man has a shuffle, dragging his feet. The more tired the young man becomes, the lower his angle of striking the ground. We could pick up from his tracks that he was tiring.

We always used the shadows in the sand to read the tracks. Always work with the sun against you as the preferred option. You want to see the shadows coming *to* you. So, early in the morning it is easier to go east; in the afternoon it is easier to go west. I have seen trackers walking backward on tracks to utilize the shadows, others next to the tracks. At midday between eleven and three, tracking is always more difficult.

But having the sun against you is ideal for tracking cows, not people. People carrying guns use the sun to hide behind. Often when hot tracks turn into the sun, an ambush is imminent. Insurgents knew they had the advantage when we had to track into the sun, and used it to anti-track or slow us down. We just had to be more alert to the bush around us. So we learned through practice to track with the sun.

Walking with the sun.

It is difficult, but for the trained eye it is possible.

Tracking is not only about footprints. It was also about the environment. Trackers have to be aware of the complete surroundings. We could establish how old a footprint was by using the indicators nature gave us. Some insects only come out at night. If you see a track and you see the tracks of a spider or other insects crossing the print, you know this track was made last night.

Similarly, we studied loose rocks. There is usually moisture underneath rocks. If it has been stepped on and loosened, the level of moisture behind the rock indicates that this man was here a long time ago—the rock is already dry. Or we looked at the leaves and grass. Grass that has been recently stepped on has a specific character. Even if someone resets the grass upright, the base of the grass will still show signs of having being stepped on. You cannot change that, even with anti-tracking. In a day or two, it becomes even more obvious.

Recently broken fresh leaves also have a specific character. Some vegetation reacts by discarding moisture. Recently crushed leaves look different from leaves crushed two or three hours ago. The hot Namibian sun quickly dries damaged vegetation. So we could establish how old a track was—ten minutes or two days.

The behaviour of insurgents also taught us a lot. A Koevoet follow-up was seldom a secret. With all the noise coming from the teams, the insurgents generally began to run. In the bush you hear vehicle engines from a great distance. At nine or ten kilometres off, the tracks might be 90 minutes old when we found where they began running, moving at about a kilometre every ten minutes, or 6 kph. With our front cutting, we could reduce this time gap very quickly.

Helicopter gunships played a crucial role in our tracking. When we closed in on an insurgent he would most likely run. When a helicopter arrived on the scene he would suddenly walk. The moment the helicopter disappeared, he would run again. This behaviour told us we were close, very close.

Insurgents slept and their fire could tell us how long ago they had been at that particular spot. Sand kicked over hot coals or a new fire burning with flames, all tell a story. In some cases, we might have been following 12-hour-old tracks; by sending forward a front-cutting team we might find the tracks were now only two hours old—somewhere along the way the insurgents had slept.

As with all things, the more you do it, the easier it becomes. The more you know about nature, the easier tracking becomes.

Then there is the feeling you develop. A tracker working every day with spoor gets to the point where the tracks 'talk to you'. You instinctively know how old a track is, even though there is limited information available. You develop a feeling for this which cannot be taught. You develop this ability only by doing it. In one incident, a bit of light drizzle confused the trackers in another team. They said the tracks were 12 hours old. When I arrived I discovered they were fresh tracks. My own and the other experienced trackers' opinions were ignored. Shortly thereafter, at a nearby kraal an old man picked up a small child and fled inside a hut. We drove into an ambush that killed one of our men.

The really good SWAPO anti-trackers also tried to mislead us during hot-pursuit follow-ups. They must have had nerves of steel. With a gunship hovering above them they would brazenly imitate us by pointing to the ground with their rifles or with sticks, just like we did. If they were 50 metres or less to the front they sometimes got away with it. Sometimes they would lie dead still in the thick undergrowth. It is very difficult to spot someone in such conditions. The insurgent would then immediately run in a circle to come back on our tracks, or he would cut behind the passing cars. The inexperienced youngsters running with the veterans usually paid the price as they would be forced to face us alone.

But even in a unit with excellent trackers, there are those with outstanding abilities, better than anybody else—men like Warrant Officer Simon Nkwezi. Although he was a leader, he often took to the ground when the insurgents began to anti-track and things got into a rut. Then there was Sergeant Lourens Mosure, a schooled man who had studied agriculture before he became a policeman. He was flown in a few times when everybody else had run out of ideas, when the best of SWAPO had got the best of us. He seldom disappointed. He could unearth things nobody else had seen. A week after Sergeant Botes was posted back to Ovamboland where he was sorely needed, Sergeant Mosure received his transfer. 'Boats' would not go without him. Eddie Marongo was another highly talented man. Luckily, he too was on our side.

Anti-tracking techniques are used by insurgents to counter your tracking abilities. Anti-tracking consists of various ways to put you off the scent and confuse you, such as walking on hard ground, getting rid of boots and walking barefoot, using rough or broken terrain such as rocks, wiping away tracks with branches, forcing civilians to wipe away their own and any unrelated footprints, or using busy paths such as ones that schoolchildren take in the mornings. Often the insurgents forced local herd boys to run their cattle over their spoor. As mentioned before, even road workers tried to eradicate tracks. On a few occasions SWAPO sprinkled water over their tracks to make them appear older.

There were many techniques; good Koevoet trackers had to stand up to the best anti-tracking tricks that SWAPO could throw at them.

Many good anti-tracking insurgents survived but many others came up against a better tracker.

Willie Roux seeks vengeance: a driver and big wheels (Omeya Nalala, 1986)

The commander of Bravo Company at Rundu, Warrant Officer Willie Roux, was a big man. As well as running the company, he also had his own team, Zulu-4 Whiskey, the 'W' derived from his name. Every year there was a competition between the companies and teams. The team which shot or captured the most insurgents received 1,000 rands, ten cases of beer, cases of cooldrink, meat and boerewors, to celebrate with a huge party. One of Willie's teams won it three years running.

Willie was a brave man with much experience. He also trained the new recruits at the Etosha training centre at the Koevoet base in Okashana. He had a very characteristic way of talking over the radio, but when he got excited the Whiskey disappeared and Willie took its place. When Willie appeared a contact was not far off: "Zulu 4, Zulu-4 Willie" was the signal that tracks had been found or hot information gleaned.

Zulu-4 Whiskey—which quickly became Zulu-4 Willie—is busy patrolling southeast of Okongo when they find enemy tracks. It is around 1000 hours. The tracks have been made by a group infiltrating from Omeya Nalala. We (Zulu-4 Sierra) are busy to their south at Okankolo near the army base, with Zulu-4 Echo to their northwest at Okongo.

At about 1200 hours, Willie calls his whole company to come and help. They are following the tracks closely. While we are on our way, one of Willie's up-front trackers detonates a POMZ and several team members are wounded. Willie arranges for a 'giant' to pick up the wounded. He leaves one car behind with them to await uplift. We arrive at the car with the wounded and begin following the Zulu-4 Whiskey spoor.

After about 30 minutes we catch up with the other Zulu-4 Whiskey cars. We find Willie in a furious mood—he wants revenge for the POMZ incident.

We are now hot on the tracks—they are running. The gunship joins us. Willie sends mine and Kallie Calitz's cars 500 metres to the front to track ahead. Drom and one of his cars track ahead at 200 metres. We find nothing; Willie calls us back. The tracks have changed direction and we would not have cut them. They are now running due north.

Willie sends two of his cars with Chappa as commander to scout about to the north. While we are on the way, to search in the same area, a battle erupts right in front of us. Kallie and I charge through the bush and we drive into two insurgents who are shooting furiously, engaged in the contact. They fall in front of the guns on the cars.

Two heads.

Ahead of us Chappa's two cars also kill an insurgent.

We pick up the enemy packs and equipment. But there are still more tracks—running. There are now two gunships on the scene. While one stays on our spoor to provide cover for the trackers, the other flies ahead to support the cars up front. While fleeing, the last insurgent throws away his backpack and a FAPLA special-unit jacket. Willie's car has now joined us at the front; he wants the last man for himself. In front of us the gunship fires short bursts. The pilot says he thinks he's got him.

"Shorty, load up your people. They've got him."

But something tells me not to get in the car.

Willie and Kallie drive ahead to where the gunship rounds were striking.

"Shorty, where are you?" Willie asks, half irritated, on the radio.

"Still on the tracks, Warrant," I say, expecting a tongue lashing.

"Well stay there! Keep following the tracks."

The air force has just killed another kudu (the second time during my time with Koevoet).

The whole tracking effort is reorganized. Kallie and I are sent ahead to re-look for tracks. We find them and they are now only 15 minutes old. The insurgent cannot be more than 2,000 metres away. My gunner, Josef Bernabe, is alongside the driver, Job Kakunde.

We drive about 200 metres and I tell them in which direction to proceed. While I am still leaning over the side of the vehicle, looking at the tracks and indicating their direction, Job suddenly swings sharply to the right. I crash against the side of the turret and latch on to the rim. The next moment something hard hits the front of the car and the right front wheel flips into the air as if it has hit a tree stump.

The car stops abruptly.

Josef Bernabe jumps out of the driver's hatch and right over the nose of the vehicle onto the ground.

"What are you doing?" I yell at him, as I straighten up and look to the right. Halfway under the Casspir lies the body of the insurgent that Job has just run over.

I report back to Willie. "Warrant, we have a VY."

"Shoot, shoot the bastard!" Willie screams over the radio. He has been anticipating a contact and is still worked up over the six casualties we suffered earlier that morning.

There is no contact, but the insurgent has fallen under the Casspir's front wheels. It is good enough.

Four insurgents, one SKS and 12 rifle grenades, two AKs and 12 full magazines, one RPG and eight rockets, three hand grenades, two POMZs and four backpacks: a good haul.

That afternoon the general congratulates us.

We are withdrawn.

Good work.

A grey area: southern Angola

This war was not a nice affair; war never is but especially not when it's a civil war. It was a brutal and devastating conflict in which little mercy was given and little expected.

However, there was a 'grey area'—and a grey area in any war is open to abuse. People would die and blood would flow unnecessarily. Our grey area was the south of Angola. In Namibia, civilized laws were obeyed, as in any normal country. The South West African Police (SWAPOL), of which we were part, maintained law and order. As soon as we crossed the border into Angola, however, there were no laws and few rules.

In Namibia we had to report all deaths and bring the bodies in for identification. This was not necessary in the south of Angola. If a SWAPO member fell here, in many cases he was left where he fell. And it was not just SWAPO; FAPLA also died if we made contact with them. They were the enemy; it made no difference if we had any doubt whether they were SWAPO or FAPLA. In our eyes they were the same—the enemy. But what did you do if you caught a FAPLA or a SWAPO in Angola? What if there was a firefight in Angola? Yes, there were contact reports—we declared the contacts—but nobody investigated or questioned our actions. Angola was lawless.

During a follow-up operation we find two SWAPO terrorists not far north of the border. During the ensuing firefight one dies and the other is captured, slightly wounded but alive. He has two shots through the side and one through the lower arm. No bones hit. Nothing serious. Initially he is not helpful but we do not have time to waste. We have a war to fight. We interrogate him and after a few blows he decides that it would be better if he cooperated. He takes us to a stockpile somewhere in the Angolan bush. He removes the anti-personnel mines around the cache and starts digging.

He removes a large number of Kenyan army uniforms from the hole. We burn the uniforms. But the team leader is not happy. He and some of the other car commanders suspect that the man knows more than he is saying. I am convinced that the man has given us everything he knows. He is interrogated once more and receives a few more blows to the head. The team leader says he is going to shoot him—he has to talk. Some of the other black members and I have a problem with this. We are fighters, not murderers. If we shoot the man, what makes us better than the communists and the way they are fighting the war against us? To shoot a man in cold blood is contrary to how I was brought up and even though there are no laws in Angola it does not suddenly mean that I am not accountable. There is such a thing as right and wrong. There is such a thing as conscience. We were all raised as Christians.

I state my case thoroughly. With my driver and a few others, we climb into our Casspir and drive a few hundred metres. As we switch off the engine we hear the AK-47 shots. A while later, the rest of the team joins us —without the prisoner.

Only a few members were involved and the rest of the team said or did nothing to stop them. Did it happen at other times and other places with other teams? It was possible and I am sure it did. Not everyone caught in Angola was sent back to Namibia. A story did the rounds of one instance when a team commander stayed behind, alone in a Casspir parked in a deserted town. With him were nine FAPLA/SWAPO prisoners. He came back alone. He apparently did not let them go.

Maybe there was also an incident or two that were not rumours.

It is this type of rumour that made things difficult for us.

I experienced both sides of the violence—SWAPO's and Koevoet's. Neither's life was worth much. Sometimes the paperwork was just too much. It is easier to fire a round in the bush.

In many cases, the bodies were left where they fell. In some cases, they were destroyed with explosives. In one case, six bodies were packed on top of each other and blown away with their own landmines and TNT. Their own weapons of terror destroyed their own identities. Justice.

SWAPO sympathizers

Most times the propaganda against us was unfounded. Sometimes a small incident would be blown out of all proportion and made to appear as if it were the norm. We were accused of invading the locals' *mahango* fields with our vehicles and destroying their crops. It is possible that a few incidents took place. If a local supported SWAPO or gave food and shelter to the insurgents, what could we do? If we came to a kraal that openly supported SWAPO and there were possible insurgents in it, we did not avoid confrontation.

What could we do?

If a lot of tracks came out of a pro-SWAPO kraal, were we supposed to drive around the kraal to look for them on the other side?

There were incidents when drivers and car commanders sometimes intentionally and recklessly drove through vegetable patches. In every war you get a quota of sadists, people with no regard for unnecessary destruction. We had a few such people; SWAPO had more.

After the war, the SWAPO people who had problems with us identified our people: "You were the one who drove through the *mahango* land that year. We will get you."

Such intimidation and murder would be the cause of many of us fleeing as refugees to South Africa. SWAPO were brutal. They did not only threaten.

Sixth sense (Epembe, 1986)

We leave Arendsnes and head for Nkurunkuru toward the 18° marker. We carry out the normal drills of testing our weapons on the cars. Everything works. Our team leader, Lieutenant Lukas Koen, contacts Zulu 4 and we are ready for war. We drive past Okongo to Elundu and TB, not far from the army base at Elundu. The next morning, we travel south to the Okankolo area. At Epembe the patrol starts in earnest when we leave the road to move in among the kraals. Two of our cars do a 360° around one of the kraals. Asser Samuel is sitting on top of one of the cars and shouts: "Stop! Stop!" Elias Katura, Abed, Josef Bernabe, Chuma and I climb off. There are tracks in the sand. Three barefoot people passed here.

On top of the Casspir Kallie loudly asks what we are looking at. However, we are so busy that we ignore him. He does not like this very much but there are times when the white commanders get in the way. I climb back into the car and discuss the possibilities with Kallie. I suggest that we should look a bit farther west.

He contacts Lukas Koen and the rest of the cars join us. A few hundred metres later I stop the whole follow-up. Between the dry leaves lies a piece of porridge. These insurgents got food in the kraal and came to eat it under the trees, away from the kraal. Unbeknown to us, we interrupted their breakfast when we arrived at the kraal. They took their food and ran. Between the leaves and grass lie the tracks. The tracks are *payife-payife*—very fresh.

The Koevoet machine starts working.

Lukas Koen calls the Zulu 2 base at Eenhana: "Zulu 2, Zulu 2, Zulu-4 Sierra."

"Zulu 2 send, over."

"Zulu-4 Sierra, three Victor Yankees, running tracks. Direction Sierra Whiskey, 45 minutes old. Golf Sierra can come, over."

"Zulu 2, Golf Sierra 18 minutes' flying time. Channel 16, white phos. Sending Zulu-4 Foxtrot and Zulu-4 Whiskey to join you."

Warrant Officer Willie Roux, the commander of Bravo Group is with Zulu-4 Whiskey somewhere in the bush. He calls us over the radio and asks for a 1,000-foot flare to mark our position. Kallie Calitz fires the flare into the air and within a few minutes they join us. While we are tracking, Zulu-4 Foxtrot also joins us. We hit a contact almost immediately. The insurgents have no chance. They have their backs to the wall and there is not much they can do. Two of them fall before our rifles, but in the chaos of the contact one of them survives and makes a break for it.

The helicopter is cancelled—18 minutes is too long.

We follow the survivor for the whole day and sleep on the spoor that night. The next morning, we follow the tracks again. Even with our tracking abilities it is difficult to catch up to him. He must have run the whole night. At about 1300 hours one of the Zulu-4 Whiskey cars misses him: he has ditched his SKS rifle, uniform and boots and is now simply a barefoot Ovambo. There is no way we can catch him. We leave the tracks when he starts walking on a footpath and we return to Eenhana.

At the army base at Eenhana we fill up with diesel and supplies. The Casspirs have taken a beating driving through the bush for two days. We have many wheels to repair. By late afternoon the three teams leave Zulu 2 and we return to the bush. We sleep outside Eenhana in a TB.

In the bush we always went to bed early. We got up early and the day was long and busy. To concentrate and run the whole day takes a lot of energy. But you cannot just sleep; right through the night we took turns at guard duty. You rarely slept through the night.

The evening after we lost the third porridge eater, I sleep between Casspir 2 and the Blesbok. The lieutenant also sleeps there. We are discussing the events of the day at about 2100 hours when Lieutenant Koen speaks up.

"Sisingi," he calls, using my traditional name, "You will see we are going to catch up with them and shoot them. Northeast of here there are three or four tracks. Tomorrow is the day."

"How do you know, lieutenant?"

"I just know; you will see."

The next morning we travel northeast, just like Lukas Koen predicted last night. At the first kraal we pick up four tracks! They are moving in the direction of Angola—direction November Echo. We start to follow the spoor. I move to the front with our car to track forward. I find the tracks about two kilometres farther on and now they are running. Lukas calls the gunships. They are 24 minutes away.

The tracks now lead in an easterly direction. They are running through an area of very dense bush. Our car goes ahead and where the bush opens up we find the tracks again. The helicopter is close by and asks us to throw a white phosphorus grenade to guide it in. We throw the grenade and everybody gathers together with the helicopter above us. We form a V-formation while the gunship's 20mm cannon covers us from above. After moving forward about 200 metres we hit a contact. We are so close to the enemy that the helicopter cannot take part in the action. In the firefight three PLAN members are killed. They have a whole arsenal with them: one RPG-7 launcher, five RPG grenades, one SKS with eight heat-strims, two AK-47s, six magazines and masses of POMZs and Soviet hand grenades. We have prevented them from penetrating deeper into Ovamboland

We hoist the bodies onto the mudguards of the Casspir and drive through Okongo to Etakaya. We sleep just outside Okongo. By the next afternoon, we are back in Rundu.

By this stage of the war we are a well-oiled machine. Every one of us is tuned to the enemy. It gets to be a sixth sense. Your eyes, ears, nose, mouth and hands—all know what to look for. But there is also another factor: people like Lukas Koen have been involved for so long that they just know.

How did he know there were tracks?

I don't know, but he knew and the proof was draped over the mudguards of the Casspirs the following afternoon.

Bush fire (Ombumbu, 1986)

In 1986 we regularly slept over at Zulu-4 Oscar at Okongo. Before leaving on patrol one morning we have an orders-group meeting. We decide to go back to the Chandelier Road, which is on the border between the two tribal areas of the Ovambo Kwanyama and the Kavango Kwangali. Cattle boys from both tribes always meet here to chat and exchange information.

At the tribal border we leave the road and drive along a footpath heading west. The footpath is well used and takes the direction of Ombumbu.

A few kilometres on we meet an army patrol in Buffels. We ask if they are aware of any insurgents in the area. They say they have patrolled up to Oshifitu, but have found nothing.

One of the army soldiers is a corporal and he asks one of our trackers where he can find Kafiya. The corporal says he knows that no one in Koevoet wears rank, but he knows Kafiya is a sergeant in Zulu-4 Sierra. The tracker directs him to me. A minute later, two corporals appear at car 2. I recognize them and they call me by my war name, 'Kafiya', which is derived from the Afrikaans *vee*, to sweep. We chat like old friends. They say that they have had a long patrol, but they could find no intelligence. I joke that they will see Koevoet shoot some SWAPO today.

If you see the gunship you will know.

They laugh.

We get back into the cars and drive to Ombumbu, where we start questioning around the kraals. From one to another we get the same answer: there are no SWAPO here; they have been living in peace for months; everything is quiet and peaceful.

But I know that Koevoet has not been in the area for a long time and everything appears *too* peaceful. When the army dominates an area, 'domination' is not always the right word. SWAPO knows where and how to take chances.

We take another footpath and drive in a southwesterly direction.

I am in Casspir 2 and we are at the back.

In passing, I notice two young local men by the side of the road.

I instruct the driver to stop. Three trackers and I get off. My instinct tells me something is wrong. Like all good policemen, I just know.

One of the older Koevoet men takes one of the young men round the other side of the car while I question the other by the roadside.

The time for games is over.

One of the trackers grabs the man by the throat and throws him to the ground and presses his R5 rifle against his neck: "Talk! Today is the day I kill you. Give us all the information you have."

The intimidation tactics work immediately. The youth says he knows of five VY at Ombumbu. They have been there for two months.

"You don't stay in Ombumbu, so how do you know what is going on there?"

"I was at the well last night at about 7 o'clock to give the cattle some water when I saw them. But why are you asking me? The other guy knows more than me."

I am about to fetch the other one when the older Koevoet member brings him to me. He has already talked. It was he who took the five SWAPOs to the well the previous evening. He also swept their tracks clean. He will show us where.

Kallie Calitz and Hendrik Engelbrecht have already told the other cars to turn around. We put the two informants in a car and drive to the well. I write down their names and their kraals before letting them go.

We start tracking and after a while stop to analyze the information we have picked up from the tracks. Five tracks, direction Sierra Whiskey, two and a half hours old—with extreme anti-tracking measures.

They know we are here.

At one spot they stood still when they heard the vehicles. After that they started the anti-tracking measures.

We call Zulu-4 Echo to join us and move forward. At a large tree we find where they stopped again. Rudolf Tiweye and I discuss the age of the tracks. They are an hour old—they are very close.

Zulu-4 Echo has now joined us and has started tracking ahead.

They call us over the radio "*Komesho! Komesho!* Forward! Forward!"

They have found the tracks and now they are running. Hendrik Engelbrecht calls the gunship on the big radio. 20 minutes' flying time—they are coming.

We join Zulu-4 Echo and the two team leaders split responsibilities: Sergeant Botes, who has the spoor, takes command of the teams on the ground and Sergeant Hendrik Engelbrecht takes over coordination with the gunship.

A car from Zulu-4 Echo is also with us in the rear of the follow-up. On the ground are some of the best trackers in the unit: Sergeant Rudolf Tiweye, Sergeant Ulombe and Constables Naftali, Likuwa, Asser Samuel and Timotheus Palata.

After a while, we find spoor missed by the cars tracking up front.

The gunship is too high to be of much help so Hendrik Engelbrecht asks it to fly lower. The helicopter flies lower and within minutes they report that they can see two trackers about 500 metres in front of the cars. It is unusual to have unprotected trackers on spoor, however, the trackers are pointing at the ground with sticks, which is normal procedure.

The gunship passes the information on to Hendrik who gives the order for us to press forward. He also asks the gunship to keep an eye on the trackers. We move in the direction of the trackers. Hendrik then orders us and the Zulu-4 Echo car on ahead. Kallie Calitz and Sergeant Sampie are in command.

With about 200 metres between us and the trackers, my eye catches the shape of an AK-47 flashing briefly in the bush.

We do not use AKs, but R5s.

"Contact," I shout.

Kallie Calitz also realizes what is happening and shouts over the radio: "Contact!"

"Straight," I shout at the driver. "Straight ahead! 12 o'clock!"

Above us gunner Bernabe in the Casspir has already started doing what he does best: in front of us the sand erupts in clouds of dust as his machine guns chew up the earth.

The cars race ahead as the big wheels carve up the ground, but the enemy has already fallen.

"Cease fire!" shouts Kallie.

Two heads.

Hendrik Engelbrecht arrives.

Koevoet trackers never work alone. An experienced gunship would have picked this up immediately. Luckily, we are experienced men who are not fooled by such a trick. Not for a second did we think the so-called trackers were Koevoet.

Hendrik turns back immediately. Somewhere behind us they have marked the place where five tracks were last seen.

The follow-up must continue.

We load up the bodies, strapping them to the mudguards before turning around and continuing the follow-up. When we meet up with the other teams they are already hot on the tracks of the remaining three insurgents.

The gunship is low on fuel and returns to Zulu-4 Oscar.

We are on the heels of the insurgents when they play another card. They set the bush alight—and at certain times of the year in the Kavango, the wind blows with gusto. They flee in a westerly direction, right into the wind with us on their heels. It does not take long for the massive flames, licking angrily over the dry veld, to reach us.

We get into the cars and drive straight through the flames.

Once more, we start searching for the tracks—but they are gone. Hendrik Engelbrecht calls a halt. It is getting late in the afternoon. When we last saw the tracks they were 40 minutes old.

Maybe it is our turn to play the last card.

Hendrik orders Kallie to take two cars in a westerly direction to search two and a half kilometres ahead. Maybe we can pick up the tracks again. Sampie is instructed to search where the bush did not burn.

I and the other trackers climb on top of the Casspir. Like all armoured fighting vehicles, it has its pros and cons. When inside during a contact, the enemy could fire thousands upon thousands of AK and SKS rounds at us and we'd be safe. Landmines—the same. Our cars could absorb a triple-cheese mine detonation and everybody inside would be fine, with the V-shaped hull deflecting the blast. But the real problem came when an armour-piercing round from an RPG or heat-strim rifle grenade penetrated the interior, with the grenade spreading deadly, red-hot shards of steel and shrapnel inside.

So we often rode on top of the cars. To experience the openness and freedom of the bush and the smell of nature were things to be cherished. But it was still war: when rockets and rifle grenades were fired at the Casspir, this was a very vulnerable position. It was safer than being inside a car with the danger of shrapnel, but you were still exposed to rifle fire.

Driving through the bush, Kalevhu and I are talking about what we will be doing at Zulu 4 that night. Kalevhu has already talked me through his six beers when he suddenly shouts, "Contact! Shoot! Contact!"

On top of the Casspir the sounds of a contact erupt—R5s shooting in short bursts. The Browning and LMG machine guns also open fire. From everywhere our weapons spit forth hundreds of shiny, hot bullets.

After some heavy firing, Kallie shouts for us to cease fire.

We get off the car and find one dead insurgent, the one Kalevhu saw, shot to ribbons, with everybody now gathering around him. We search the area and find an RPG and RPD. Either this guy loaded himself to death or he has friends who are close by. We start searching and find two of them hiding in some bush. They are armed with a Scorpion machine pistol and a Makarov—but they are cornered and to resist will cost them their lives. They are not ready to die so they surrender.

Another day—two contacts.

Three dead and two prisoners, three POMZs, one AK-47, one RPD, two

RPGs, one SKS, a Makarov and a Scorpion pistol less to worry about.

The people of Kavangoland are today a bit safer.

There is still enough light and we drive to Ombumba where we find an army platoon at the wells.

With the dead strapped to the mudguards and their clothes flapping in the wind, we sing a song of heroism and triumph.

SWAPO are not afraid of the army but they are afraid of us. We interrogate the prisoners later and they give us valuable intelligence.

One of them will later join Koevoet.

He will become a good friend of mine.

The sensations of war

To anyone who thought this war was an idyllic, low-key affair in a far-off African land, I can tell them the opposite.

Do you know the sweet, coppery smell of blood? It is a smell that you never forget. The blood of a human smells differently from other creatures—it is the smell of a soul. If you have smelt it once you will never forget it.

Do you know what the intestines of a man smell like when he has been shot to pieces?

And how quickly the bloated blue flies come to feast?

Have you seen the damage a Browning can do? The damage done by a five-0 or a 20mm to the human body is difficult to describe. It breaks the body.

Do you know what a man looks like when one of these bullets has blown his head off? We picked up many heads. It was gruesome work.

The smell of machine-gun ammunition and diesel smoke, the smell of rifle oil. The smells of rat-pack food: chicken briyani, meatballs in sauce out of a can, warming over a fire made of African hardwood.

The sensation brought on by adrenalin. Do you know what fearless men sound like when they have been wounded by a POMZ? Even the bravest take it badly.

Do you know what it feels like to keep on living when an RPG rocket takes the life of your friend next to you?

The sensation of hearing: the noise machine guns make, the turning of Casspir engines and the *whoo, whoo, whoo* sound of the Mercedes engines. The chattering of radios during a contact blending with the clattering sounds of the helicopters.

Have you ever experienced the fine dust on your skin created by the big Casspir wheels churning up the dry sand?

The burning sweat in your eyes on a hot African summer's afternoon?

One week retraining (Arendsnes)

From time to time, even the best trackers lose tracks. When this happened we had to report to Zulu 4. At one stage, the commander of Zulu 4 was Major Josie Engelbrecht. He was a difficult man. His teams were not allowed to lose spoor. After this happened once too often he called us over the radio.

He was in a foul mood and his words were clear: "If that man has gone to ground, then you take a shovel from the Blesbok and dig him out! If he has flown, tell me, and I will send a *Vlamgat* [Mirage] or an Impala and they will find him! You will find him! End of story! I don't want to know about it—over and out."

We could not dig him out, nor could the air force shoot him because we could not find him.

Back at the base, he was waiting for all the team leaders—black and white, warrant officers and sergeants. "I want to chase the whole lot of you away! You are useless. You cannot stay on a track! What are you here for? I will get rid of the whole lot of you!"

The next morning should have signalled the start of a week's rest for us. But we first have church parade, after which Sergeant Hendrik Engelbrecht asks his team to stay behind. He calls the senior team members together in front of the storeroom. We have to make a plan. Things cannot go on like this. We decide to do some retraining.

We won't be going home this time round.

During the following week, we do intensive retraining. We practise shooting, night shooting and fire and movement. We deploy some of the turned insurgents and follow their tracks. We even use prisoners and follow their tracks. The air force is sympathetic and sends a gunship to practise with us. We practise follow-ups with Casspirs and on foot.

We start seeing the gaps. We have too many trackers on the ground and they are walking over the tracks. We change the tactics. In a silent follow-up we now only deploy 12 men on the tracks—two on the tracks, four to the left of the tracks, four to the right and two behind with the radio. Those on the sides of the tracks serve as protection elements. They look at the trees, bushes and ground for possible ambushes and obviously on the ground for the dreaded POMZs. Support follows if necessary.

The tactics when following-up with a vehicle also change drastically. Now we have just five trackers on the ground. Here, as well, too many people on the ground take the focus away from the trackers and obscure the tracks. Having too many trackers on the ground during a contact is also dangerous for the Casspir drivers. If we hit a contact we have to be able to call upon the maximum firepower of the vehicle's machine guns. A ricochet from a 12.7mm or 20mm bullet is always dangerous for people on the ground. With fewer people on the ground the drivers can use their cars as mobile destroyers and the gunners can do their work, unconcerned about shooting their own people.

After a week's hard, intensive training implementing the change of tactics, we are back at base. SWAPO will pay with their blood for our lost rest days. The good news is that Josie does not want to chase us away any more.

When we go on patrol the next morning we are motivated and ready. As we drive out of the base we sing spontaneously—fighting songs, songs of war.

The new tactics were to place much pressure on the experienced trackers and I too would be working under far more demanding conditions.

Recces with chevron-patterned boots
(Okadidiya, December 1986)

One morning, we commence a patrol after sleeping near the army base at Elundu. We decide to move south to work the Chandelier—or 'White Road'—area. The Chandelier Road runs from Rundu to Okongo and then farther west into Ovamboland, where it becomes known as Oom Willie se Pad (Uncle Willie's road). At the Chandelier Road, we turn east. After about four kilometres, we turn off the road, heading in a southerly direction. This is a traditional Ovambo area.

We start making inquiries about activity in the area. Who has been seen and who has been doing what? At a *cuca* shop I talk to the owner. He was open later than usual last night. The party was rough. There were soldiers here—army. They were dressed like PLAN and had AKs. They had a lot of money and spent freely. They were apparently Recces in disguise, acting as if they were SWAPO. He takes me to the tracks on a footpath.

But the army does not wear chevron-patterned boots! We gather the team together. Piet Neethling calls up Zulu 2 and informs them of five tracks. Zulu 2 dispatches Zulu-4 Echo to join us. Sergeant Botes and his team are only a few hundred metres f-away; with his vast experience he takes over command and regroups the teams. With our initial forward tracking effort we find the tracks at the point where they start running. Botes calls for a gunship, but there isn't one available. They are busy elsewhere. It is the high season. December is the onset of the rainy season when SWAPO saturates Ovamboland. The air force sends us a Bosbok reconnaissance aircraft. Once more, we track forward and run into two of the five. We shoot one and capture the other. Before we can start chasing the other three, it starts raining. The tracks vanish and the insurgents live to fight another day. Rain was often PLAN's salvation.

We hand our prisoner over to Zulu 2 at Eenhana.

We would get to see him again.

POMZ incident (Okadidiya, December 1986)

The next week, we go out with Lieutenant Lukas Koen. We stop at Eenhana and pick up our new friend, the recently captured insurgent. He willl almost certainly have an interesting fact or two for us.

He takes us back to the Omupako *cuca* shop where the SWAPOs buried their equipment and ammunition. He speaks of a large tree nearby. But there are many large trees. Eventually we find the right one. Lukas Koen gets on the radio and tells the team to be careful. The insurgent says that many of his friends are operating in the area.

Casspirs 1 and 3 start searching in the vicinity of the tree. I am in Casspir 2 and together with Casspir 4 we begin looking farther off. In the car with me is Steven Sander. It does not take us long to find where the insurgents were when we arrived. As usual, they start running when they hear the cars coming.

Lieutenant Koen decides to use the tactic of overwhelming force. He calls together all the Zulu 4 teams. Sergeant Botes's Zulu-4 Echo, Zulu-4 Foxtrot and Zulu-4 Whiskey are all close by.

We start tracking in earnest.

One of the Zulu-4 Echo drivers is known as Peter—nicknamed after the reggae musician Peter Tosh. He is also a very good tracker and when Zulu-4 Echo has problems sticking to the tracks he gets out and hands over the car to another driver.

Two of our cars and two of the Zulu-4 Echo cars are sent up front. Myself, Steven Sander, Peter Tosh and John Sam work together with four others.

We are on the tracks.

The next moment one of the trackers detonates a POMZ. Steven and I dive to the ground. When the dust settles, we see wounded and dying trackers lying all around us.

John Sam is dead.

John Sam is the war name for Kapanya Natta, an ex-PLAN commander.

He was captured the previous year and decided to join us. He was a brave man.

The ever-willing Peter Tosh is badly injured, another four less so. Lieutenant Koen calls Zulu 2 and they send a 'giant' to come and pick up the wounded.

Four slightly wounded, one critical and one dead.

Steven Sander and I shake off the dust. Why we were not wounded we do not know.

I was involved in five POMZ incidents. Three times I would just shrug off the dust.

The fortunes of war are something we do not understand. If it is your day you walk away without a scratch; if it isn't, you are dead. This is a dangerous game and the risks are so much greater on the ground following a track.

A teacher in camouflage uniform (Ekoka, 1987)

It was sometimes difficult to understand the Koevoet policies. Once we had to sleep in the bush for three weeks. The Security Section, 21-Echo, had a base at Okongo. They evacuated the base and Zulu 4 took over and called it Zulu Oscar. We patrolled the area and every night for three weeks we slept in a temporary base just outside the existing base. 'Koevoet does not sleep in a base if it is not their permanent base' was the rule. So we slept just outside a Koevoet base with more than enough space for all of us. When we needed rations we would then go back to Rundu and return to the bush outside Okongo.

One night at about 2300 hours we heard rockets, mortars and small-arms fire to the north-east of Zulu-4 Oscar. The army had a base near there at Enyana. The next morning, early, at about 0400 hours, we left our TB, headed north-east and found the place about 90 minutes later. Just as we thought, the army is also on the tracks. None of us want to leave, but Lieutenant Koen is with us. He decides that we should leave the army, cut to the front and intercept the spoor. We successfully 'stole' the army's spoor a few kilometres away.

We will follow the tracks with two teams, Zulu-4 Echo and Zulu-4 Sierra. We find five tracks and follow them. The tracks are going south. We cross the Chandelier Road at 17° 30. Near Ekoka, Lieutenant Koen calls the gunships. We are near the five insurgents.

The gunship joins us after a few minutes. The teams of Warrant Officers Oupa and Willie Roux are also there. Lieutenant Koen does not know the pilot and enquires over the radio whether he has provided support before. The pilot says that he has—it would prove to be a lie. The gunship was too high to make a difference. The cars on the ground usually described to the pilot who they were.

"Gunship, I am Zulu-4 Sierra 1. I am in front with the trackers. Do you see me?"

"No," comes the answer.

"Gunship, drop—you are too high." It was difficult for the helicopter to see the big identification numbers on the noses of the Casspirs in the dense bush. And impossible to provide support fire in the right places.

The lieutenant again asks the gunship to drop lower and when he does not drop low enough, the lieutenant loses his temper. "If you do not want to cooperate, you can leave!" Now the helicopter drops to a useful height. He is also at risk, but it takes a lot of pressure off the trackers. Now the eyes can see much further ahead. The lieutenant asks the gunship to fly ahead to do aerial reconnaissance. The gunship has gained height again.

Lieutenant Koen calls the gunship: "Can you see what is painted on the front of this Casspir's nose?"

The gunship does not answer.

The lieutenant is not happy. Then another gunship arrives. This pilot is experienced. He takes over and shows the new pilot what to do. He keeps low and circles in front of the trackers. Not long after that we find an insurgent and capture him. The insurgent was a teacher who had been kidnapped by SWAPO. He did not want to fight or die. Pressed into a war he had no interest in, he surrendered.

Lukas Koen was a man who ate from one pot with his trackers, who drank from the same water bag with us. He was an officer, but he was one of us. He did the same things we did. We would walk through fire for him.

Unfortunately, we lost contact with him after the war. It would be good to see him again.

POMZ destruction: Omboloka, Onalumono, Omundongilo, the grace of God (1987)

If there was one thing that we were more careful of than anything else it was the POMZ anti-personnel mine. I have seen grown men go crazy and disorientated, reacting like they are being attacked by a huge swarm of bees and cannot get away. Some cry, others swear, some mumble incoherently. They want water, some want their wives and others want their mothers. I have seen drunken men who have been nowhere near a drink—drunk from pain and shock. I was a trained medic, having completed a two-month course in 1987. I know the word for 'mother' in every language that is used in Namibia and southern Angola:

Ovambo—*meme*
Kavango—*niyineye*
Nyemba—*ngangele*
Afrikaans—*ma*
English—*mother*
Himba—*mama*

We are patrolling south of Omboloka and east of Okongo when we are informed of three enemy tracks, which are said to be three days' old. We send the cars out in front and it does not take them long to find the tracks. It turns out they were made late the previous afternoon, but there are six not three sets of spoor. We track up front and after a while we cut the tracks again—they are now just four hours old.

They are leading to the Angolan border, past Omboloka kraal right on the Jati. The other cars join us and we progress further. The tracks are now just 60 minutes old. Herman Havenga, our team leader, contacts Zulu 4 who in turn summon all the teams in the area to link up with us: Zulu-4 Foxtrot, Zulu Papa, Zulu Lima, Zulu Uniform and Zulu-1 Hotel. During the course

145

of the morning, all the teams gather at our position. The tracks have now crossed the border and are moving parallel to it in a westerly direction. The insurgents run behind each other in one another's tracks.

Warrant Officer Attie Hattingh of Zulu Uniform is now the senior man on tracks. He has much experience and is an excellent leader. He decides to put just seven men on the ground with one team of cars to the left of the tracks and one team to the right. It is relatively easy to follow the tracks: six people running behind each other advertise their path. The tracks are now about 30 minutes old, so Attie calls in the gunships. It is 25 minutes' flying time from Eenhana to our position.

We move forward. The next instant there is a huge explosion among us trackers on the ground. Noise and dust. Someone shouts "Contact!," but it is cancelled. A tracker has triggered a 'Jumping Jack'. A Jumping Jack is an anti-personnel mine similar to the POMZ and activated by a trip wire. This one jumped about a metre into the air before it exploded.

Still groggy and on the ground, I examine myself: my ears are ringing, my eyes are full of dust and sand but everything is still where it should be. I do not feel the warm, sticky touch of blood. There is nothing wrong with me. But next to me are three wounded—one of them critically so.

The bush is dense and there is no place for the gunship to land, so the Casspirs create an LZ by flattening bushes and small trees. The gunship lands and picks up the wounded. On the way to Ondangwa the seriously wounded man dies.

Another gunship has replaced the casevac helicopter. We start again on the tracks when five minutes later there is another BOOM!, this one right next to me. The same as before. Once more, I examine myself. Once more, I pick myself up from the dust. This time, it is a POMZ and it has wounded five of us. Again, I do not have a scratch on me.

My luck is surely used up for the day.

Once more the cars flatten an LZ for the helicopter. Three seriously wounded men are taken away. The air force later sends a giant to fetch the others. But now the insurgents' luck has also run out. Ten minutes after the Puma has left we hit an ambush. Two of them are killed and the rest flee. Zulu Lima finds the tracks but the bush is very thick. About an hour later there is another explosion. Another POMZ! Four wounded. The air force sends in the giant again. In the firefight shortly after, another two of the initial group of six insurgents are killed.

We are now near Onalumono. It is late in the afternoon. There are two insurgents left when we make our TB for the night. The POMZs have really hurt us today: eleven wounded and one dead for four dead insurgents.

Early the next morning, we pick up the tracks. They were made at midnight. We follow them and find where they made a fire; it is still burning strongly. They must have heard us and started running.

The tracks change from northwest to east. Attie and Herman Havenga decide to play their trump card. "*Epalyondjamba!*" Elephant stampede! All the cars form up in a sweep line and we charge forward. The cards are now on the table. This is what we have; now you show us what you have!

Over the radio come the words "Attack! Attack!" We did not speak English over the radios. However, one of the Zulu Lima cars has a turned insurgent on board and when they hit the contact he is at the radio and let fly with the English version (that he'd learned in Tanzania). During the firefight one insurgent is killed, while the other disappears between the huts of the Omundingilo kraal complex. When we start searching we find a weapons cache: weapons and equipment for five men, including rifles, RPGs, magazines, rockets, uniforms and backpacks.

Our tally is five insurgents, but they were paid for with our blood—eleven wounded and one dead. I have dusted myself off twice today.

The grace of God was with me.

At least today we have something to show for our efforts. Many a time we suffered POMZ or Jumping Jack casualties with nothing to show for our troubles.

We climb into our cars and drive to Rundu, past Okongo on the big road.

The local population

Being caught up in a guerrilla war was a precarious predicament for a
civilian. The local population always lost. It was no different in Kavangoland,
Ovamboland, Kaokoland and southern Angola. Thousands of them suffered
because of SWAPO. They were accused of being informants for Koevoet,
that they were spies for the security forces and that they were undermining
the 'revolution'. They were beaten, raped and murdered. Their animals were
killed and they were robbed.

The flip side also held true. The security forces accused them of giving
food to the insurgents, wiping out their tracks and running their cattle over
spoor and feeding information to the insurgents. The result was that the
security forces drove through their *mahango* fields and flattened their fences.
Or they were sometimes slapped and assaulted.

Many a time we questioned local people who claimed they knew nothing,
only for us to drive slap-bang into an ambush mere metres from the kraal.
Then the kraal would pay. Often we captured an insurgent who had been
staying in a specific kraal for months—a kraal we'd visited plenty of times in
the interim and had gleaned nothing..

The attitude of many locals was philospohical: Koevoet assaults and burns,
SWAPO cuts throats. Would you rather face the rifle butt of a policeman or
the bayonet of an insurgent? What is your choice? If SWAPO was hiding in a
kraal you kept quiet—maybe you would get away with it. If a firefight broke
out at a kraal, the kraal would burn, but what were the options?

When two elephants fight the smaller one gets hurt—it is the law of nature.
Unfortunately, it also happened in northern Namibia.

The locals were caught in the middle.

POMZ (Ongolongela, 1987)

Three teams, Zulu-4 Foxtrot, Zulu-4 Echo and our own Zulu-4 Sierra are working in the Ongolongela area. Zulu-4 Foxtrot has picked up the tracks of four VY and called the other two teams to join them. The tracks were made at around midnight. It is still early and we all start following the tracks.

But these guys are clever. They are experienced. They try to throw us off and mislead us. They begin anti-tracking measures almost immediately. They use every trick in the book to cover their tracks. They walk on hard ground, wipe away traces of the tracks with branches, and walk in one another's tracks.

They are good.

We are struggling and the going is slow, but we can determine the general direction. Then Sergeant Drom of Zulu-4 Echo has an idea. We will take out the 60mm mortar and fire a salvo about 2,000 metres ahead. We are also experienced. If we fire, they might think we know where they are. Then one of a few things might happen: they may stage an ambush and fight it out, or they might bombshell and each escape in his own direction; they might abandon the counter-measures and start running; they might hurriedly lay anti-personnel mines to hurt us, to demoralize us so that we might stop following them.

SWAPO weren't the only experienced ones in the bush.

Now we will force the matter.

Drom's men fire five mortars. Thump! Thump! Thump! the mortars sound as they leave the pipe. The cars form a sweep ine.

"Forward! Walk like elephants! *Enowambo! Epala lyondjandba!*," comes a voice over the radio, in Afrikaans and Ovambo.

Everyone understands what is happening.

Half the cars keep to the left of the tracks and the others to the right. About 300 metres farther on, the whole line stops; the tracks have turned 90 degrees. The cars in front are called back. They will not find the tracks there. The tracks now run directly north. The commander of Zulu-4 Sierra, Herman Havenga, calls Zulu 2 which is on standby with the helicopters at the Eenhana base. The operational commander of Koevoet, Major Willem Fouché (Whiskey Fox) is at Eenhana. Whiskey Fox does his job and the gunship is on its way.

Once more, the whole line is brought forward.

"Forward!" one of the team leaders shouts.

We move slowly. There are many trackers and support personnel on the ground. On top of the cars the gunners sit ready behind their guns. The bush is thick; the PLAN members cannot be too far away. When we fired the mortars ten minutes earlier, they were no more than 300 metres ahead of us. We've moved less than 100 metres when there is an ear- splitting BOOM!

"Contact!" comes over the radio.

But there is nothing further.

"Cancel!" the order comes.

The experienced SWAPOs have played their trump card. The POMZ anti-personnel mines they planted have caused devastation. In the sand and among the bushes lie 13 wounded. Nearly everyone who was in the vicinity of the POMZ is wounded.

Herman Havenga jumps out his vehicle and starts helping the medics with the wounded. Three of them are critical. Everyone is marked with a black marker; the name and blood group of each man is written on his forehead. Then the giant arrives, the Puma helicopter, with a doctor on board.

Casevac—a word associated with pain and blood.

Now the fat is in the fire. The follow-up continues. Two other teams join us. Zulu-1 Hotel and Zulu Uniform were on their way when the mine incident took place, which gave them time to catch up. Now the gunship is also above us. We pick up backpacks that have been dropped in a hurry.

But night is approaching. PLAN have won this round.

The next morning, we have to settle the score. Very early, by first light, we are back on the tracks. They ran during the night and could not anti-track.

Our front trackers catch up to them quickly. They are beginning to tire. But where previously there were four sets of tracks, now suddenly there are five. Somehow a PLAN terrorist has made a fatal mistake by meeting up with his comrades during the night. After about three hours we make contact and with overwhelming firepower, two of the five are killed.

We get ready to follow up again. There are so many teams and trackers involved that we are afforded the rare luxury of following individual tracks when they bombshell.

During the course of the day the last three also die.

Five VY—but the price is high: 13 wounded trackers. This hurts us.

But this day belongs to the leaders of the teams. These hard men have fought in hundreds of contacts. They are experienced and they know the job. They had a feeling what PLAN's next step would be. They were always one step ahead of the enemy. Even a blow to the nose, such as the POMZ explosion, did not unnerve them. They merely dusted off their clothes, wiped the blood away and followed the tracks with renewed vigour.

We worked with Drom and Herman every day. They were excellent. Willie Roux from Zulu-4 Whiskey was our senior non-commissioned officer, a dedicated man who instinctively took charge when he arrived at a scene. Sergeant Potgieter of Zulu-1 Hotel was also a man who knew his stuff.

Then there was Warrant Officer Attie Hattingh. He was an excellent team leader. In his day he could walk and keep up with the best of the black trackers. He was undoubtedly the best white tracker in the unit; he was not scared to be on the ground. He could organize an entire follow-up from the ground. Attie became a legend in the unit and would stay until the end. After the war he kept in contact with many members. At his private security company he employed mainly Koevoet members. They respected each other and their mutual trust made it easy in a very difficult profession.

Attie was a man without equal.

Two cars, five insurgents (beacons 28–30, 1987)

Four teams, Zulu-4 Sierra, Zulu-4 Echo, Zulu-4 Foxtrot and Zulu-4 Whiskey drive to the border north of Okongo. We all get out and the company commander, Warrant Officer Willie Roux, conducts a prayer parade.

We are here to cut off a large group of insurgents who have been picked up by Zulu 3, the intelligence unit of Koevoet at Oshakati. From their informants and prisoners they are able to form a clear picture of SWAPO's intentions. Many a time we would act proactively on their information, almost literally one step ahead of SWAPO.

Once again, this is information from one of their sources.

Willie Roux says the intelligence is hot and we have to be careful. There are many SWAPOs in the region and we have a large area to cover. We will work in teams of two and will not be far from each other—each team within five kilometres of its nearest sister team. For a time though, each team will be on its own. We will have access to reinforcements, but not immediately.

We get back on the cars, R5s loaded and at the ready, our webbing loaded with several full R5 magazines. Zulu-4 Sierra and Zulu-4 Echo head in a northwesterly direction, the other teams northeast into Angola. After about seven or eight kilometres, Zulu-4 Echo calls the base at Arendsnes on the big radio. Ten to fifteen Victor Yankee tracks are moving in a southerly direction—north of beacons 29 and 30. They ask us over the small radio if we have received the transmission.

We have. We change direction and catch up with them.

At the site of the tracks we get off the vehicles. The senior black team member is Warrant Officer Nkwezi, then come Warrant Officer Lang Paulus, Rudolf Kamanga and myself. Nkwezi takes us to the tracks.

"How many are there?" he asks me.

"I don't know, ten to fifteen, maybe. They are walking over their tracks and there are boots and bare feet all mixed up together," I reply.

"I think you are right; ten to fifteen," he retorts.

We pass the information on to Willie Roux and he decides on our strategy. All four teams will take part in the follow-up. The other teams come and join us. There are many trackers on the ground. With us is a white policeman, Phillip, whom we are training. He mans a Browning.

We proceed about 500 metres when the enemy group scatters and bombshells into three groups of five each. They have dropped their backpacks and are running. Now we can count better. There are fifteen. Warrant Officer Roux decides to group Zulu-4 Sierra and Zulu-4 Whiskey together and follow one group of tracks leading west. Zulu-4 Foxtrot and Zulu-4 Echo follow another group heading east.

Roux calls for gunship support; arrival time on the scene is given as 25 minutes. The tracks now lose direction and turn in a circle straight back onto ours.

They are trying to throw us off.

We follow the circle, but in the dense bush some of the cars decide to circle to the right with the tracks. Maybe the insurgents have decided to break the circle and break away to the left, I think to myself. I shout to my driver to break left and Rudolf Kamanga, the driver of our vehicle, Casspir 3, does so immediately. We are right. Fifty metres after breaking to the left the first RPG-7 comes at us. In the thickness of the bush the RPG gunner misses. The SKS and AK-47 rounds hit the steel armour plating around us. More rifle grenades and small-arms fire follow. All the grenades miss. Another Casspir that has broken with us is car number 3 of Zulu-4 Whiskey. Warrant Officer Epafullas and his men give us support with their machine guns.

Our car hits a tree and stalls. Rudolf Kamanga has trouble starting the engine. In the turret the Browning handled by Phillip has a stoppage. For a moment all looks desperate, but on the ground the other trackers and I move forward aggressively. The Zulu-4 Whiskey car is with us and together we smash right through the ambush position.

All five PLAN members are killed. One whole group is accounted for.

It was a chance we took, but we got away with it. With only one mobile car, 15 of us have overcome the enemy with aggression and daring. This says much about our training, and especially the dedication of men such as Hendrik Engelbrecht.

We gather up the five bodies, and start collecting their weapons. The rest of the two teams sweep the area with us. Two RPG launchers, one PKM machine gun, one SKS and an AK-47. The insurgents were also in possession of two Jumping Jacks but we placed such rapid and intense pressure on them that they did not have time to lay their lethal mines.

One of the dead is a senior PLAN commander, Mushandi, with the war name of Chad.

Willie Roux is very proud of us.

A gunship with a ringside seat (Angola, 19 August 1987)

We leave from our Zulu 4 base at Arendsnes, near Rundu, for an operation in Ovamboland. Our point of departure in Ovamboland is Okongo. We cross the Ovambo–Kavango border at 18°. At the border we test-fire the big guns on the Casspirs. If they have been tested and they work, we are ready for war. We are on our way to Okongo. If the discipline and style has been casual before, we are focused now.

We are ready for any SWAPO—whether he sees us first or we him.

The area to the north of Kavango is controlled by Unita. When SWAPO come they come south through Ovamboland before turning east into the dense bush of the Kavango. They infiltrate quietly and in large groups.

The area north of Ovamboland in Angola is controlled by FAPLA and their Cuban buddies. Otherwise there is no one here except when the South African army is in control. Here SWAPO, who are mainly Ovambo, come in greater numbers, but cross the border in smaller groups before blending in among the local population, who are also Ovambo. The chances of us walking into small splintered groups or single insurgents are much better in Ovamboland: there are simply more SWAPOs here.

That night, we sleep at Okongo, outside the base in a TB, of course. The next morning, we turn the vehicle noses north to the Jati. There are no boundary fences. We cross the Jati at beacon 29. Ovamboland is flat and has very little in the way of prominent natural features, so there are man-made beacons every five kilometres, constructed for navigation and reference. The whites call the place 'Beacon 29', but the Ovambo know it by its traditional name, Onayimbungu.

With us is our sister team, Zulu-4 Echo. The two groups are under the command of Sergeant Drom van Rooyen of Zulu-4 Echo. When we cross the border, Drom gives the grid reference and direction to Zulu-4 Oscar over the radio.

It is early in the morning and we drive many kilometres until we get to

Eheke, the place where the Recces were given a bloody nose in 1977. But the large SWAPO base was destroyed and never rebuilt. There are people living in the area so we start with the usual drive-and-question tactics—stop; question the population; no information; move on and look somewhere else. By late afternoon we have still found nothing. We make a TB and sleep overnight, 30 kilometres inside Angola.

The next morning, we start well and find three tracks, but there are problems with Drom's car. Only three cars of Zulu-4 Sierra deploy this time: car number 2 under Constable Cassie Carstens, car number 3 under my command and car number 1 under Warrant Officer Mbonga. As Drom cannot continue, he transfers command to his senior black WO, Warrant Officer Simon Nkwezi. Drom instructs the teams to follow the tracks while he fixes his car. Zulu-4 Echo now also has only three cars. Except for the fairly new and inexperienced Cassie, there were no other whites in any of the six cars in the follow-up.

Three VY tracks walking together: two large, experienced men and a younger, smaller spoor, obviously a novice. We can deduce from the tracks that the other two want to be rid of him. We find backpacks that they have stashed. Just after this, the two break away from their pupil. They have eventually got rid of him—must have threatened him with death. But we are looking for the two experienced PLAN members. They know we are tracking them. That is why they hid their backpacks: everything heavy has to go. Now speed and counter-tracking measures are of the essence. Warrant Officer Nkwezi lets Drom know that we have found the backpacks.

The jackal is out of the burrow.

The gunships can come. Send them, the pair cannot be far away. Zulu 2 says the flying time for the gunships is 28 minutes; when they approach us we must throw a phosphorus grenade to guide them in.

On this morning, I am in the front-cut car. The driver is Sakkie Kaikamas, who is on a patrol as a driver for only his second or third time. He is barely 18 years old. I am in command of the Casspir and a veteran at twenty-two.

Behind, with the group at the tracks, are Warrant Officer Nkwezi, Sergeant Rudolf Kamanga and some of the other experienced men, like the driver, Frans Mundjango.

When things start getting busy, we cannot keep Drom out of the picture for long. I hear him calling me over the radio: "Shorty, you find those terrs for me today?"

"Yes, sergeant," I say.

"Simon, throw red smoke."

Drom can already hear the gunships from his position and guides them onto the follow-up. Warrant Officer Nkwezi throws a red smoke canister. I am tracking up front. Drom has already told the gunship that I am in front.

Then the gunships are on the radio: "4-Echo, gunship."

"4-Echo, send gunship," says Warrant Officer Nkwezi.

"Gunship, I am going to stay with Shorty up front. Gunship two will stay with the group."

Again, Drom comes on air. "Shorty, the front gunship is yours. Do the business."

In front of me the trackers are on the ground. They are searching tirelessly for every piece of broken soil, each broken blade of grass, each small shadow in the sand.

Then the gunship speaks to me. "Shorty, gunship."

"Send gunship."

"Gunship. In front of you is a herd of cattle with one man chasing them but he looks like a young herder."

"Gunship, Shorty, keep him in sight. I'll get to him now."

The few trackers up front get in the Casspir and we crash ahead through the bush, with the other cars some way behind. We find the herder in very dense bush. It is too dangerous to get out of the car. We shoot probing fire into the bush near him with the heavy guns. Our driver drives around him a few times until we are sure there is nobody near him.

We climb out and the constables deploy in a circle in all-round defence.

I question the young man but he says he knows nothing, that he is merely looking after the cattle. But it is difficult to establish an identity in Angola. No one has documentation. I grab him and yank him toward me and see the strap marks on his shoulders. He also has marks on his feet that could have been made by boots. My patience is wearing thin. After a few minutes I am tired of him. I grab him by the shoulder and slam my fist into his chest. He starts to sob.

I scream at him threateningly, "Why are you lying to me? I wanted to spare your life, but I am going to kill you now!"

He pleads with me not to kill him. I am sure that he is the younger one of the three.

I order the trackers to search the area; not long after they locate his equipment: an AK, seven magazines, three hand grenades, two POMZs, three water bottles, a Kenyan camouflage uniform and boots.

I let the rest of the team know that I have captured one, and return to them. They have lost the tracks in the interim. Warrant Officer Nkwezi tells me to bring the prisoner to him. He questions the man. Not long after the SWAPOs had hidden the backpacks, they bombshelled. I take the man to Drom's vehicle; he has almost caught up with us. He is driving slowly and stopping often. I leave the prisoner with him and return to the front again.

In the meantime, Warrant Officer Nkwezi instructs us to do a 360-degree search.

Sergeant Kamanga, Warrant Officer Mbonga and I drive about three kilometres farther and arrive at a kraal. Outside is old man; when he sees us, he starts crying. No old man normally starts crying when he sees a Koevoet Casspir.

There is a snake in the grass.

I climb out and the frightened old man immediately volunteers information: the PLAN members threatened to beat him to death when they return.

"What about my children? Who will look after them?" he sobs.

I put my arm around his shoulders and console him.

"Don't worry, they will not come back. I will find them."

I take the radio and call up the two teams. Drom is also now with them.

"Zulu-4 Echo, Zulu-4 Sierra, this is Shorty."

"Send," Drom answers.

"Sergeant Drom, I have two tracks, one hour and thirty minutes old. The gunships can stand by."

It does not take the teams long to start following the tracks—once again without Drom. Warrant Officer Nkwezi gets out of his car with a radio and joins the trackers on the ground. He orders me to track up front in my car and tells Rudolf Kamanga to take over command of the teams in the command car.

I move a few kilometres ahead—nothing. Then I search again. Still nothing. Am I missing something, I think to myself? Then I look even more carefully, searching in front of the oncoming cars—and there they are! Two sets of tracks. But they have changed course 90 degrees.

The cars all assemble on the new line.

But not before Warrant Officer Nkwezi scolds me: "You have to wake up! These terrs were lying here looking at you! You missed them! You drove right past them!"

Unknowingly, I had driven past an ambush. But they never attacked. They did not spring the ambush. We are lucky.

Warrant Officer Nkwezi calls up the gunships. They are 27 minutes away. It is the same gunship as before and he calls me. I am about 450 metres in front of the teams. We find a POMZ that has only been half set. There was not enough time to do the job properly and half a POMZ is not worth much. We could have had problems if the insurgents had not panicked. The gunships are three minutes away when Warrant Officer Nkwezi orders us to move quickly ahead—the gunships will provide cover when they arrive.

About 100 metres in front of us is a kraal. The next moment, the unmistakable sound of AKs shooting: *Zing! Zing! Zing!*, the bullets fly over our heads. Those of us with the front cars are in the line of fire. We jump back into the cars. Our gunner on top behind the Browning is Josef Bernabe. He puts down heavy fire into the bushes between us and the kraal. Our young driver speeds ahead, but in the chaos the Casspir lands on a hidden tree stump. We cannot move forward or back—we are stuck. Bernabe is still firing with all he's got. The rest of us jump out and fire into possible hiding places. We start fire and movement. The gunship is directly overhead now, but he cannot fire because we are too close to the enemy.

We move in and find two dead SWAPOs.

After the contact, the gunship lands and the pilot asks to see me. He fumbles in his pocket and takes out R100 and gives me the money. He says I did well. One terr captured and two dead. He saw everything: I must go and buy myself a beer.

"We don't drink on patrols," I tell the pilot.

"It does not matter; I will work with you any time. You know what you are doing," he says.

Special Unit (K) Kavango, Rundu, 1985
Zulu-4 Sierra

Front from left: Special Sergeant Gilbert Haure, Special Constable Ignatius Shikongo, Sergeant Kallie Calitz, Sergeant Hendrik Engelbrecht (team leader), Constable Piet Neethling, Medical Ordnance Lance-Corporal S. McMurray (South African Medical Services), Special Sergeants Paulus Mberema and Rudolf Kamanga; 2nd row: Special Constables Blasius Kutenda, Lyuma Mateus, Siambi Kufuna, Jesaya Domingo, John Sam, Makai Kanzara, 'Rocco' Dimbu Kosmos, Special Sergeant Sisingi Kamongo and Special Constables Frans Makina and A. Fernando; 3rd row: Special Constables Obed Vilho, Johannes Poulus, Listo Kanguni, Timutus Palata, Amos Mgwara, Efalistus Mangundu, Assel Sirunda, Amandus Muronga, Joseph Mukupi and Moses Ulombo; back: Constables Josef Bernabe, Uliwa Tjiumbu, Eduard Muhembo, Matheus Feresiano, Tjoakim Kasinda, Max Kamberuka, Elias Katura, Matheus Tjangano, Richard Karukete, Job Kakunde and Naftali Rikuua.
Photo Kallie Calitz

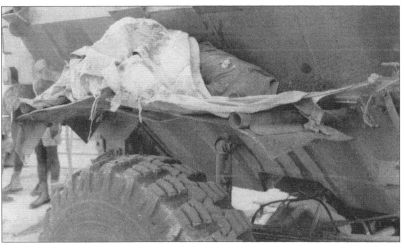

The body of an insurgent. No place inside, so sometimes on the front bumper but most of the time draped over a mudguard.
Photo Attie Hattingh

Camouflaged uniforms and red flags on a car after a contact, in an attempt to prove that the police did not kill innocents. A police parade through a village was designed to intimidate prospective SWAPO recruits and persuade sympathizers to reconsider. *Photo Kallie Calitz*

Zulu-4 Sierra senior NCOs: Warrant Officer Gilbert Haure (left) and Sergeant Ignatius Shikongo.
Photo Kallie Calitz

A deadly combination: a Casspir and an Alouette gunship, with its 20mm cannon. The second man on the right of the Casspir displays an orange dayglow, to make him more visible to airborne helicopters. *Photo Attie Hattingh*

A gunship lands on the Chandelier Road, also known as the 'White Road'. *Photo Kallie Calitz*

Omaheva on the day the army pushed Koevoet off spoor. One of the dogs was killed when its throat was slit by a concealed insurgent.
Photo Kallie Calitz

Sergeant Kallie Calitz behind twin .30 Brownings: a level-headed leader. Unshaven, he is filthy from the dust, wears a headband to keep the sweat from his eyes and has shiny new gloves, compliments of an air force gunship gunner.
Photo Kallie Calitz

The author, Sergeant Sisingi 'Shorty" Kamongo (left), Constable Joseph Mukupi and an unknown captured insurgent. Many young insurgents were abducted from school and saw little sense in fighting for the SWAPO cause. *Photo Kallie Calitz*

Trackers in extended line searching for spoor. *Photo Kallie Calitz*

"White phos, channel 16." The gunship is near. The smoke generated by white phosphorus was visible for miles from the air. *Photo Robert Brand*

A typical Okavango kraal, with pole fence.
Photo Kallie Calitz

A kraal burns in southern Angola. It could have been an accident caused by a tracer round. *Photo Kallie Calitz*

Landmine. Casspirs were tough vehicles, easy to repair. Within a few hours this car would be mobile again, fitted with a complete new differential and back suspension. *Photo Attie Hattingh*

Sweep operation in southern Angola. A Mike-4 Echo car on its way to assist, detonated a mine and was destroyed by fire. The next day a second Mike 4-Echo car suffered the same fate. The two cars were both recovered and limped back across the border two days later. *Photo Kallie Calitz*

Follow-up operation in eastern Ovamboland. *Photo Kallie Calitz*

Rural scene at a pan at Opepela, with a Casspir in the background. *Photo Kallie Calitz*

The rainy season and the sand became mud and the flat *chanas* instantly became sodden pans, bringing out the mosquitoes in force. Digging and pulling cars out was a constant occurrence. Thunderstorms saved the lives of many insurgents as the rain would obliterate their spoor. *Photo Attie Hattingh*

Zulu 4-Sierra cars. Car number 2, Zulu-4 Sierra 2, has Sergeant Rudolf Kamanga standing, with Sergeant Shorty Kamongo sitting on the side of the second car. *Photo Kallie Calitz*

A trigger-happy gunship gunner made it Air Force: 1 – kudus: 0; the other score was Koevoet: 0 – SWAPO: 0.
Photo Attie Hattingh

Interrogation of a suspect. Things sometimes got heavy-handed, depending on who was in charge.
Photo Attie Hattingh

Taking a break. Zulu-4 Sierra and Zulu-4 Whiskey in western Kavangoland. Warrant Officer Willie Roux is on the left with a Zulu-4 Whiskey comrade on the right. *Photo Kallie Calitz*

Below: Warrant Officer Attie Hattingh's Zulu Uniform after a contact. The car took a bullet to the driver's armoured front window. *Photo Attie Hattingh*

Above: In the later stages of the war some cars were equipped with 20mm cannons. The weapon seen here above the co-driver is an LMG. *Photo Attie Hattingh*

Zulu-4 Golf lent Zulu-4 Sierra a car when one of latter's detonated a landmine.
Photo Attie Hattingh

A temporary base (TB) after a storm.

A Zulu-4 Sierra car during a follow-up where the insurgents set fire to the veld. *Photo Kallie Calitz*

A captured insurgent digging up his own landmine on 'Oom Willie se pad' (Uncle Willie's road) between Okongo and Oshakati. *Photo Attie Hattingh*

Negotiating another pan during the wet season: prime insurgency time with denser vegetation, plenty of water to drink and rain to wash away tracks. *Photo Attie Hattingh*

A temporary base with the ubiquitous bivvies, which kept out *most* of the water: many rainbows in the wet season and many a wet night in the fine, sticky sand. *Photo Attie Hattingh*

The man who swung the battle at Opepela: Warrant Officer Attie Hattingh. With a few rag-tag teams he charged, cavalry style, a dug-in SWAPO mortar position and after a heavy fight destroyed it. His action saved the pinned-down cars a few kilometres away from being wiped out. *Photo Attie Hattingh*

Opepela, 23 dead insurgents.
Photo Herman Grobler

The bush at Opepela was flattened to allow the Puma to land. The car in the centre is a Wolf from Zulu Foxtrot. *Photo Herman Grobler*

Opepela, the aftermath, with the dead strewn over the battlefield. In the background is a Wolf. *Photo Herman Grobler*

The April 1989 SWAPO insurrection. Was it a massacre? More than 300 SWAPO cadres died as did over 30 policemen. *Photo Herman Grobler*

Trackers on a footpath with a .30 Browning in support, near the Ovamboland–Kavangoland border. The cars usually drove next to the path to avoid landmines.
Photo Piet Benade

Arendsnes at Rundu, the headquarters of the Kavangoland (Zulu 4) teams. The parade ground is in the foreground.
Photo Piet Benade

An Ovamboland car from Zulu Sierra working with Bravo Group from Zulu 4 in southern Ovamboland. This photo was taken by Piet Benade seconds after the Zulu Sierra car detonated an anti-tank mine; the dust has not yet settled. The car was propelled eight metres forward from the point of detonation (arrow) but nobody was injured, testament to what a hardy vehicle the Casspir was. *Photo Piet Benade*

After questioning a kraal. Around the kraal are *mahango* fields, with the cars parked some distance off so as not to damage the crops. However, the crops grew thick and were ideal hideaways for ambushes. Unfortunately, firefights often broke out in the crops which created much animosity. *Photo Piet Benade*

An army medic attends to the wounded after a POMZ incident. Every team had an army medic attached; they did great work and saved many lives. *Photo Piet Benade*

Koevoet cars and army Ratels in a sweep-line formation to root out the hundreds of SWAPO insurgents. SWAPO's treacherous invasion cost them dearly with more than 300 being killed. Thirty-one policemen and soldiers were also lost. Piet Benade is standing behind the guns of the Casspir in the foreground. Shortly after this photo was taken the extended line was dropped and individual cars pursued individual tracks. SWAPO bled heavily. *Photo Piet Benade*

Special Constable Masonde and members of the Zulu-4 November team parade along the villages in eastern Ovamboland after another successful contact, displaying captured RPGs, SKSs and rifle grenades.
Photo Piet Benade

Warrant Officer Willie Roux, Bravo Group commander, and two smartly dressed Unita officers meet just north of the border.
Photo Piet Benade

Casualty evacuation of wounded Bravo Group members after a POMZ incident. "Three times I was evacuated in a Puma. Nice it never was ... blood and pain." *Photo Piet Benade*

The same casevac: for medical treatment at Ondangwa or 1 Military Hospital in Pretoria. *Photo Piet Benade*

Questioning a kraal south of Okongo, eastern Ovamboland. Constable Petrus Ipinge is in the centre (with cap). *Photo Piet Benade*

Puma helicopters played a crucial role, saving many wounded Koevoet policemen. Once on the helicopter your chances of survival were very good, with a doctor usually on board during casevacs. *Photo Piet Benade*

North of the Kavangoland border, Unita, the anti-communist rebel movement, dominated southeastern Angola. SWAPO suffered horribly at the hands of its erstwhile ally which made the job of the South African security forces so much easier. Meetings between Koevoet and Unita were not officially sanctioned but took place nonetheless. Here Sergeant Piet Benade of Zulu-4 Whiskey shakes hands with a Unita colleague. *Photo Piet Benade*

Bravo Group members, Piet Benade and Chappa Strauss, on top of a Casspir. 'Chappa' was the Kwangali nickname for the freckled Strauss, meaning guinea-fowl. The white members named his car 'The Ambulance', for when he was sitting on top his red hair reminded them of the red light on top of an ambulance. *Photo Piet Benade*

Titus Kambalanu, Thomas Muhwika and Piet Benade smile for the camera. *Photo Piet Benade*

After Koevoet lost spoor on several occasions in 1987, the unit was retrained in a major overhaul of tactics. The change put huge pressure on the experienced trackers and only a few stayed on the ground, with the majority banished to the safety of the cars. The job became even more dangerous thereafter. *Photo Piet Benade*

"The grass gets damaged when elephants fight." The local population was in an impossible position. *Photo Kallie Calitz*

Terrorism and intimidation come in different guises. The landmine was one such guise.
Photo Attie Hattingh

An Alouette gunship takes off after refuelling on an operation. A Blesbok fuel transporter is in the background.
Photo Attie Hattingh

Alouette airborne.
Photo Attie Hattingh

A tracker investigating a possible sign, the dayglow patch on his cap clearly visible. *Photo Kallie Calitz*

An unidentified Koevoet member showing off a captured AK-47 after a successful contact. *Photo Attie Hattingh*

"My little brother." An insurgent, wearing a jacket given him by Koevoet members, recovers his 82mm mortar bombs from a cache. He is no longer a foe. Many captured insurgents switched sides and more than 400 POWs were released after the war. Conversely, captured policemen and soldiers were simply murdered by SWAPO. *Photo Kallie Calitz*

The same insurgent. Koevoet were not only paid for enemy personnel—dead or alive—but also for captured weapons. *Photo Kallie Calitz*

Inside a Casspir.
Photo Attie Hattingh

During follow-ups trackers often ran, a dangerous practice because of ambush and mines. On a road such as this ambushes were common. The fact that there is another car up front explains why the trackers are taking the opportunity to sprint forward. *Photo Attie Hattingh*

The tough Sergeant Sampie Potgieter who joined Koevoet from 32 Battalion, at the site of a landmine explosion. *Photo Kallie Calitz*

A wounded insurgent being treated immediately after a contact in southern Angola, 1986.

Zulu-4 Sierra cars regrouping after a successful contact near the Chandelier Road. *Photo Kallie Calitz*

Above: A Koevoet team inspects a bridge destroyed by a landmine. Unfortunately for the insurgents they always left tracks and Koevoet had outstanding trackers.
Photo Attie Hattingh

Taking a break somewhere in the bush are Special Constables Daniel Muku (sitting left), Ben Sinangu Shuna (against the tree) and Petrus Ipinge (standing).
Photo Piet Benade

Zulu-4 Whiskey trackers seen here are Special Constables Z.P. Mingeli (mechanic at Rundu) and Motihanus Hamutenya, Special Sergeant Makina Yikuma and Special Constable Ndumba 'Shorty' Nakanyika. *Photo Piet Benade*

Inspecting a captured weapon in the bush. Zulu-4 Whiskey members from left: unknown police national serviceman, Blackie Swart, Warrant Officer Willie Roux (with hat), Bielie Ferreira (head slightly bowed and turned away), Piet Benade, Johannes Petrus and an unidentified tracker. *Photo Piet Benade*

In the thick bush of Kavangoland are an unidentified tracker, Hiskia Masuna and Mathias Mahina.
Photo Piet Benade

Nge, the scorpion insignia
of Koevoet battle team
Zulu-4 Sierra, at Rundu in
Kavangoland, 1984–89.

The medal issued to all finishers of the Dinamika
Springbok Vasbyt 10/25km run, July 2009.

A kraal burns.
Photo Kallie Calitz

Left and below: The equalizer: an Alouette gunship. The moment the gunships arrived overhead in the bush the odds turned heavily in Koevoet's favour. Visibility from the air combined with impressive and precise firepower was something the teams welcomed and the insurgent dreaded, for their deaths were generally imminent.
Photo Kallie Calitz

A Koevoet team meets up with Unita in southern Angola. The tall smartly dressed man with the red scarf is WO David Absalon, senior warrant officer of Zulu Uniform. He was one of many ex-Unita soldiers who joined Koevoet over the years. He was a born leader and a fearless warrior. *Photo Attie Hattingh*

"Put that thing down before you hurt someone" (Onanime, 1987)

We are chasing five tracks in the thick bush between Onanime and Oluwayi. Warrant Officer Willie commands three of the teams: Zulu-4 Whiskey, Zulu-4 Echo and Zulu-4 Sierra.

We make contact and two of the group of five SWAPOs are killed.

Now there are only three left.

We clean up the contact area as Warrant Officer Willie decides to follow the other three in a sweepline formation because of the dense bush.

The tracks run northeast and we are again hot on the trail. The tracks suddenly change direction and in an attempt to get back on them Warrant Officer Willie's car finds itself on the far right flank of the line.

He shouts to his driver to stop.

While he is busy explaining to the driver what he wants, he looks to his right, away from the sweep formation. Scarcely three metres from the Casspir stands an insurgent aiming an SKS with a rifle grenade right at him—rifle butt in his shoulder, finger on the trigger, ready to fire. There is no time to swing the machine guns around—they cannot turn at that angle in any case.

And so the warrant officer does the only thing he can.

He shouts at the young insurgent, "Put that thing down before you hurt someone! If I have to get off here, I am going to beat you to death! Put down that thing!"

With his dirty red face, long red beard and roaring voice, he is an intimidating sight to the young man. The young SWAPO lays down his rifle and raises his hands in the air.

We load the boy into the Casspir and give him cold water from the water bag. I question him. He is only 17 years old and was abducted from school by SWAPO three years earlier. He isn't at all impressed with the war.

That's tracking—even the best trackers sometimes miss a sign.

All the trackers had missed this insurgent in the bush. Luckily for us,

Willie saw him by accident. If he had not "put that thing down" someone would definitely have got hurt.

As it was, through Willie's quick thinking, two lives were saved: his and the boy's.

This incident passed into Koevoet legend

I was part of it.

Six insurgents at Oshana Shanalama
(Cuanama, Angola, 1987)

We cross the border at Big Omulemba and drive northeast in the direction of the zero line. Later that afternoon, we TB deep inside Angola, all four of the Bravo Company teams of the Kavango.

Early the next morning, we have the usual prayer parade.

Willie Roux issues instructions: look for information. Make sure. This is enemy country. There are many of them. Be alert. Don't take chances. Follow up on clues.

We move toward Oshana Shanalama, or Cuanama. We arrive at a water hole where there is an old man and a few other people watering their animals. Although we are deep into Angola, we come here so often that we know the local population.

The constables each take a local by the arm and question them separately.

The old man is mine. He asks me for R30 and some tinned food before he will help me. I say I don't have money but I can help him with food.

"Well, I have not seen a PLAN in three months."

I know he is lying. I grab him by his shirt. "You are making me angry. If you don't want to help I'll get some of my young men to help you remember. I have information from Rundu that says you are helping the PLAN insurgents. I am not here to play," I say threateningly.

He laughs in resignation: my tirade has worked. He points with his one hand to the north where an old Portuguese town was once situated. "You will not see the end of the war," he says to me dejectedly, like somebody caught in a situation where he does not want to be.

"There were six armed SWAPOs next to that large tree by the ruins. They should still be around."

I and the other trackers get back in the cars. I take out a ration pack and toss it to the old man.

We drive to the tree and get out. Six tracks, just like the old man said.

I call Willie Roux to come across.

He joins us and calls up Zulu 2. The gunships can stand by.

We start following the tracks, all four teams. We normally don't track too far up front when we are in Angola, but with four teams in place we have enough firepower to do it this time round.

The tracks run south along a footpath.

At a *chana,* my car and one other drive through it to the other side and pick up the tracks again.

They are running.

Willie Roux calls up Zulu 2. The gunship is on its way—30 minutes' flying time. The insurgents bombshell into groups of two. Our two cars, number 3 Zulu-4 Echo and we, Zulu-4 Sierra 3, move forward a faction on one set of tracks and immediately make contact.

"Contact! Contact!"

We are right on top of them.

We throw red smoke so that everyone can see where we are. The contact is such a chaotic mess that insurgents and trackers literally look one another in the eye. From the hatches of the cars the machine guns chatter furiously. Josef Bernabe is behind one. With all his experience he does not miss. I shout at him to stop as he is in danger of hitting our people with his ricochets.

I shout at the drivers to look for the insurgents and to run them over.

But there are more than two insurgents in this firefight. In a stretch of land of about 200 metres in length, there are six of them. As the other cars approach the scene, they too drive headlong into the contact.

Somewhere an RPG explodes and then another. Cars are all over the place.

The gunship is laying down searching fire around the perimeter. It is too dangerous for his 20mm cannon in the contact area itself as he might hit us.

One of our cars misses an insurgent who is lying dead still and not firing. He has frozen in the mayhem. Chris Cloete sees him and from his car dives on top of him. He knocks the AK-47 right out of his hands. Cloete picks him up by the throat—just like a professional wrestler does with an opponent.

But the insurgent does not fight back. It was this SWAPO's first and last contact. To freeze in your first contact is something that happens in any army in the world.

Another insurgent might have hurt us badly; Chris could have taken a barrage of bullets in his chest.

Once again, everything is quiet and we count five dead. One is the SWAPO commander with the fighting name of Driekwarti. We gather up RPGs, AKs, a PKM, an SKS and armour-piercing grenades, backpacks, landmines and a whole lot of POMZs.

We suffer two wounded: one man from Zulu-4 Echo and one from Zulu-4 Sierra. It might even have been by friendly fire.

We will never know.

The gunship lands and takes them away.

Sakkie Kaikamas: one driver, four rockets (Omuramba Odela, 1988)

Sakkie told me this story, as well as the account on page 167.

The start of the dry season in 1988; Kavangoland is quiet. Ovamboland is quiet. Sakkie is 18 years old and is one of the drivers of the Zulu-4 Echo team. As a tracker, he already has nearly a year's experience, but behind the wheel of the steel giant, he is still fairly new.

They TB at Okongo and in the morning drive past Odela in a westerly direction. Then they turn north at Efinde where they will begin their questioning. In this patrol Sakkie is in car number 1—the group leader's car. Drom van Rooyen is the commander. He wants Sakkie close by. The commander of car 2 is Sergeant Pieter 'Chappa' Strauss. *Chappa* is the Kwangali word for 'guineafowl'. Chappa is a man with many freckles, hence the reference to the multi-spotted guineafowl. The whites called his car the 'ambulance': when he sits on top of his car with his red head, they said it reminds them of the red light on top of an ambulance.

Chappa has heard that there is enemy activity at one of the kraals which is why they are on the way to the kraal at Efinde.

When they get to the kraal, Chappa talks to the informant. The information is vague. He has heard that there are SWAPO members in the area. He does not know how many. He does not know where, just that there are a lot of them.

They drive away without any concrete information. What are the chances that there would be so many insurgents at that time of year? At this stage, Drom and Herman Havenga are constantly making jokes about the 'contacts' they had been in. Dangerous and irresponsible jokes, as Sakkie would later learn.

They arrive in the area of Omuramba Odela and spread out over the veld to see if they can find any tracks. Everything is quiet and, except for the information from the informant, there is no indication of anybody in the area. They take a chance. They deploy a sweep line stretching over a few hundred metres, when suddenly Sakkie drives right into an ambush of about 30 insurgents.

"Contact! Contact!" Drom shouts over the radios. But he has to shout a second time before Herman hears the urgency in his voice.

Everywhere around Sakkie fighting erupts. An insurgent right in front of him fires an RPG rocket at him. He barely misses. He reloads and fires again, but Sakkie swings the car around and the rocket flies past in front of the vehicle's nose. From another direction another RPG operator fires over the roof of the Casspir. The third rocket also misses. Between Sakkie and the insurgents is a large, dry fallen tree. He can't go forward because he is scared the tree will break the axle or the shocks and he might get stuck and become a sitting duck. If that happens the SWAPOs could overrun Koevoet.

The other cars start arriving at Sakkie's Casspir, offering support The battle is fierce. Rounds from AKs and SKS rifles hit the cars like a hailstorm. Above and next to Sakkie the gunners fire desperately at their attackers. R5s are firing through the gunports on the sides of the Casspir. Empty magazines drop to the floor and cartridge cases fly around the car. The smell of the gunfire is heavy.

Then the first RPG operator fires another rocket—the fourth. He misses—Sakkie does not know how; he thought he was about to die. He could not miss—but he did. Could he have been nervous? Could he have been suffering from 'shooting fever'? The rocket flies past harmlessly. One over, one in front, another one over and the last one to the side.

The incompetent SWAPO RPG operator in front of them eventually falls before the Koevoet guns. The other one is also shot. The contact breaks off and the insurgents flee for their lives.

But the action is not over—the Blesbok has disappeared and does not answer his radio. Could he have been overrun? Did the insurgents get him? While the cars mop up the site, the teams search for him. The Blesbok has vanished.

Meanwhile, Zulu-4 Sierra joins them. A gunship arrives from Zulu 2 and also joins in the search. Eventually they find the wayward Belsbok and bring him back. His radio was broken and in the dense bush he lost the rest of the teams and simply carried on driving.

With the support of Zulu-4 Sierra they continue to follow the insurgents' tracks. Not too far away they find three insurgents. They have been left to cover the retreat, to give their comrades time to escape. The teams crash through the ambush position and all three are killed.

What a waste of lives.

It starts to rain and the tracks are lost.

They try once again—a car from Zulu-4 Sierra and Sergeant Blackie (Riaan) Swart's car 3 drive to a nearby kraal. They are two minutes away from the teams when Sakkie hears the sounds of another contact. They hurry in that direction but when they arrive the battle is over.

Another one dead.

That was their last action of the day. Five heads with plenty of equipment. The group of 30 has been broken and scattered.

Herman and Drom would never make jokes about fake ambushes like that again. Koevoet had prayer parade every morning. Their communist-inspired enemies did not. Sakkie lived through four RPG rocket attempts that day. One was enough to kill them all—and the last one had his number on it. But he had prayed that morning.

Today Namibia is a country with freedom of religion, not ruled by communist atheism.

Koevoet did make a difference.

Sakkie Kaikamas, Casspir driver: action before breakfast (1988)

They leave Okongo in a northerly direction and enter Angola at beacon 28. They turn northwest and drive to the Onalumono area where they start questioning the local population; one of them says he saw a group of about 200 PLAN members two weeks earlier. The story is a bit much to swallow, but Drom van Rooyen calls the teams together and they decide to put the informant in a car and go and have a look. They are already in Angola and it is not a bother.

They load the man in a car and drive to the indicated place in the bush. Yes, there are tracks and there are many, but they are two weeks' old. The driver of the Blesbok gets out and takes a few tins of food from the back of the vehicle which he gives to the man.

They follow the tracks until nightfall and make a TB to overnight. The next morning, they continue on the tracks. The tracks run due south toward the border, the area whence the teams had come two days earlier. Along the road they question the kraals. The story is always the same: yes, there were 200 PLAN insurgents on their way to South West Africa. That night the teams sleep on the Jati on the Angolan side.

The next morning, they cross the border. The insurgents have wet the tracks with water from their water bottles to make it look as if the tracks have been rained on: an anti-tracking trick which, unfortunately for them, Koevoet is familiar with.

Just across the border, Zulu 4 sends Zulu-4 Foxtrot and Zulu-4 Whiskey to join them. They are on the tracks for the whole day, bundu-bashing. The terrain is punishing on the cars—branches, flat tyres and sand. The grills of the cars fill up with leaves and grass and the cars overheat. Every now and then a car has to hang back to cool off.

That night, they sleep in the bush near Efinde.

On their fourth morning on the tracks they enter much thicker bush. After an hour they find where the group based up for a few days. They are now near Oruwaya. The tracks lead away from the SWAPO TB, still heading south. At the White Road, the Chandelier Road, the tracks suddenly turn east. Near 18° the tracks turn north and then west again. This lot knows Koevoet is onto them. They are running the teams in circles.

Warrant Officer Willie Roux is not going to take any chances and calls the gunship at Zulu 2. When tracks start moving in circles the chances of an ambush are increased. Willie calls a halt to the whole tracking effort and they wait for the helicopters. After about 45 minutes the helicopters are above. The tension is unbearable. Sakkie's heart beats in his throat and he is sweating. To possibly have 200 insurgents waiting in ambush is nerve-wracking. Where are they and who will fire the first shot when the ambush is sprung?

They move forward again—but the long wait has given the SWAPOs an opening. Instead of springing an ambush, they have bombshelled. Now there are about 15 or 20 groups and each has gone its own way. Koevoet will be lucky if they come across one or maybe two groups today.

Sakkie's team begins to follow a group moving in a southerly direction. Once more they arrive at the White Road, but they won't catch up with any insurgents today—darkness is closing in. They mark the tracks and drive to Okongo at Zulu-4 Oscar, where they spend the night.

There are two teams at Okongo that night: Zulu-4 Echo and Zulu-4 Sierra. The senior black commanders have a meeting.

"Why did the *shirumbu* [white commanders] stop when we were close to the large group today?"

"We were ready for them."

"The decision to wait for the helicopters effectively made us miss the contact. If they are scared we must get other commanders. We cannot work with cowards as commanders."

After a while, they call Herman Havenga and Drom van Rooyen.

Herman and Drom must explain—I translate. They explain that it was not their decision. Warrant Officer Willie Roux made the decision. The senior black commanders are not convinced. "Willie Roux made a bad decision. Why does he decide on his own? Why did they not stand up? Why were our opinions not taken into consideration? You are brave men, but you folded under the pressure today."

It is a day when the team leaders lost much credibility. (Willie Roux explained later that he could not attack the big group, as he knew an ambush was imminent and that the insurgents were probably dug in, which later proved to be true. Koevoet casualties would have been unacceptably high and unnecessary. Koevoet, in fact, achieved its objective, i.e. to break the large group down into more manageable smaller groups.)

The quarrel with the white commanders does not signal the end of the meeting. The war must go on and Koevoet has to sweep the area clean of insurgents. They will return to the tracks tomorrow, both teams to the same place. The chances that the insurgents will have slept there are slim. They will have fled during the night. We will split the cars into two groups—one from each team—and send them to search for the tracks.

They conclude the meeting. They inspect the cars and fill up with diesel and water. They don't know when they will get another opportunity. The next morning at 0430 hours they drive out of the base.

They wait for the sun to rise on the tracks.

Drom and Herman lead the search. At the first kraal that two of the cars visit, they obtain information. It is 0630 hours. Sergeant Blackie Swart passes on the information to the team leaders. One enemy slept there—there are his tracks—he is running. After the previous evening's confrontaion, the white team leaders will not again be accused of being cowards. Herman Havenga calls Zulu 2. They send a gunship—20 minutes' flying time.

But this time the teams do not wait.

The tracks are *payife-payife*—hot, very hot.

They proceed without helicopter support.

The follow-up begins to look like a race. Sakkie is driving the Casspir as if on a tarred road, but there isn't even a dirt track. They are bundu-bashing.

The insurgent starts running in circles, around the teams over his own tracks—sometimes they surely pass within metres of where he is hiding.

Then Herman calls, "Contact! Contact!"

Immediately R5s and machine guns open up.

"Cease fire! Cease fire!" Herman shouts seconds later.

It is only 0700 hours.

He is dead—no he is alive! In the chaos of the contact, there is uncertainty whether the insurgent is alive or dead. He is alive. The team climbs out and one man carries him to Sakkie's car. The medic gives him morphine and puts him on a drip.

"Don't kill me."

Sakkie gives him water and he starts talking. There were 200 of them who crossed the border. Yesterday there were 30 in the group that Koevoet was chasing when it got dark. They scattered when they heard that Koevoet was near. They all plan to rendezvous today at Oshifitu.

The gunship arrives and the team throws smoke. He lands, but today he is not here to kill. They load the insurgent as a casevac onto the gunship and send him to the base at Okongo.

They do not have time to waste—they have to get to Oshifitu.

B Company should have already been withdrawn from the field, but with all these tracks there is no chance for any immediate withdrawal; certainly not when taking into account the intense events of the previous day. Alpha Company is already in the field; while Sakkie and the teams are on their way to Oshifitu, the cars of Zulu-4 Juliet join them.

At Oshifitu they start tracking 360 degrees around the kraals. Some of the trackers find where the insurgents washed their clothes. In the middle of being tracked and during the night these insurgents washed their clothes! These are no ordinary insurgents—these are disciplined soldiers.

At the entrance to a kraal they find fresh tracks.

"*Payife*—they have just been here, three of them!"

Blackie passes the information on to Herman Havenga. They are southwest of the complex. They fire a 1,000-foot flare and the rest of the teams gather on them. They follow the tracks further and next to Sakkie, car 1 of Zulu-4 Juliet suddenly shouts, "Contact! Contact!"

Herman Havenga is behind the gun on top of his car and blasts one insurgent into eternity. Another falls under the guns of car 1 of Zulu-4 Juliet.

They get out and examine the area. Two dead. The list of weapons reads:

1 x AK-47 and seven full magazines

1 x SKS and eight rifle grenades

4 x hand grenades

2 x POMZs

3 x Jumping Jacks

2 x backpacks

A variety of uniforms

These SWAPO members are from a special unit, the Typhoon unit. They are the best that SWAPO has. They were on their way to the white farms in the south.

It is 1100 hours and the teams have already had two contacts.

Zulu 4 calls them back. The Ovamboland teams are also here and Sakkie and his teams can now go and rest. They drive across the 18° and Herman and Drom get out. They start laughing along with the other team members. It has been a difficult week. The tension is gone. They started off with 200 tracks, nearly lost them all, only to make contact twice before 11 o'clock in the morning. Two heads and one prisoner.

But there are still many others out there before they can cosider the job done. When they arrive at Arendsnes the teams sing spontaneously. Now they can rest—SWAPO cannot.

The Alpha Company teams of Zulu 4 and Zulu will make sure of that.

Eleven insurgents at Oshakati Cuca (Eenhana, 1988)

The trading complex just outside Eenhana was more than just a *cuca* area. It was a general trading centre with a lot of drinking places. From time to time we even bought spares for the Casspirs at the heavy vehicle parts shop that was also situated there.

The problem was that the insurgents also drank here—and when they were drunk they were braver than usual. Then they'd shoot at vehicles on the road, most of the time army or police convoys, but sometimes anyone who happened to be passing by. It was like the Wild West, Indian country, but with Ovambos.

One of the Zulu-4 Foxtrot cars went to Oshakati *Cuca* one morning to fetch some spare parts. When they arrived some of the 'resident' insurgents spotted them and began firing rockets at them. Luckily they all missed. The driver sped away to Eenhana to report the attack.

Zulu 2 went into action and the whole Bravo Group of Zulu 4 was called to inspect the area. The idea was to cut the insurgents off and make contact with them before they could cross into Angola at dusk.

We hurriedly leave Okongolo where we are patrolling.

Zulu-4 Foxtrot are already on the tracks and a while later Zulu-4 Echo and Zulu-4 Whiskey join them. The tracks show signs of running and are moving north toward the border. They are now in the Omundongilo area. We are coming from some distance away and drive to where the rockets were fired and here we start following the Casspir tracks.

We only catch up with everyone at Hakafiya. The tracks indicate that the insurgents are still running but it has become too dangerous in the fading light. The sun is going down and the Bravo Group commander, Warrant Officer Willie Roux, gives the order for the men of the four teams to stop and make a TB. All 160 men make a TB with 16 Casspirs and four Blesbok armoured supply trucks—a formidable laager.

By 0500 the next morning, we move out and start tracking again. We get to the Jati. At the border the insurgents spread out and we can count the tracks for the first time—eleven in total. They are still running north.

Willie Roux gives our position to Zulu 2 and we cross the border into Angola. After two kilometres the group splits up into one group of five and one of six. We and Zulu-4 Whiskey take the tracks of the group of five; we head northwest. Zulu-4 Echo and Zulu-4 Foxtrot take the group of six; they head northeast.

After a few kilometres, we lose the tracks. I am in command of car 2. We move up front with one of the Whiskey cars. We arrive at a footpath and start searching. We find the tracks, but they have crossed the footpath and are moving west into the bush, away from the direction in which they were going when we first started following them. But whereas the previous tracks were last night's, these are fresh—very fresh. Between where we lost the tracks and our position here, they must have slept somewhere. The other trackers join us and agree with me.

The tracks are very fresh.

Warrant Officer Willie joins us, and Herman Havenga and I discuss the situation with him. We were right on top of them when they heard us, which is when they decided to change direction. Willie tells our two cars to scout ahead—two kilometres ahead.

We and car 3 of Zulu-4 Whiskey find the tracks quite soon. The insurgents are now just 20 to 30 minutes in front of us. I let Herman Havenga know that the tracks are *payife, payife*—he must call a gunship. Before the gunship arrives we lose the tracks in a *shona* filled with water. We are not fish and cannot see in the water.

Two hours later, we find the tracks on the other side of the *shona*. Once again, Chappa and I from car 3 are sent two kilometres farther to the front to try our luck.

We find the tracks and Willie Roux instructs me to fire a flare so they can see where we are. I climb off the car and fire the flare. The teams link up with us within minutes. The tracks are running, all one behind the other. They want us to run as well; they want us to run into the muzzles of their AKs or to activate an anti-personnel mine through recklessness.

Running would put many lives in danger.

We have been in action too long to be sucked into a trap—we are veterans of many such follow-up actions. We load all the trackers onto the cars except the experienced men. The man in command on the ground is Hiskia, an old hand and a gifted tracker.

They run on the tracks but they are careful. They look for the spoor but they are also looking for unnatural lines—such as a taut nylon wire. There are no straight lines in nature.

The next moment Hiskia's hand shoots up. "Stop! Stop!" he shouts.

Everybody stops immediately. I jump off and go to him.

He is speaking Okavango and is patting his chest. *"Tura mutjima."* (Be still my heart.)

A few centimetres in front of his feet is the barely visible trip wire of a POMZ. His sharp senses and keen sight have saved the lives of four trackers. Willie Roux and Herman Havenga join us.

We put the safety pin back in the POMZ.

The follow-up can continue.

The tracks are now very fresh. The gunships are on their way, but it starts raining. There is a huge storm. We try, but the bird has flown the cage—everything is washed away. Once again, the rain saves the enemy.

As it is in Africa, the rain sometimes comes in isolated showers. It rains in one spot and a few kilometres away not a drop falls. Toward the east it is dry and we hear the sound of a contact coming from that direction. The helicopter that was on hand to help us is dispatched to the other contact.

After a few minutes' radio silence a casevac is requested. Five insurgents have been killed, but there are casualties on our side. One man is dead: Warrant Officer Felix hit by an RPG inside a Casspir.

All the teams return to Okongo.

This day was a turning point in our war.

In the gunship was a photo-journalist. When the gunship arrived overhead the contact area he wanted a nice photo of the action. Instead of shooting the insurgents the pilot and gunner tried to position the helicopter to get some good action photos for the journalist. The result was that one car drove past an insurgent who blasted it through the side with a rocket. The shrapnel killed Warrant Officer Felix. For the sake of a photo we lost a very good man. We decided among us—black and white team leaders—that we would never allow a photographer on one of our patrols again.

Photographers were welcome to come and take nice action photos—when we were playing soccer.

A hero, a wound, the death of a good boy (Ongolongela, 28 March 1988)

We move from Arendsnes in Rundu, past Nkurnkuru to Mpunguvlei over the border of Kavango and Ovamboland. The border is at 18° east. We sleep at Okongo. The next morning, we hear that Naas van Zyl has had a bad dream. We hear him telling the whites about it.

Naas says to them: "I think I am going to be killed today."

We go on patrol and progress to Oshifitu. Naas is in command of our car and second in command of the team. This day the team consists of 36 black members, four white commanders and a white medic. I am second in command of the Casspir and senior tracker of the team. I am 22—an experienced, fit young man. I can stay on a track from morning to night, 12 hours—seven to seven.

Not far from Oshifitu I can see that Naas is not his usual self. He is quiet and appears anxious. I ask him what is wrong. He says that he does not want to spook the team. Nothing is wrong. But the other constables notice. They ask me what is wrong and I tell them not to worry, Naas will be fine. He is just a bit quiet this morning.

We arrive at a well where there are a few people gathered. We question them. With me is Josef Bernabe, the Angolan and former Unita soldier. He came to Namibia seeking a better life than that which Angola could offer. He ended up with Koevoet. The unit was grateful for his wealth of local knowledge and experience.

We are called over the radio.

We quickly get into the Casspir and drive to where Zulu-4 Foxtrot is waiting for us. Zulu-4 Foxtrot has found tracks. They say there are seven tracks about three days' old. Our team is on the western side of a big kraal complex, with Zulu-4 Foxtrot at the other end, to the east. We move toward them, but by the time we get there they are already gone.

After about three kilometres we catch up with them. Zulu-4 Foxtrot is moving along the tracks, but we stop so that we can have a look at the spoor.

Something is not right. Naas van Zyl climbs out and asks what the problem seems to be. I tell him to wait where he is while I approach the other trackers, Asser Samuel and Abed. We study the tracks together. It is very clear that these tracks are not three days' old, but last night's tracks. While we were questioning the people at Oshifitu it had rained—a few drops, very little— and these tracks are a bit wet. One of the spoor is that of an old adversary, Mamubona, a veteran local SWAPO commander. We move forward on the tracks and arrive at another kraal complex near Ongolongela.

Warrant Officer Willie Roux and his team Zulu-4 Whiskey also join us. Over the radio he instructs Sergeant Herman Havenga, team leader of Zulu-4 Sierra, to take three Casspirs to the southeast of Ongolongela and Drom van Rooyen to send one of his Casspirs with us. Asser Samuel asks me why we are going to track ahead if we are not sure of the age of the tracks. It could be dangerous.

Naas also looks uncomfortable with the proceedings.

The three Casspirs from our team and the Zulu-4 Echo car drive behind each other past the kraal, with our car bringing up the rear. An old man picks up a child. The other trackers and I are edgy. I shout at the driver to stop. I want to talk to the old man, but Naas says we press on. The warrant told us to track ahead and Naas does not want trouble with him. The other cars are already a few hundred metres ahead of us.

We drive off.

We are about 300 metres from the old man's kraal, when a PLAN insurgent initiates an ambush with an RPG-7 rocket. We were right from the outset! The tracks *are* fresh, not three days' old—last night's!

The rocket crashes through the small armoured window on the left, on the gunner's side, and explodes inside the Casspir. SWAPO also fire at us with SKS rifle grenades. (The SKS looks like a hunting rifle and many of the white policemen dreamed of having such a rifle as a hunting weapon.) It sounds like a hailstorm on a tin roof as AK and SKS rounds slam into the steel hull of our lone car. The bulletproof windscreen shatters into whiteness; not pierced, but damaged so one cannot see through it any more.

Inside the car there is pandemonium. The RPG explosion has killed Naas outright, virtually cutting him in half. The driver, Daniel Muhuli, has been wrenched from the steering wheel and stumbles blindly to the back, heavily wounded and in shock. The car is stopped right in the middle of the killing zone. I am also badly wounded by shrapnel; I am bleeding all over my body and legs. There is blood in my eyes.

I am now in command of the car. Before I can take over command a wounded and bloody Josef Bernabe jumps behind the Browning on the roof. He shoots with withering determination into the ambush position. This saves our lives. I regain my senses and grab the radio but it has been destroyed: useless. Above me the sound of the big gun is ear-shattering—Thud!— Thud!—Thud! the bursts sound as Bernabe fires like a man possessed.

Then everything goes quiet. Like lightning, Bernabe drops from the top of the car. I think he has been shot, but he jumps behind the steering wheel of the Casspir and drives it wildly out of the killing field. The other Zulu-4 Sierra Casspirs now join us and start milling around the contact area. It snaps the enemy's resolve and they break off contact.

A Puma comes to fetch us and we are taken away, first to Okongo. The sickbay there, however, cannot treat the large number of badly wounded men. We are stabilized and sent to Ondangwa and then to Pretoria and 1 Military Hospital in Voortrekkerhoogte. While I am lying in the dressing station at Okongo, I hear over the radio that the tracks have been lost. It has started raining.

By the time we reached Ondangwa, the big boys in the unit had found the tracks. The next day Sergeant Francois du Toit and Zulu Quebec would find and wipe out five of the group who took part in the contact.

A stupid mistake—carelessness—would make a man's premonition of death a reality and get him killed. The tracks were entrusted to inexperienced trackers. The commanders were in a hurry and left their judgement to the wind. Naas van Zyl should never have died. One piece of shrapnel took the life of a very good man.

But the loss could have been much greater. Had it not been for the cool, calm performance of Josef Bernabe, the casualties could have been far worse. His aggressive action saved the situation and when he could not continue firing, he took the Casspir out of the danger zone. His performance was, to say the least, heroic. He saved the situation with a calmness of spirit and neutralized the ambush single-handedly.

The hero of the day was undoubtedly Josef Bernabe

He was a man among men.

Settling the score (Ongolongela, June 1988)

It is the winter of 1988. The Kavango teams of Zulu-4 Echo and Zulu-4 Sierra are working near Efinde. We pick up the tracks of a suspected insurgent moving in a southerly direction. We cross the Chandelier Road and come back to the area near Oupile. Farther south we find the large kraal complex of Ongolongela, where I was wounded a few months earlier.

Our team commander, Sergeant Herman Havenga, gets out of the car at the complex and talks to an old man. The old man is evasive. He looks uncomfortable. Yes, he did see six insurgents. They were standing next to the road when he saw them last. We move off a bit and find the tracks on a footpath—the six who were allegedly next to the main road. Six insurgents in dense bush can prove a difficult challenge. Herman Havenga asks for help. The two teams of Zulu 4 are now supported by Zulu Tango, Zulu-1 Juliet and Zulu-4 Foxtrot.

The hunt is on.

The tracks run south, then east, before turning north. I am the tracker in front of the front-cut car. Constable Bernabe, the hero of the previous contact in which I was wounded, arrives and calls me over.

"Sergeant, one of the six is a SWAPO commander."

"Who?"

"Mamubona."

"How do you know?"

"I asked at the kraal and they gave me his name."

I search among the tracks and yes, there are his tracks. Unmistakably Mamubona's tracks. I have seen these tracks before. Mamubona was there the day I was wounded three months earlier, the day Naas died.

The day of reckoning has come.

When the tracks turn north we know that the insurgents are aware of us. I feel unsafe because I know an ambush is a strong likelihood.

We are not trotting on the tracks anymore and the cars pass us.

The Casspirs with their firepower and armour must handle the fight now.

Fifty metres after they pass us, rifle fire erupts, then the sound of an RPG rocket exploding. One of the Casspirs is burning. Two SWAPO insurgents are killed in the firefight. Nobody on our side is hurt. We leave the burning Casspir and its crew behind and follow the other four insurgents.

Mamubona is one of them.

Usually they bombshell, but not today. A few hundred metres farther on there is another short, violent firefight. Another two SWAPO members are killed. There is no escape and we capture Commander Mamubona alive.

He has fought hard—a brave fighter.

The man responsible for my wounds is out of the way at last. We return to Okongo and sleep there that night.

The next day, we are back at Arendsnes with our old enemy, Mamubona, in tow.

He will languish in jail for the remainder of the war.

The whites

The whites in Koevoet who served with us in the bush were good men. Most of them were genuinely interested in, and cared for, us. But there were some who changed drastically when they were back at base, and we did not always understand them. Like the ones who washed their clothes with petrol!

One man stood out above the rest: Lukas Koen, a deeply faithful Christian with a strong sense of justice. He was promoted to officer, yet even as a lieutenant he was not 'above us' when we were in the bush. He always stood up for our rights. Some of the whites were not prepared to stand up for us; they refused to confront the officers on our behalf. But Lukas Koen was not scared of anybody; he believed in his people and our cause. He often sent the whole Bravo Group home when we'd done a job well. (There were two groups in Koevoet, which alternated between deployment in the bush and resting up at base or at home. Bravo Group was made up of Zulu-4 Sierra, Zulu-4 Echo, Zulu-4 Whiskey and Zulu-4 Foxtrot, while Alpha Group consisted of Zulu-4 Delta, Zulu-4 Hotel, Zulu-4 Juliet and Zulu-4 November. Lukas treated both groups similarly and fairly.)

There were some critical requirements in being a member of Koevoet: discipline, understanding, obedience, bravery, knowledge and leadership. If you did not possess all these factors, your life would likely be very short.

The ability of the commander was central to everything. Willie Roux was the senior warrant officer of Bravo Company. He was one of the most competent leaders in Koevoet. Zulu-4 Sierra, Zulu-4 Whiskey, Zulu-4 Foxtrot and Zulu-4 Echo were his responsibility. He had wide-ranging abilities. As an instructor, he was without equal. He was a policeman first and foremost; he taught his students to investigate, to question—to separate the chaff from the wheat; he taught us to be analytical, but he also knew the bush, and even the black trackers, people of the bush themselves, respected his abilities.

There were others like him. Bravery was the core quality—young Steven

Sander, Sampie, Kallie Calitz, Mossie, Kassie, Nattie 'Drom' van Rooyen, for example. Drom was a big man, as his name suggests, but even with his massive frame, he could run on tracks with the best of us.

Then there was Herman Havenga, later team leader of Zulu-4 Sierra. As his senior black sergeant, he and I worked together very closely. He was loyal to us until the end—a great team leader, who listened; a brave man who never stood back for anything.

And then of course our founder, trainer and commander, Hendrik Engelbrecht. His nickname was 'Kwang' because of the respect afforded him by the Kwangalis who served with him; he was a man who deserved the highest of respect.

Sadly, he died before publication of this book. A tragedy indeed: another victim of the war.

But we will never forget him.

Rescue and treachery
(Ncagcana, March 1985; Eenhana, 1988)

We are patrolling out of Nepara near the Kavango–Ovamboland border. We arrive at Ncagcana, where at one particular kraal there is a large festival in progress; the people are very drunk, but everything goes off without incident—a good kraal party, where it feels good to be welcomed.

The next morning, we obtain information that SWAPO arrived at the party just after we had left and abducted a female teacher. They first raped her and then took her with them the next morning when they moved out at about 0400 hours.

There are five VY tracks. The teams of Zulu-4 Sierra and Zulu-4 Echo go after the tracks and by 1000 hours the contact is over. Four of the five insurgents are killed. We capture a lot of weapons and equipment.

The woman is in a bad condition. All five of the insurgents raped her. They also stabbed her in her thighs with their bayonets. Our medic does what he can and gives her an injection for the pain. Then we take her to Okongo. At Okongo a casevac helicopter is already waiting for her. The air force takes her to the aid station at Ondangwa, where she is treated until she is well enough to return home.

She recovered fully and started teaching again, at a school in Eenhana.

One day at Eenhana, we are called to the school. The teacher thanks us and gives us four cases of beer and cases of cooldrink. She thanks us in front of everyone assembled and says that the people of Koevoet saved her life.

A few months later, we happen to be at Eenhana again and come across the same woman. But now she wears a SWAPO T-shirt and is busy telling anyone who cares to listen that Koevoet is a bunch of murderous thugs. During the latter part of 1988, SWAPO was openly canvassing, spreading its particlar brand of politics withour fear of repercussion. At the time it was already clear that, before too long, the South African military involvement in Namibia and Koevoet would be things of the past.

People have short memories and forget the crimes perpetrated against them and trauma inflicted upon them. To save their skins, it is easier to switch sides.

This is a natural human condition.

The same thing happened with the National Party politicians in South Africa, who were to sell us out by denying their involvement, sweeping our contribution under the carpet.

We were cast aside by the woman teacher, by the politicians and by our own senior policemen.

Loyalty was to become a dirty word, clad in the yellowness of treachery.

The political tide is turning (late 1988)

By the end of 1988, the political tide is turning. Up until recently, most of the people have supported us; we receive their goodwill and their blessing in our relentless efforts to stop the spread of SWAPO terrorism.

But that is all changing.

It is obvious that the wholesale intimidation of the local population by SWAPO's political commissars is having a severe effect on the way in which we are perceived by the tribespeople.

One morning, while patrolling near Nkurunkuru, we stop at a kraal. I enter and talk to an old man we know well, and whom we have regularly visited over the years. This time he is uneasy about us being here.

I explain to him that things will be soon be easier for the people, that things will get better: nobody will have to carry identification documents; anyone will be able to freely move around, anywhere, even at night; everyone, SWAPO and Koevoet alike, will be integrated into the same police force; the war will stop.

"They say that you are murderers. You supported and fought for apartheid. You will never be allowed into the new security forces. They will kill you," he says.

"What about people like Festus and the other PLAN members who have committed murder, here, in your very own kraal?" I ask him.

"Festus is dead, and he was as mad as all you people who started this war."

We leave and a few kilometres farther on, meet a young man. We engage him in conversation and chat about the future.

"Which political party do you support?"

"We are policemen. We do not get involved in politics. We are here to protect and to serve the people."

He continues on the same lines as the old man.

It is very obvious that SWAPO is busy with a massive 're-education' programme. Our home base, our support base, is rapidly being eroded and we do not have the tools to counter the onslaught. The South Africans cannot, and do not step up to the plate.

Our security and our future are in the balance.

Our lives are in the balance.

We drive back to Nkurunkuru.

At the base, two of the young constables come to me. They have heard everything. "Sergeant, if you fight, we fight. If you go to South Africa or Angola, we also go."

They would stick to their word.

The macro-politics: a Koevoet tracker's view (April 1989)

The battle of Opepela was my biggest contact ever. It took place on 2 April 1989. That day has often made me think of the dynamics of a sports team, a partnership where there is harmony, where you have one captain, but a leader who listens to his players.

Koevoet was a unit that was in complete harmony. That was why we were so successful. Although there were officers back at base, essential decisions were made by the men in the bush, on the ground—experienced trackers of all ranks with skilled team leaders coordinating everything. The team leaders commmincated on-the-ground information to the operation rooms, which in turn deployed more teams and helicopters, but the tactical situation was entrusted to the teams. If there was a contact, the team leaders were in control. No one else. They had a lot of experience, they were excellent fighters with an intuition for job at hand.

1 and 2 April 1989 were different from anything we had experienced before. Normally SWAPO ran when we were closing in. This time it was different. On the way to the target areas where the insurgents had crossed the Angolan border we found SWAPO supporters dancing and singing in some of the kraals.

Some of them shouted, "You won't be coming back! You are driving to your death."

When we came back they were not so cocky.

At that time the radio was full of war: "SWAPO has invaded northern Namibia; insurgents and security forces in heavy battles; terrorists flee back over the border; widespread contacts across the country."

That was the time when we were under the control of the UN, under the direct control of Marthi Atthisari, not the South Africans any more. Atthisari must have choked on the fact that he had to fight his favourite pets, SWAPO, with their biggest enemy, Koevoet. There was a time when the pro-SWAPO UNTAG literally begged us not to chase and attack their friends, the

SWAPO insurgents when they fled back across the border. UNTAG was the United Nations Transitional Assistance Group—the so-called peacekeepers who owed their dubious existence to the implementation of United Nations Resolution 435.

Resolution 435 made provision for the army to be confined to their bases, the air force could not operate their helicopters and we had to revert to our role of ordinary policemen. All our heavy weapons had to be removed from the cars and our khaki uniforms were replaced with standard police grey ones.

With all these restrictions we still managed to hit SWAPO hard. Our success did not mean a thing to the UN. They totally ignored the fact that Namibia was not deteriorating into yet another chaotic, war-torn African state. Their sole ambition was for their favourite—SWAPO—to take power. SWAPO's war atrocities, what today would be known as 'crimes against humanity', were completely and conveniently ignored. The murders, kidnappings, landmines and rapes perpetrated by SWAPO faded into irrelevant history, not least of all because this is how most OAU members themselves had attained power in their own blood-soaked African countries.

What *was* loudly remembered, however, was that we, Koevoet, were the baddies, because we stood against the Soviets, the communist Eastern Bloc, the Cubans, the Western liberals and the rest of Africa. The fact that there were other Namibians—other Namibians who did not support SWAPO—was never taken into account.

We did not fight for the white people. We did not fight to uphold apartheid. We fought for ourselves and a free Namibia. We fought against a one-party Marxist dictatorship of the type SWAPO would have implemented had they come to power earlier, like many other examples in Africa and Asia during the 1970s and 1980s—Frelimo and Machel in Mozambique, and the MPLA and Neto in Angola being two of the most glaring examples.

Prelude to death: on the road to Opepela (1 April 1989)

Although we knew that SWAPO would launch an attack as soon as their freinds UNTAG took over in 1989, our hands were tied. We had had to put away our big guns and maintain a low profile. However, when Zulu Foxtrot caught a SWAPO pathfinder on 31 March, the cat was out of the bag.

But we were not prepared for what was to come.

We saw no action for many months. SWAPO was quiet.

But no one trusted SWAPO, not for a second.

On the afternoon of 1 April, we leave Rundu, pass through Nkurunkuru and overnight at a temporary base nearby. The next morning, we travel north through Okongo to the border. At the Jati we join some of the other teams already waiting for us. The situation is dangerous. There are more SWAPO tracks than any of us have ever seen. Maybe 250 or more.

Eventually there are seven teams which begin the follow-up. But not all the teams are complete. Some of the cars still have to be re-equipped with their machine guns in preparation for the coming battle and are still in the maintenance workshops at the Eenhana and Okongo bases.

We form a line that extends two to three kilometres and start on the tracks. At a deserted kraal I ask a lone old woman where all the people have gone. She says they have fled and that SWAPO has moved through here. SWAPO told her to warn us that there are not enough of us to deal with them, that we should bring in massive reinforecemnts. But there are no more teams available. Our teams are fully preoccupied in dealing with the SWAPO incursion that has spread like a cancer right across the region.

In every case we are vastly outnumbered by SWAPO.

Some of the trackers differ on the age of the tracks. However, it is clear that the insurgents are carrying heavy packs. They have come, but not in peace. They have also come to stay. By early afternoon we get to a kraal in the Opepela area near the Odila River.

Some of us are wondering why we haven't test-fired a few mortars. Maybe

Sergeant Grobler is a bit inexperienced, what with such a large battle group on his hands. Maybe he is not convinced that we really are on the verge of being ambushed. I'm convinced that some of the old hands would have handled the situation differently.

At Opepela the battle that has been threatening all morning, erupts. It is a massive ambush that appears initially to work well for the enemy in the dense bush, which restricts the movement of the cars; visibility is down to a few metres. The commander, Sergeant Herman Grobler, is badly wounded and his car is shot out immediately. His heroism that day would become legendary. Other cars are also seriously damaged and two of Zulu-4 Hotel's cars are also shot out. In one case both the driver and the gunner of a car are killed. We cannot get gunship support because under Resolution 435 there is peace and in peacetime gunships are not necessary. Only helicopters to transport injured policemen are allowed to fly.

It is a desperate fight for survival. Mortars explode behind us but soon start falling among us. We are in a very difficult situation, especially as so many of the cars are immobile and out of action.

The man who would eventually turn the fight in our favour, Warrant Officer Attie Hattingh, arrives on the horizon like a shadow. He was not part of the follow-up because his car was in the process of being repaired and refitted with its machine guns at the base workshops. However, he was already on his way to us when the contact began. With him are his own teams, and several rag-tag pick-up teams that he managed to scrape together back at base.

He had decided to drive cross-country to our position, and arrived about five kilometres to the south of the battle, right in the midst of the SWAPO mortar position. After some heavy and desperate fighting he and the few cars under his command managed to neutralize the numerically superior enemy in the heavily defended mortar position.

SWAPO's protection element is now out of action and, as a result, the mortars stop raining down on us. We are now able to clean up the ambush position with comparative ease. The whole firefight has lasted about three hours.

After much pleading with the operations room for a casevac helicopter, we eventually get a Puma to come and extract the wounded. There are many wounded. We flatten the trees with the cars to clear a landing zone for the Puma. We gather up more than 20 SWAPO corpses from the contact area. Many more will die as they are carried away by their comrades in the days to come.

It is sunset by the time the wounded and dead are flown out.

Could the day have been different? Yes, our teams were not ready for action. If all our cars had been ready and equipped as normal it would have been a different story. I don't know why we didn't fire a salvo of mortars at the projected target site or at least 2,000 metres in front of us like we usually did. Maybe we were scared that we would hit the locals. If we had had gunship support our casualties would have been much lighter.

With this battle at Opepela we unsettled SWAPO's nerve. They thought they could cross the border and set up base camps in Namibia with impunity. They did not believe for one minute that we could stop them so firmly and aggressively. This is the chance they took, a chance that cost them dearly.

After this contact, SWAPO split up into several smaller groups and scattered in all directions. We hounded them relentlessly over the next few days and wiped them out, group by group, insurgent by insurgent. Many of them threw away their weapons and equipment in an effort to blend in with the locals. But we still hunted them down and killed them.

The Namibian war was never pretty, but its dimensions had now changed radically. It would be bloodier than ever. We literally shot terror into SWAPO. We were still the champions. Like a stampeding elephant herd, we still trampled the insurgents at will. As Bravo Group, we still were able to leave our mark. And we at Koevoet were ironically a UN force!

Bravo, Group Bravo!

An army captain (south of Opepela, 3–4 April 1989)

SWAPO began their treacherous incursion on 1 April 1989. What should have been a time of peace was now a time a war, the likes of which northern Namibia had never seen.

On 3 April we drive through Okongo, past yesterday's battlefield at Opepela, to Etakaya. At Etakaya a number of army Ratel 90s join us. A captain is in command.

We start following the tracks of 60 VYs. They are moving southwest and come from the direction of Opepela and Onaway. There are two teams from Zulu, five from Zulu 4 and a squadron of Ratels from the army. We chase the tracks the whole day, but we cannot catch them.

By nightfall we make the biggest TB I have ever seen. We make fires to prepare dinner. As always, the Koevoet TB is noisy. Next to us the armour soldiers are digging in for the night. The shovels come out and each soldier digs a hole to sleep in. There are no fires and they do not make any noise. This does not really help because their neighbours do not believe in noise control. It gets too much for the captain. He approaches the nearest Koevoet member and asks who the commander is. The captain is directed to me.

"Please douse the fires and keep quiet!" he says.

"Captain, I have been with Koevoet for six years and have never been scared of SWAPO. They do not attack our TBs. They allow us the rest. Go and sleep peacefully. We also don't put guards out."

The captain asks my name.

"Sergeant Kamongo," I reply.

He turns away, shaking his head in frsutration and goes over to where the white Koevoet members are braaiing meat—another kudu that did not survive the war. They also give him an answer he does not like. He returns to his lines in disgust.

By 1900 hours the army armour men are in their sleeping bags with guards posted and fields of fire laid out. By 2200 hours we are also almost quiet—

with dozens of plans and ideas formulated of what we will do to SWAPO when we find them.

Early the next morning at about 0400 hours we have the usual prayer parade. The armour men also take part.

But all is not well in the SADF—the army captain is not happy.

He confronts Willie Roux after the parade about our noise during the night, calling us reckless. He wants to take it further when we all get back to base.

Willie gets annoyed very quickly. "Captain, we are not scared of SWAPO—they are scared of us. Before this day is over, you will see. They are going to run. They are going to throw away their backpacks and rifles. Mark my words, before this day is over!"

When it is light enough to see, we start on the tracks. There are a lot of Casspirs, Wolfs and Ratels in the follow-up. Up front, in the centre is a small group of trackers. I am one of them, the lead tracker of the follow-up—point man in American terminology.

We find an old man at a kraal where the tracks have recently passed. "Son," he says to me, "they say I must tell you that you are too few. Today you are all dead. They are heavily armed and carry heavy loads. I am sorry for you."

"Grandfather, before the sun goes down today, they will be running. They will run past your kraal. You will see this with your own eyes."

"I have never seen SWAPOs who have given me messages for Koevoet that say, 'tell them we are going here or there'. They always want to hide. They say they will get you at Onalusheshete." He finishes off with a nervous laugh and claps his hands, as though he sees himself as the unwilling bearer of bad news.

Behind me are 250 men waiting for the two of us to finish our chat.

I give the information to Warrant Officer Willie. We carry on tracking.

By 1200 hours we are about 30 minutes behind the enemy. With the moratorium on gunships temporarily lifted the previous day Willie calls Zulu 2 and they dispatch gunships—24 minutes' flying time. After 15 minutes we move forward. The contact is now mere minutes away—we can feel it.

When the helicopters arrive ten minutes later, the planned ambush dissolves. Where there should have been an ambush, 60 insurgents are fleeing in all directions. They bombshell into groups of three to five.

But the day is far from over.

The helicopters have broken the insurgents' nerve. Against a Casspir you still have a chance—but against a fire-spitting 20mm cannon from above you have no chance. It is death and destruction, nothing less.

Willie Roux is now determined. The recent deaths of our friends at Opepela are still fresh in his thoughts. Many of us wear the black arm bands of mourners. SWAPO will pay with blood for our men's lives. Willie takes the radio and asks to talk to Zulu directly—the general. He wants to split his cars up into pairs and follow these small groups in this manner.

The general says fine.

The gloves are off.

SWAPO is prepared to make war—but only until 1200 hours, 4 April 1989. They have come to take over the country through the barrel of a rifle. Elections and democracy are not on their agenda—the military base at Onalusheshete is. However, their plans are now a shambles.

We start chasing the tracks and everywhere we pick up backpacks, equipment and ammunition. Anything that could hamper their flight is dumped by the insurgents in an attempt to save their necks. In some places we even pick up AKs and RPGs. We follow the tracks, with the sounds of machine-gun and small-arms fire all about us. SWAPO is bleeding, but the army is acting according to their manual—too carefully according to ours. They are holding up the mission with their caution. We have experienced literally hundreds of this type of contact over the past ten years. We are not scared of small groups. We do not need an army captain delaying us! Some of the senior team leaders complain to Zulu and the order comes through to ditch the army.

It is a wise decision. We can now fight at our own pace.

SWAPO die everywhere. On that day of 4 April there was just one security-force death—an army Recce operator attached to one of the teams. The enemy lost over a hundred. It was a slaughter—but this was SWAPO's gamble. It was an expensive and bloody error of judgement.

The SWAPO incursion in April 1989 was not a good idea. It cost them many lives unnecessarily. UNTAG begged us to leave their pets alone—even though they did not think we would be able to regroup and re-arm so quickly.

They forgot we were the most successful anti-insurgent force of our time.

Did SWAPO come in peace? They were very well armed for people coming in peace. The battles of that first week in April were the heaviest of the bush war.

Peace?

On 9 April 1989 the remnants of the SWAPO insurgents vanished with their tails between their legs back across the Angolan border, and the battles and skirmishes fizzled out.

The war was at an end.

Twenty-three years of armed struggle was over.

But for the Koevoet men it was far from the end of the road.

Where the trouble all began: communist propaganda depicting Marx, Engels and Lenin in an abandoned southern Angolan town. The only legacy of the communists was destruction and death, as can be seen by the buildings and, fittingly, the billboard.
Photo Attie Hattingh

Below: Another southern Angolan ghost town over the barrel of an LMG. The burned-out wreck of a Soviet-supplied military vehicle is in front of the building in the centre.
Photo Attie Hattingh

The inside of a Casspir. Koevoet members faced the conundrum of where to put enemy corpses. *Photo Attie Hattingh*

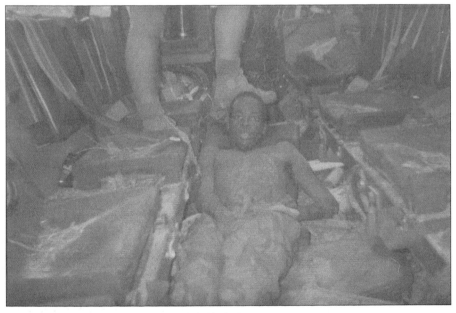

A wounded insurgent inside a car. *Photo Attie Hattingh*

Blesbok armoured-support vehicle: the logistical hub of a Koevoet patrol.
Photo Attie Hattingh

Willie Roux and Hendrik Engelbrecht.
Photo Willie Roux

Warrant Officer Willie Roux: "Put down that thing before you hurt someone!" *Photo Willie Roux*

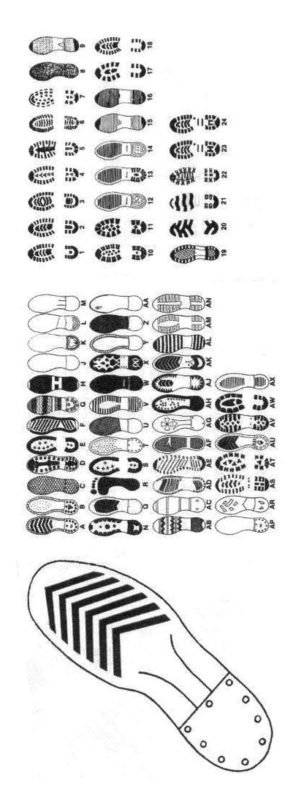

The art of tracking. The SWAPO chevron-pattern boot and other enemy boot prints on the left, with security-force prints right.

Another landmine blast, with no damage to the hull.
Photo Attie Hattingh

Zulu-4 Sierra at the wreck of a FAPLA truck on the Jati after it was attacked by Unita, 1989. Sergeant Shorty Kamongo is in the centre with the black T-shirt which reads 'Nge', the scorpion, insignia of combat team Zulu-4 Sierra. By 1989, the truce between South Africa and Angola had been instituted but the war between Unita and FAPLA raged on unabated.
Photo Willie Roux

Zulu-4 Whiskey driver Constable Shikare Kamalapi behind the 'five 0' and 'three 0' combination.
Photo Willie Roux

A Puma helicopter landing in the bush at last light. The LZ has been was flattened and cleared by Casspirs to allow the helicopter to land. *Photo Herman Grobler*

Ovamboland teams at a temporary base, with dinner under the car on the left. *Photo Attie Hattingh*

Harvested *mahango*, the staple grain in northern Namibia and southern Angola.

Zulu Foxtrot car and Puma after a contact. *Photo Attie Hattingh*

One of Sergeant Francois 'Toitjie' du Toit's Zulu Quebec cars after a landmine blast. The V-shaped hull could withstand the blast of three anti-tank mines simulataneously without serious injury to the crew and passengers. A blown-off wheel hub was a minor irritation.
Photo Attie Hattingh

Investigating terrorist activity at a local store, a *cuca*, somewhere in eastern Ovamboland.
Photo Kallie Calitz

Below: Koevoet convoy on the Chandelier Road.
Photo Attie Hattingh

Sisingi Kamongo in front of the house donated to him by Fabricated Steel Manufacturing, with the shack he used to live in at left, August 2010.
Photo Leon Uys

Vingerkraal, near Warmbaths (now Bela-Bela): the farm an agent'sold' to ex-Koevoet members. He might have won the court case but one day he'll be presenting himself before the Almighty ... *Photo Leon Uys*

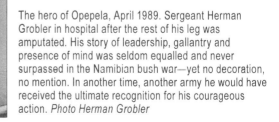

The hero of Opepela, April 1989. Sergeant Herman Grobler in hospital after the rest of his leg was amputated. His story of leadership, gallantry and presence of mind was seldom equalled and never surpassed in the Namibian bush war—yet no decoration, no mention. In another time, another army he would have received the ultimate recognition for his courageous action. *Photo Herman Grobler*

Opepela at dusk with the 23 SWAPO corpses in body bags. *Photo Herman Grobler*

Major Willie Ras's Puma at Opepela. The bold decision to overload the helicopter saved many lives, including Herman Grobler's. *Photo Herman Grobler*

Herman Havenga, team leader of Zulu-4 Sierra, in 1988, with Naas van Zyl. Naas was KIA a few days after this photo was taken. He'd had a dream that he would be killed. The man on the right is Nande Bernabe, brother of Josef Bernabe, the hero of the contact in which Naas was killed. "I cried a lot for Naas."
Photo Herman Havenga

The inside of Naas's car after the ambush in which he was killed. The RPG came through the left front window with the shrapnel from the glass and steel virtually cutting him in half. The radio was also destroyed. Sisingi Kamongo and most of the others in the car were injured; Kamongo spent three months in hospital recovering.
Photo Herman Havenga

Typical SWAPO chevron-pattern boot print.
Photo Louis Bothma

An Alouette gunship covers a Casspir with its 20mm cannon. *Photo Attie Hattingh*

A Koevoet patrol awaiting orders at Okongo. *Photo Attie Hattingh*

Twenty years later in July 2009 on Delville Wood Day, the Voortrekker Monument Running Club held a race to honour Herman Grobler for his bravery during the battle of Opepela. Awaiting the start of the race is Herman Grobler (Zulu Foxtrot), Francois du Toit (Zulu Quebec, scripture-reading and prayer), Inspector Charl Jordaan ('The Last Post'), Pipe-Major Craig Herwill (South African Irish Regimental Association, 'Flowers of the Forest') and Leon Bezuidenhout (organizer). *Photo Marna Kriel*

An authentic SWAPO photograph of an insurgent with an SKS rifler and rifle grenade. The photo was given to the author by an ex-PLAN member. *Photo anonymous*

A Koevoet policeman helps a villager draw water from a well at Oshana Shanalama, southern Angola, 1986. *Photo Kallie Calitz*

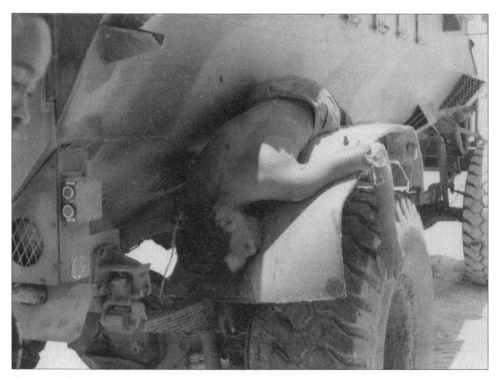

The corpse of an insurgent strapped to a mudguard. *Photo Attie Hattingh*

Koevoet trackers on spoor. If the spoor was clearly visible, recent and open, the trackers could follow it at a brisk trot. *Photo Attie Hattingh*

Herman Grobler as a police recruit, 1983.
Photo Herman Grobler

Sergeant Herman Grobler takes a break on top of a car during his earlier days with Koevoet in 1986. "I have no regrets. I lost my leg but I lived my dream."
Photo Herman Grobler

A Casspir in a TB at dusk, with guns facing out. By dawn the TB would be gone. *Photo Attie Hattingh*

Another Portuguese-style southern Angolan town abandoned and destroyed. No one back in South Africa knew that police teams were operating deep inside Angola. *Photo Attie Hattingh*

"They said I must tell you, you are too few, today they will kill you all." Old Ovamboland woman at her kraal fence. *Photo Kallie Calitz*

Getting information was one of the crucial factors to success. Civilians were either pro-SWAPO or pro the security forces— then there were those who were involved, just by being there. *Photo Attie Hattingh*

Even in the midst of a war in Africa, football was universally played. Here a Koevoet patrol drives over a football pitch in eastern Ovamboland. *Photo Kallie Calitz*

The idea of a civil war (Rundu, 30 October 1989)

On 30 October 1989 three hundred of us assemble in front of the stores at Arendsnes with our rifles. I have an R5 rifle and two pistols, one without paperwork. They will not get that one. As a sign of solidarity and also to say goodbye, we dance and sing.

Then we move out—never to return to the base again.

Koevoet, the most feared of counter-insurgency units, has disbanded.

Demobilized.

As a group, we are still a target; not only in the eyes of our old enemy, SWAPO and the UN, but also at another level—the political level. Outside the gates a former Koevoet warrant officer is waiting for us. He is working for the DTA, the Democratic Turnhalle Alliance, the South African-supported political party standing against SWAPO in the elections. We are given DTA T-shirts and are recruited immediately.

I go home with the question in my mind of what will happen if SWAPO win the election. Would there be a second war? At home in the Kavango the DTA are strong. Some of the people start calling me 'major'. We have our own teams made up of former police and army members. Everyone has been demobilized. We have our own rank structure. We have our own informers and are well informed of what is going on across the region. Among the SWA police there is much sympathy for those of us who have been demobilized.

We in the DTA are so strong that our message sweeps across the region. We are prepared to fight to avoid the ravages of communist oppression. By this time, the Cold War is on its last legs, with the USSR imploding. However, where we are in this little corner of southwestern Africa the old enemy is no less intimidating or violent. The fact that the USSR is falling apart means nothing here: there are no sophisticated media in the Kavango. If SWAPO wins the election, the war will resume.

The election takes place early in December 1989. SWAPO wins, the DTA comes second. But our option to fight has evaporated. We have no weapons and most Koevoet members have already fled. Many have crossed the border into Angola to join Unita, the pro-Western liberation movement, South Africa's allies against the Cuban communists. Others in Ovamboland and Kaokoland have already fled to South Africa.

I do not have much choice. SWAPO supporters are becoming more and more aggressive and arrogant. They want blood and there are not many of us left.

We have a secret meeting one night to decide what to do. We weigh up all the options. There are a couple of possibilities. We can stay and take our chances—which might cost us our lives and our blood. Unita is another option, but they are struggling and the South African support they rely on might not last too long. The only other option is South Africa, but it is far away. Alternatively we could go to the South African enclave of Walvis Bay. We debate for many hours until I realize that some people at the meeting are not quite so anti-SWAPO any more. The meeting has suddenly become a dangerous place. SWAPO also have their informants. I cannot trust anyone any longer.

Now we are all on our own.

My choice is Walvis Bay. As a Koevoet leader, I am blacklisted with SWAPO. I cannot take the chance. I am 26 and could still start a new life in South Africa. I leave my house and family behind, my wife and my young daughter.

They should join me later, which unfortunately never happened.

From Rundu to Walvis Bay and beyond, 1990

I decide to go to South Africa. My first goal is Walvis Bay. I take a taxi from Rundu to Windhoek. There I find a warrant officer who had also been in Rundu, who wants to help me. He is in charge of the single quarters in Windhoek. He takes me to a room and gives me some food. To anyone who is curious he introduces me as sergeant. Our story is that I am here as a witness in a case. The other policemen relax and respect me. Other former Koevoet members also arrive. The number of 'witnesses' grows. The warrant officer explains that we will not be here for long.

After three weeks, I leave for Walvis Bay with four other former Koevoet members. At the border a group of SWAPO political commissars are waiting. We are warned before we get there. We stop the vehicle a few hundred metres before the border and I bury my bag next to the road. Inside are the last few bits of Koevoet uniform I have left, all the photos I took during my six years' service, as well as my notebooks that I also used as diaries. Six years' worth of battle information. As far as I know, I was the only Koevoet member to keep such a record. But my life is on the line. Inside the bag I also bury my AK-47 and a Makarov pistol. My police 9mm Berretta I'd given to one of my friends who decided to stay behind at Rundu. I brought the AK-47 back from a patrol in Angola.

We cross the border without incident, but we could not have risked trying to smuggle such contraband. SWAPO is busy tightening the screws on former Koevoet members. I could lose my life.

After a week in Walvis Bay, 13 of us fly to South Africa to start a new life. We fly from Walvis Bay to Lanseria airport near Johannesburg—but it is not easy. Nobody is there to meet us. We have no passports, but we say we are from the police and they let us through. By 1700 hours we are all standing outside the arrivals hall. Some of the others are unhappy. A few white soldiers pass us and ask us what we are doing here. I explain that I am Sergeant Kamongo from Koevoet and that I would like to talk to their commander. They take me to an officer, but he does not know what to do. with us, so he phones the SAP headquarters in Pretoria and hands me the telephone. At the other end of the line is a black person, but he speaks Zulu, a language I have never heard before—except from Brenda Fasie's songs. I only talk Afrikaans, and so we get nowhere. Eventually he hands the phone to an Afrikaans sergeant and the situation improves. The sergeant says he will send a vehicle. A police vehicle with two white policemen arrives later. They buy hamburgers and cooldrinks for us and then leave us there! We go back to the airport lounge and I see a framed article about the SWAPO April invasion on the wall. I burst out laughing.

"Why are you laughing?" the others want to know. They are quite sour. I show them the article and they laugh too. Here we stand, the heroes of this very invasion, and nobody cares. We are actually more in the way than anything else.

Our laughter attracts the attention of the airport police and we have to explain who we are and why we are laughing. We find new friends. By 2200 hours a police truck arrives at last and we are taken to a nearby police station. Once again, phone calls are made and this time it is Colonel Willem Fouché, the last operational Koevoet officer, on the line. He explains that we have to sleep at the police station. He will send someone to come and fetch us early the next morning. A police station is not a hotel, so they book us into the holding cells and we overnight after our fingerprints have been taken!

The next morning we are 'released' and they give us coffee. There is no mention of transport. At about 1000 hours, I am sitting on a rock at the gate of the police station when a small bus drives in. Inside are a number of white policemen.

Someone yells from inside the bus, "Stop! Stop!"

I recognize him immediately as one of Warrant Officer Willie Roux's car commanders from Zulu-4 Whiskey.

"Shorty! What are you doing here?" he wants to know.

I explain our situation.

"Where are the others?" he asks.

"Around the corner."

"Go and fetch them. I'll be back now."

I call the others and we go back to the rock. Minutes later, another minibus arrives with the sergeant from Zulu-4 Whiskey driving.

"Where are we going?" I ask him.

"Moordkop," he says.

I had never heard of it.

At last we are on the way to somewhere. After about 40 minutes, Sergeant Herman Grobler in another bus catches up with us. Even with his artificial leg, he drives quite well. But the Zulu4-Whiskey sergeant does not want to let us go. He is determined to complete his mission but he lets a few of us get onto Herman's bus. Herman stops at a shopping centre and buys food for all of us—beer as well. By the time we get to Moordkop we are very jolly. We sing and chatter.

At Moordkop there is a wonderful reunion. There are hundreds of people, but most of the able-bodied men are on deployment. We are allocated a place to sleep and sworn in as 'Special Constables' in the SAP.

Two weeks later we join the rest of the unit where they are conducting operations in KwaZulu-Natal. They are staying at a TB on a farm and are sweeping the area. We locate hundreds of stolen cattle, goats and sheep. It is hard work, the Drakensberg Mountains are tough. I receive my first pay cheque in the South African Police in August 1990—R70.00 (about 10.00 US dollars). It is very little, but the criminals are not in the same league as SWAPO. Unfortunately, there is no 'danger pay'.

After everything we experienced in the bush war this is child's play. Finding cattle in the mountains of Natal is easy. No one sets POMZs or shoots at us. The men of Zulu now work among the Zulu!

The effect of the teams now being deployed in the rural areas is wonderful. Dagga plantations are found and destroyed, game poaching and cattle theft are almost entirely eradicated. We find many firearms. We help solve many murders. If the culprit leaves a spoor, we follow him and track him down. Our crime prevention and investigation is making a huge difference; in our area of operations crime almost ceases. The story gets round that we are here. Word of our success spreads like wildfire across Natal and criminals think twice before committing a crime in our area.

Our contribution to the overall safety of South Africa and Namibia should never be underestimated. With our lives and our blood we created a stable environment in which the politicians could work toward peace. Unfortunately, the very same politicians betrayed us. They indeed had the power to accommodate us, but the name 'Koevoet' unfortunately had unpleasant connotations for them, and their skins. When they'd got what they wanted, they cheated us financially, robbed us of our prospects and discarded us.

All this, however, can never change what we know in our hearts: that we helped bring about change and create a better South Africa and Namibia. Whether someone important will have the courage to one day tell our story, remains to be seen.

A sacrificial lamb (Vingerkraal, 1993–1994)

By the end of 1993, we were working hard in the South African Police. We had stopped the surge in farm murders dead in its tracks. In areas where we operated serious crime was virtually non-existent. We were supported by the law. We took many criminals off the streets and locked them away. We were a success. If a problem area existed we were ready to get stuck into it and clean it up. Sometimes we were deployed within hours. If you left tracks, we were on your heels. We would get you.

We were in demand in many of the police districts. We stopped cattle theft on the Lesotho border, made farms safer in the Eastern Cape, chopped up and destroyed huge dagga (marijuana) plantations in Zululand and stopped cattle theft on the Tugela River. We even made an impact in the towns. At one stage, we were working in Midrand between Johannesburg and Pretoria. The criminals left. Criminals are funny: if they know they are being watched they stop. We, Koevoet, the political dilemma of the police, became the success story of the police.

But our enemies were never far away. For some politicians we were the sacrificial lambs. What we had achieved was not important. We were Koevoet and we had to go. The writing was on the wall in late 1993. We were 'offered' severance packages, but were not really given a choice. Take it and leave or, well, take it and leave. In two areas the district commanders found ways to circumvent these clumsy attempts, to their everlasting credit. In Cape Town and Pietersburg 30 of us stayed on in the police. Most are still there.

The picture at Rooiberg, where we were later deployed, was none too pretty. Clashes between top police management and the loyal former team leaders increased. In all, we were promised R63 million in the way of severance packages by Louis Pienaar, the previous Administrator-General of South West Africa. These funds were duly transferred to the South African Police. We were faithfully promised we would get our money.

We signed the papers, received our leave pay; we were finished with the

South African Police. We bought the farm Vingerkraal with our leave pay. The agent cheated us. It transpired later that the 'selling contract' turned out to be a 'ten-year lease contract'. He subsequently defended himself in court, but his 1994 verbal statements and his written contract did not tie up. He may defend his so-called 'contract' in court, but less likely before the Almighty.

We never received the R63 million. When the ANC government came to power, the staff at Police Headquarters were too scared of their new political masters, and refused to make the payments. Monies due to us were withheld by spineless policemen who were only concerned with their own future in the newly named South African Police Service.

By now we were all South African citizens. There was no chance of turning back. We were part of South Africa and that was it.

Unemployed, but citizens.

By 1994, we were all finished with the police.

But our experience as bush fighters was in demand. Many of us joined the South Africa security company, Executive Outcomes. Some of us went to Sierra Leone, Angola, Iraq and Afghanistan. Some of us were also involved in the failed *coup d'état* attempt in Equatorial Guinea and would spend some years in a Zimbabwean jail. But this kind of work was scarce—the money was good but based only on success. I was personally never involved with Executive Outcomes or active in the countries mentioned above, but my tracking skills were well utilized within South Africa.

Farm protection, burglar on a bicycle (Levubu, 1997)

I am working in farm security on the farms in the Levubu district, east of Louis Trichardt, not far from the border with Zimbabwe. Our company has a contract with the farmers of the area. Four of us, all former members of Koevoet, are on duty one Friday morning when we are called to a crime scene. It is about 11 o'clock.

We arrive at a farmer's house and the South African Police Service already have two men on site. They are busy taking statements. I call the farmer to one side and ask him to give us more information. He shows us. The perpetrator broke in through a window, then fried himself some meat in a pan in the kitchen, drank the farmer's beer and took his whisky and some of his clothes. The farmer thinks he left the scene on a bicycle.

We start looking for bicycle tracks. At about 1 o'clock we find bicycle tracks on a small footpath near the house. We start our old technique of forward tracking. Two members follow the tracks and two go up front in the Nissan to look for tracks. We make quick progress. At 4 o'clock we find a man on a bicycle wearing a beautiful suit near Mayilula, nearly 30 kilometres from the farm. The bicycle tracks are the same as the ones we started tracking on the farm.

We perform a citizen's arrest and load him on the pickup. We hand him to the police at the Levubu police station. The man is identified by the farmer, as is the beautiful stolen suit. Upon further investigation, the police discover that the man is on a wanted list in the area. He is tied to many other cases.

When one does good security work the farmers do not renew their contracts. But criminals are patient. Weeks after our contract was terminated, the criminals were back.

Well, actually another lot—ours were all in jail.

Smuggled away like a thief in the night (Gravelotte, 2002)

After the war, Marius Espach of Zulu-4 Echo went back to Phalaborwa, where he had been a detective, until the day he became tired of the police and formed his own security company. He hired me and a few of the others. We worked on the game farms to the east of Tzaneen, bordering the Kruger National Park.

Game theft and poaching was a huge problem and the farmers were unprepared for the onslaught. The poachers were very good and the farms were very big. The security people who were there before us could not solve the problem.

One night, the dogs start barking non-stop on the farm where we are staying. At 0200 hours I wake up the guards to go and have a look. But it is dark and we don't see anything suspicious. At first light we start looking for tracks in the area. When the farmer eventually joins us we have already been tracking five tracks for some time. The perpetrators have brought their own dogs with them. We are chasing tracks made by people and their animals.

A bit farther on we find a place where two impala have been slaughtered. The skins and horns are hidden under a bush. We carry on and find the carcasses hanging from a tree near the road, ready to be picked up later. We leave a guard hidden in the bush about 100 metres from the site—just in case they decide to be brave and come and collect the carcasses in broad daylight. I am sure we would see them that evening anyway.

By 1900 hours, we are in place for the night's work. I asked the farmer to place two stopper groups in pickups some distance farther down the road. I and two of my men wait about 50 metres away in the bush, ready for action.

At 2100 hours two men come walking down the road. Nearing the carcasses, they start looking around to see if anyone's watching. Minutes later, a pickup stops next to them and they start loading the carcasses. I phone the farmer and the poachers drive right into their roadblock.

We catch all four culprits.

Back at the farm we all go to bed—we have been up since 0200 hours that morning. Poachers will not bother us again tonight.

However, that day, Marius, the owner of our security business, has come to the area to have a look-see and gets involved in a discussion with some farmers at the local farmers' bar. At 0200 hours the next morning there is a knock on our door. It is Marius.

"Get up! Get up! We are leaving," he whispers.

I do not understand. Later I would hear that one of the farmers was so impressed with our tracking abilities that he wanted to make us all an offer the next morning, an offer we would not be able to refuse. Marius could not afford the loss to his business if he were to lose us, so he smuggled us out of there like thieves in the night. We were worth too much to his business to lose.

A champion bull (Tzaneen, 2003)

I am commanding five former Koevoet members performing farm security on three farms around Ofcolaco, near Letsitele. One of the farms is owned by the chairman of the local farmers' society, Theo de Jager.

One evening, the farmers' society has a meeting where one of the farmers, Ernst Helm, is very unhappy. He bought a champion bull a week ago at a show. He paid a huge sum for the animal. The bull is called Blum-Hofklaus, a champion Simmentaler. The bull spent a few nights in the kraal and then it disappeared. It is now the third day and Ernst's investment is still missing.

Late that evening, the chairman comes to the rooms where we are staying. He wakes me up and tells us that early the following morning a farmer will come and pick us up, and we are to go and search for the bull. The next morning, a farmer collects us in his pickup. I and one other man accompany him.

We stop at the farmhouse and an elderly white woman comes out. She is from Oshakati in Namibia and is visiting her daughter. She speaks fluent Kwanyama. After talking to us, she tells her son-in-law: "You will have your bull back today; these people know their tracking."

We take our leave and go to the kraal where the herders are waiting for us.

We question them. They say they are also trackers and that they followed the tracks to the tarmac road. The bull was then taken away on the tarmac road—it must have been stolen. I ask them to show me the tracks—I want to see for myself. After a while, they show me the tracks. It was likely an attractive bull to the farmer but I can see that one front hoof is slightly twisted and one back hoof is bigger than the other. It is not normal.

I start following the tracks where they leave the kraal along the footpath. My tracker and the farmer's tracker walk ahead, apparently tracking, but I follow the bull's tracks step by step. The two trackers keep to the footpath, but the bull's tracks turn off the path. Not where they are walking. They lose the tracks. The tracks don't lead anywhere near the tarmac road but in the direction of the dense bush on the farm. The other trackers see me turning away and come back to me very embarrassed. I tell them to walk behind me. They know nothing about tracking.

We pursue the tracks all the way to the edge of the farm. We find hair on the boundary fence where the bull broke through the barbed-wire strands. The tracks are four days' old. We keep following the tracks. I find places where the bull laid down on different occasions. Where the bull grazed recently, we find dung and it is still warm, not older than 30 minutes. But now there are also other cattle around. I walk up to them, about 200 metres away.

Among them is a huge bull. It has a little yellow disc in its ear with a number. I compare the number on the disc with the number the farmer gave me. We have found him. I phone the farmer on my mobile phone.

By 1400 hours I have solved the R40,000 riddle.

The farmer arrives; he cannot believe that I was able to follow tracks that were four days' old. I explain to him that I was in Koevoet for years and finding a bull is easy. I have been doing it since I was a child.

When we arrive back at the farmstead the farmer gives me R400 for a few hours' work. It is far more than I received several years ago from Koevoet when I found the B10 and its bombs.

The farmer's mother-in-law also comes out and says. "I told you, these men know how. Do you see?"

I never told the farmer that his champion bull actually had deformed feet. I started off by tracking cattle as a child. Finding Blum-Hofklaus, the champion Simmentaler bull, would be my last-ever tracking job.

An invalid (2004)

The POMZ explosion I was involved in on 18 February 1986 would haunt me for the rest of my life. There were 15 wounded. I was one of the five seriously wounded. We were flown to Ondangwa, and from there to 1 Military Hospital, Pretoria. Both my feet and legs were peppered with shrapnel.

In the rainy season, the POMZs were particularly dangerous. The outer steel casing rusted, and the rusted metal of the shrapnel created an ongoing cycle of infection and sores. Even after I returned to my duties, I regularly had to visit the doctor for treatment of infections and abscesses.

Owing to the amount of shrapnel I had in me, as well as the positioning of where some of the steel was lodged, the doctors decided it was not possible or safe to remove it all from my body. The left side of my body suffered more than my right and my left leg regularly caused me to return to the doctors. From time to time it swelled up alarmingly, so much so that I could not use the leg.

Even more serious was a particularly large piece of metal very close to my spine, which was too close to the nerves to be removed. Taking it out would mean the end of the use of my legs.

In 2002 I was back in hospital again. Elim Hospital transferred me to Pietersburg Hospital. Here the specialists had a look at me. I explained to them the origin of my injury and they gave me a letter to submit to the police. The letter stated that my injury was very serious and asked the police to compensate me for the injury to my legs.

In November 2003 I was working for Marius Espach. We were going into a store at Elim, near Louis Trichardt, when my legs simply gave way from under me. I had not done anything unusual: I was just going to buy a Coke. All feeling in my legs was gone.

I was taken to Elim Hospital and they immediately sent me to Pietersburg. At Pietersburg I saw the same specialist.

He remarked, "I thought I would have seen you sooner."

They tried everything in their power to revive my legs but nothing worked. I was an invalid. Over the following year, 2004, I was continually in and out of hospital. The result was that I was sent to George Mukhari Hospital in Ga-Rankuwa. Once in the spinal unit I realized that this was it, there would be no turning back. I had to learn to use my new wheelchair. It was a new life for me. I had to learn how to dress, how to go to the toilet, how to get out of bed. It was a humbling experience.

Life was tough. I was sent home. Suddenly, my new South African wife did not love me that much any more. She left me. I went back to Vingerkraal. At Vingerkraal there were no roads, no amenities. I lived in a shack. Then the local government asked if anyone was interested in being resettled closer to Radium. My aunt and her husband, Daniel Kambungo, took up the offer. I talked to Daniel, he agreed that could I move my shack next to their new RDP house. I lived for four more years in that shack with a dirt floor before a certain company heard about my plight and donated a prefabricated steel house.

I was now eligible for a disability pension. I applied and it became my main source of income. The same pension a beggar gets if he is run over by a car while begging. The specialists' letter that I submitted to the police was never answered. I received not one cent in compensation nor one cent from the police as a pension.

In 2010 I heard that someone was willing to write our story. I knew I had the ability to write down my feelings and experiences, so I started to put them to paper. On the day we, the old Koevoet veterans, met Leon Bezuidenhout I had a fair amount written down already. After that very stormy meeting, I gave Leon my drafts. A day later he came back and asked for more. For the next six months, I dug into the memories of my past and put them down on paper. It was only when I wrote them down that I began to realize what a remarkable life I'd had, because of one factor: my ability to analyze shadows in the sand.

Looking back

While conducting a follow-up operation near Gcava in western Kavangoland in 1985, Zulu-4 Echo and Zulu-4 Sierra captured a PLAN commander. His fighting name was Secondere. Many of the captured insurgents were turned easily, but there were also the die-hards, the hard-core fighters who believed in their cause and why they were fighting. This man was one of them.

While sitting in the back of the Casspir he looked down at his legs. He never looked at his captors. Then he started talking.

"SWAPO will rule this country. Those of you in Koevoet will enjoy the new government because they will understand you. How do you feel in your hearts because you are being forced to fight your brothers? You are fighting for money."

"No, we are policemen enforcing the laws of the country. We are paid for it, but we also have to make a living," one of the trackers answers.

He laughs, "You don't know politicians; you don't know politicians."

He was sentenced to jail in the Naimwandi prison, but escaped after three months and went back to Lubango in Angola.

Secondere was right. SWAPO would govern Namibia and some of our former members would join the new Namibian security forces. We were naïve. We did not understand politics.

Democracy is sweet for the citizens of Namibia today; the people should enjoy it. They suffered so much during the war and they deserve a free country. May the country never collapse into a state where one party turns into a dictatorship. Too much blood has been spilt to allow that.

What was the end result of the war between Koevoet and SWAPO? The world must know that this was a war between brothers. One brother fought on one side and the other brother on the other side. I know of one case where a Casspir flying a white flag drove into the FAPLA base at Ongiva in Angola, to inform a Koevoet member's brother in FAPLA that their father had died.

It was a war in which politicians and foreigners suppressed and used black

Namibians for their own ends. On the one side were the Soviets and their communist lackeys, and on the other the South Africans who were still practising apartheid.

We were in the middle. What could we do? Which side was right? Luckily, the Cold War is over now.

The elephant bull charged and the opponents stood fast. With RPG-7s, SKSs, AK-47s and rifle grenades, SWAPO stood up to the charging Casspirs and Wolfs. It takes courage to stand up against such a charge. Most of them fell before the onslaught. That was the way of the war. One SWAPO insurgent shot three Koevoet policemen during a follow-up operation in March 1983, all on his own. He was a brave man. He died in the contact. I have the greatest respect for the enemy. They were also my brothers.

We suffered POMZ mines many times. Sometimes there were five explosions in a row, one after another. But a Koevoet follow-up never faltered as a result of a POMZ detonation and SWAPO never stopped trying to unnerve us. To walk in the sand knowing the next POMZ might kill you took a brave man indeed.

We cried for our friends and respected our enemies.

We were enemies and we were brothers.

Today, all are just brothers again.

May the war be forgotten and the brave deeds of our countrymen be the only memories that endure.

Everybody believed they fought the good fight—and they are all right.

This is my story.

—Sisingi 'Shorty' Kamongo
nom de guerre: Kafiya Maumbo ('Sweeper of the kraals')

Emwenyo modili

Shiwana mwalelepo emwenyo modili
Omeme mwalelepo emwenyo modili
Otate mwalelepo emwenyo modili
Shiwana nomutila—Emwenyo modili
Vakwetu nomutila—Emwenyo modili
Oshili nomutila—Emwenyo modili
Shiwana mwalele—Emwenyo modili

Still alive

My people, you can all sleep safely, and you are all still alive
Mothers, you can all sleep safely, and you are all still alive
Fathers, you can all sleep safely, and you are all still alive
My people, you should not be worried, you are all still alive.
My friends, you should not be worried, you are all still alive
Truly, you should not be worried, you are all still alive
My people, life continues and we are all still alive.

(Koevoet song of comfort)

Appendix I

'A fortunate time'

by Francois du Toit as told to Leon Bezuidenhout

Francois du Toit was a sergeant and team leader of Zulu Quebec. These are a collection of stories by the most successful Koevoet team leader of his time.

Do you believe?

As a member of Koevoet, I was a Christian—in name only. It was my religion, but it was not what I lived. I was a businessman: death was my business. The tactics and firepower of Koevoet made for good business. Normally if you write this type of stuff in a military book you might easily be classified as an extremist or crazy. I've been there and done that (post-traumatic stress disorder); it was ugly. However, there were two incidents which happened while I was with Koevoet which played a huge role in my life: not about a change in my consciousness but about real experience—like the sun and the moon coming up. I later related these incidents to a psychologist. He first said I was mad and then after further discussion he reaffirmed his original diagnosis.

I was really, really mad!

Nico Swiegers and I met in Oshakati and became friends. He was a member of Zulu Whiskey. He was in town to get his Casspir fixed; I was in town for administrative purposes. The following day we got into his Casspir and drove back to Okanjera police base where I was seconded for three months. During that time, I was still a member of the Special Task Force. Naturally, being thirsty travellers, we took a bottle of White Horse whisky for the long dusty road back. Nico drove and I rode 'shotgun'—behind the guns on top of the car. The White Horse did not last long.

Some distance from Okanjera the Casspir came to a jerking halt. Both of us got out. The brakes had locked and were red hot. This didn't deter Nico with a half bottle of White Horse under his belt. He placed both hands on the red-hot brake-drum; the brakes were very hot—even for a man stronger than he thought he was. He burned both his hands badly. We climbed back into the Casspir and I treated his hands as best I could. I took a tool and uncoupled the brake pipes to get the brakes released. Nico's hands were so badly burned that I had to drive.

At Okanjera we found a medic and he skilfully treated Nico's hands. We had another drink in the canteen before Nico had to leave. I offered to drive him back to hook up with his team, which was working in an area not too far from the base and stay with them for the week in the bush. However, Captain Vorster, who was in charge of Okanjera base, refused. I challenged his authority to go and the he threatened me with a *bospek*—something like a court martial, only worse: if you were found guilty you were returned to unit immediately. This was the last thing I wanted. The bush and Ovamboland were my life.

Nico decided to push the pain barrier and drive back to his team, alone. We said our farewells with an understanding that we would catch up with each other in town next time round. I was pissed off with Captain Vorster.

We slept three to a room. My bed was right opposite the door, although there was no door in the frame. I fell asleep and after a while something woke me. As I opened my eyes there was this dark shape in the doorway and it was moving toward me. I had a mosquito net over me but the next minute this thing grabbed hold of me. I was lifted up and violently thrown, bed and all, against the opposite wall, so hard that the bricks in the wall crumbled and broke. I was totally speechless and scared shitless. It was extremely weird. All my hairs stood on end and my whole body was a mass of goose bumps. The apparition slowly withdrew from the room. I pulled the bed back to its original position. Not one of my roommates said a word.

The next morning just before noon, I was sitting by the ops radio when I heard that ZW was in a firefight with SWAPO. After a long stretch of radio silence, Ben came on the air and asked the radio operator at Zulu (Oshakati) to call the general to the radio. When the general was called it was always serious: death—somebody was dead. When the general asked Ben who had been killed my nose started to bleed profusely.

Ben replied, "Nico, sir. Nico was killed in action."

The RPG hit the car diagonally from the front and sliced through it like a hot knife through butter. Right through the steel. His legs and mid-section were blown away. There was no hope. Death must have come quickly.

The truth hit me later: the Grim Reaper was annoyed that night. I should have been in that car. I wasn't—and he came looking for me. I spoke to one of my roommates about it later, but he clammed up. People might think we were both nuts.

Why did Captain Vossie not want me to go? He didn't know himself. Later, years after the war ended, we bumped into each other a couple of times in the mall in Potchefstroom. Each time there were tears. If people thought we were crazy, it was okay. We were alive: the dead could not cry. I believe Nico was a born-again child of God. But at that stage in my life I had no idea what that meant. I would've certainly landed up in hell if I had been the driver.

The second incident happened a few years later. We were following tracks when we realized that contact was imminent. I called in the gunships. We drove forward slowly. One of the cars was diagonally in front and to the left of mine and I could not see what was going on in front of him. The bush was dense. The next moment we drove right into an ambush. Everywhere shots rang out. My .50 was thumping away; the radios were all screaming. Everybody was swearing and making a racket. The R5s clattered.

Suddenly I was in another world—outside my body. I was looking down on the fight from above the helicopters and I was screaming over the radio, "Kokkie your two o'clock! They are sitting at your two o'clock behind the tree! Your two o'clock—shoot!" I saw the whole scene from above. But I was in my Casspir about 200–300 metres behind him. It was so weird. I saw myself shouting these orders over the radio. "Your two o'clock, behind the tree. Shoot!" Kokkie fired and the SWAPO fell dead over his RPG.

Suddenly I was Toit again. I was back, consciously in my body, so to speak. After everything settled down Kokkie came to me and asked me how I knew about the RPG operator. I could not explain it. They would think me nuts. Later, when I told the psychologist, he thought so.

I later realized that my experiences were not so unusual. There have been many cases similar to mine recounted by men in stressful situations. There is a long list from the First Word War, for example. I could never divorce myself from the spirit world. It was always there—I just didn't acknowledge it. I wasn't so crazy after all.

A weekend off

Koevoet had its own plane. It was available to transport officers to urgent meetings and pick up medical and logistical supplies. The plane flew all over Namibia and South Africa, to Pretoria or wherever.

By 1988 the war was losing steam and I was in love. My girlfriend lived in Pretoria; the airplane was due for service at Wonderboom airport. The pilot, Chris, and I came to an agreement that if General 'Sterk Hans' (Strong Hans) Dreyer said it was okay, then I could go with Chris to Pretoria. I would be back on parade on Monday morning. Both of us went to see the general. The pilot said that he was going to Pretoria to have the plane serviced at Wonderboom over the weekend and would be back by seven o'clock Monday morning. He also mentioned, in passing, that he needed a co-pilot and that Sergeant du Toit would fit the bill. Sterk Hans lost his cool and said, "Fuck off" to me, while waving his arm in the general direction of where I should fuck off to. Now I believe I'd had that coming for a while, but had long since stopped being afraid of senior rank, not even of the most frightening general in the police. In any case, the general's response was ambiguous enough for me. So when the plane took off, the co-pilot was in his seat.

Sterk Hans looked for me over the weekend. On Monday morning I appeared on parade, just like the pilot had promised.

"Du Toit, where were you the whole weekend?"

"Pretoria, general."

"Who gave you permission?"

"You did, sir."

"I never said that!" The general was now clearly worked up.

"When I asked you on Friday, sir, you said 'fuck off' and pointed in the direction of Pretoria—so I went."

It was too much—the whole parade collapsed in fits of laughter. Sterk Hans had lost this one. He saw the futility of the situation and left it alone. I also suspect that he had a great sense of humour. And after a couple of years of bullets and blood, I feared no one. My rebellious nature had come to the fore again: no general was going to keep me away from my girlfriend.

Fun with FAPLA, 1986 (a true story told about Toitjie)

This story was told to the author by two policemen who were there the day it happened.
I asked Toitjie about it and he laughed—so it must be true.

The relationship with the Angolans—and particularly FAPLA—changed several times during the ten years of Koevoet's existence. There was a time when FAPLA was nothing else but the enemy. Then it changed to neutrality during the 1984/5 ceasefire. It then changed again: we were allowed to follow SWAPO but had to avoid contact with FAPLA and were only allowed to engage if they fired first. Then later they became the full-blown enemy again, only to be followed by another ceasefire in 1988/9.

During the middle period we were allowed to enter Angola if we were following SWAPO tracks. But there was a snag. We were not allowed within five kilometres of a FAPLA base. That would have been fine if we'd had better navigational aids (these were the days before satellite navigation). Our main aim was always to get within five kilometres of the coordinates where we thought we were. If a helicopter got within general range, a white phosphorus grenade was usually sufficient to get him onto our position. Angola is very flat in the south which makes navigation extremely difficult. We used the sun, distance travelled and time travelled to establish our whereabouts.

One day, our two teams, Zulu Uniform and Zulu Quebec, were following the spoor of two insurgents running deeper into Angola. We were already way past the big FAPLA base at Ongiva when the two teams suddenly drove into a trench system—a FAPLA base!

Things immediately got very interesting. The spoor ran right into the FAPLA base. Behind a bush barely higher than a metre, outside the trench, a FAPLA soldier was 'hiding'. He had a loaded RPG launcher and was aiming it at D.B. Koch's car. D.B. himself was sitting behind the car's five-0. D.B. lifted his gun and took aim at the RPG operator. The RPG operator then ducked behind his 'cover'. The fins of his spare rockets, shoved into the back of his combat belt, made him look like a porcupine in a bush. Then D.B. lowered his gun, just for the gunner to aim again and for D.B. to raise his barrel again. So the two of them continued to play, against the backdrop of more 'serious' matters.

Sergeant du Toit instructed his teams to cover him and climbed out of his car. He walked to the closest FAPLA soldier and asked where the two SWAPOs had disappeared to. Through one of the black Koevoet interpreters, the FAPLA soldier indicated that he did not know, but he would get the commander to come and explain. He set off to find his commander.

In the meantime, the unarmed Toit was inside a FAPLA trench inside a FAPLA base. He snatched an AK-47 off the closest FAPLA soldier and in typical boot-camp instructor's style, started doing an inspection of the weapon. He was "appalled". In a rage he shouted in Afrikaans to the enemy soldier, "How the fuck can you fight us in a war with such a dirty weapon? Look at this thing. It is filthy! Look at the rust! Where is the gun oil? What do you fucking think of us? How the fuck do you think you can beat us with a weapon in such a state? Clean the thing!" He shoved the weapon back to the shocked soldier. He took the next soldier's weapon. The same thing happened. He was in a rage. Very upset. There was no translation needed.

It was when he grabbed the third rifle that a soft voice from somewhere in the bowels of the trench, said in fluent Afrikaans, "Sir, you should not get that angry with us!" Somewhere, the FAPLA soldier had learned Afrikaans!

By now the base commander had arrived. He was next up.

"Where are the SWAPOs? You are harbouring them!" Toit shouted in Afrikaans with the translator at his heels. But the commander refused to say where they were. So the raging Toit shouted to the commander, "I am going to Ongiva [the FAPLA HQ] to find out, and they better have a good explanation, otherwise we will flatten this place!"

We climbed back into the cars. We were not five minutes away from the FAPLA base when we received a radio call from Oshakati. "You two teams better lay low; FAPLA has scrambled MiGs and helicopters to defend Ongiva! We intercepted their radio conversations. Some South Africans threatened to destroy the place. Please lay low." The radio operator was not aware of the preceding ten minutes.

For the rest of the day our two teams sat camouflaged under the Angolan trees, unable to move, with Cuban-piloted MiGs and Mi-8 helicopters screaming overhead, searching for the would-be attackers of their HQ.

It had all started as a bit of fun with FAPLA.

A transfer or two

I was temporarily 'transferred' twice because I had allegedly screwed up. I was innocent both times.

I was in the Special Task Force in 1982. One Friday afternoon two of the other guys were riding around on a motorbike. At one stage, the thing did not want to start so I helped them fix it. Later, when I had already left, the bike ran out of fuel. The police had lots of fuel. So the two men helped themselves to five litres. On the Monday we had to go to Ovamboland to train new Koevoet members. For punishment the two guys on the bike and the 'mechanic'—me, and I wasn't even there when they took the fuel—were sent to Ovamboland for an extra three months. Like the little boy whose mother says, "You have been naughty; instead of one packet of sweeties, have two." They could have just asked me: I would have volunteered.

The second time was after a drunken evening at the guesthouse in Oshakati. I'd had a few drinks with my mates, but left early. On Monday morning at parade, the general asked in a stern voice, "Du Toit! What the fuck did you do Friday evening?"

"Nothing, general."

"Go and fetch that chair in my office."

I took off and went and fetched the general's chair behind his desk. I was on my way back with the chair on my head when a lieutenant realized there was going to be big trouble. He came to me and said, "Are you crazy? Not that chair!" and took me back to the general's office and showed me another chair. But this particular chair was in pieces. It was a bar stool from the guesthouse. I went back to the parade with the planks.

The lieutenant was a hero—he saved Sterk Hans from having a heart attack. I really did not know a thing about the fight that broke out at the guesthouse later that evening and also nothing about the chair that was in the line of fire—collateral damage. Yes, I did chuck a piece of ice at the barman earlier in the evening when he gave me Klipdrift brandy instead of Red Heart rum.

There were three of us who were transferred to Opuwo in Kaokoland—to the hot mountains in the desert. For three months with almost no action. It was a setback.

Cleaning up a mass murder at a kraal

SWAPO tried to control the moral high ground internationally and the world supported them as the only representatives of the people of Namibia. In truth, they were nothing more than a Soviet-supported terrorist organization. It was also true that they were a nationalist grouping, but the same can said for Nazi Germany. SWAPO tactics were nothing more than terrorism. Their hands were never clean.

One afternoon, we received a message that we had to go and investigate a shooting at a kraal. Only Rolf Gevers and I went. When we arrived, we immediately saw that this was not just a shooting—it was murder, mass murder. Outside the kraal 14 people lay dead. Women, children and men. Everyone in the kraal was dead. SWAPO had come over the border in the afternoon, rounded them all up, lined them up against a wall and shot them. The only 'mistake' the villagers had made was that one of the men from their kraal was in the police.

Rolf and I gathered the dead and loaded them into the back of the truck. They were already in full rigor mortis—stiff and bloated. We loaded them onto the truck one at a time. It was packed very high when we picked up the body of a woman. While loading her we must have bumped the corpse because the next instant she voided her bowels all over my arms and clothes.

We drove to the morgue at Oshakati only to be told that it was nearly full and that the bodies would all have to be loaded into the two remaining fridges. Then came the task of loading them into the drawers.

That afternoon and evening would stay with me for a long time. If they murdered a policeman I could understand, but these were innocent civilians. They used Maoist and Stalinist methods to intimidate the people and force them through fear not to support the security forces. They could always find a victim to murder, kidnap, intimidate, or find a place to plant a mine to kill the innocents. SWAPO was a bloody and merciless enemy.

This behaviour toward the population, and especially toward the families and supporters of the security forces and other opposition parties, would eventually lead to a backlash. Many a time the boundaries between right and wrong faded to a faint line in the sand.

A few days after the incident, our team is out on patrol. We are chasing the tracks of a suspected insurgent. From the tracks we can deduce that he is carrying a heavy load. A while later, the tracks disappear and suddenly there are barefoot tracks among the tracks of some young people. The trackers say that the tracks belong to the insurgent. We follow the tracks and catch up with a group of schoolchildren. At the time it was not unusual in Ovamboland to find a person in his twenties in school uniform. One young man is only wearing half a school uniform. The trackers say he is the one. We take off his white school shirt and there on his back are the marks of the heavy backpack he dumped a few minutes ago. We let the schoolchildren go.

The Ovambos try to get information out of him but there is no reaction. The trackers hit him but he is stubborn. I lose my temper; it feels as if I have lost my sanity completely as I join the interrogation with fury. I grab a branch from a lala palm lying next to the road and start hitting him hard. The terrorist realizes he is about to be killed by this six-foot-four policeman. He jumps up and starts running away. We follow him, me to kill him and the rest to stop me from killing him. I catch up with him and keep hitting him with the lala palm. The branch tears his shirt to shreds. The sharp sides of the palm branch rip the blood and skin from his back. A few paces from the road he falls to the ground in a *mahango* patch and starts digging like a madman. I keep on hitting him. Then he unearths a Soviet SKS, heat-strims, a backpack and a landmine.

I stop hitting him. We question him further and this time he cooperates.

Afterwards I take him to the other side of the Casspir.

I remember an afternoon a few days previously. How the insides of a woman burst all over me. How I had to break the bones of children to fit them into the freezers at the morgue in Oshakati.

The impostors

You get men who think they are Rambo, those who want to be Rambo and those who think they were Rambo. In the last category every respected Special Force in the world has a Roll of Dishonour: people who say they were a member of their forces, but who could only dream about it and now misuse the Special Forces' names with false war stories—this while they most probably never did anything other than admin duty. The current and ex-members of these forces cannot abide these people.

Koevoet is over. We are all back in Pretoria and are doing 'special' duty. I am working at Vlakplaas. One afternoon a few of us are in a bar just outside Nelspruit during an operation. We have not achieved a lot today, but we will try again tomorrow. After a beer or two a few burly men come into the bar. We start chatting. It is clear from their hairstyles that they are security-force members.

"What do you do?" I ask one big boy.

"I'm in the police," he says.

"What unit?"

"Special Task Force."

"Really," I ask eagerly. "Which selection course group were you in?" I was a member of the elite Task Force, so I'd know.

"Evaluation group number six," he says.

Then a short and bloody fight breaks out. A fight between the top student of Special Task Force selection course 6 (me) and a 'Unit 19' boy, who says he was in Selection Course 6 and was definitely not. Sorry about his nose.

He may have been part of Unit 19's reaction force, but to wear your pistol in a holster on your leg does not make you a 'Takie'.

Precisely one week later, Flip Fouché and I are sitting in a bar in Pretoria central in the Sanlam Centre. Next to us is a man and we start chatting. Inevitably, the bush war comes up.

"Yes, I was also there," says the stranger.

"Where were you?" I ask.

"Koevoet," he says.

"That's interesting. Which group were you with?"

He stretches out his hand and introduces himself. "Toit du Toit of Zulu Quebec," he says.

I cannot believe my ears.

Next to me Flip has been following the conversation with half an ear. I tap him on his shoulder and say, "Flip, here is someone interesting I want to you to meet. Meet Toit du Toit of Zulu Quebec of the Koevoet team Zulu Quebec."

The stranger puts out his hand to Flip and repeats, "Toit du Toit of Zulu Quebec, Koevoet."

Flip explodes and headbutts the 'Koevoet' man on behalf of the real Sergeant Toit du Toit. Blood is everywhere.

It was quite clear the guy had read Jim Hooper's book very thoroughly. But he had not taken the time to memorize the photos of Flip and me in the book. Nor was he to know that he would meet both of us in a bar in Pretoria one night. I mean, what are the odds?

Long odds and inattention to detail would lead to more blood and yet another broken nose.

'Courage, blood and treachery'

by Herman Grobler as told to Leon Bezuidenhout

Herman Grobler told his story to Leon Bezuidenhout. This is a short overview of Police Sergeant Herman Grobler's involvement in the Namibian bush war, 1982– 1989. Most of the account is sourced from Herman Grobler, personal interview, January and February 2009, Pretoria; Herman Grobler's personal documents, including statements taken two months and two years after the Battle of Opepela; and official police documents.

A policeman soldier

The following story of courage and endurance should not be viewed separately from a proud past spanning three centuries. The story of Herman Grobler tells of how an ordinary policeman was forced by time and circumstance to become a soldier. Members of the South African Police had for a long time been exposed to this unique situation of policemen acting as soldiers. But by 1995 the SAP was 'demilitarized', which would mean the end of an era.

Herman Grobler, the boy from Ovamboland

Herman Grobler's story is similar to that of many other boys of his time, and yet in a sense differs. Only about 5 per cent of the 400 white policemen to fight with Koevoet were genuine 'Southwesters' (Namibians). Herman was a true Namibian, born in Windhoek in 1963. His father was the electrician in the little village of Oshakati, the administrative capital of the then Ovamboland, along the Angolan border.

He went to primary school in Oshakati before the war really started intensifying during the late 1970s. His best friend from school, Bertus Louw, and his mother were murdered on their farm by insurgents. Bomb shelters and bunkers became part and parcel of going to school in Oshakati. When he was older, he went to high school in Windhoek. He took up electronics as a subject. At times in one's life one makes a seemingly insignificant decision, and that decision eventually plays a significant role in one's future. His choosing electronics proved to be just that.

"I always wanted to be a soldier, but as a Southwester, different from other white South African men who all had to do national service, Southwesters were subject to a draft system. If you were lucky or unlucky enough you had to do two years' service. I was unlucky. I missed the draft."

"Very disappointed" is an understatement.

"My sister had a few young men-friends who regularly came to visit her. They were police detectives. So my destiny led to the police. I joined the force, but I was too late to make the 1982 intake to the college. As an untrained policeman, I was banished to the back of Oshakati police station, where I spent a whole year.

"The following year I was sent to train at the police college in Pretoria." But again, Herman was exempted from counter-insurgency training. Southwesters were not COIN trained. Therefore, he was posted back to Ondangwa to become a detective. Herman was to investigate complaints against the police and the army. It would make him very unpopular in some circles, including Koevoet.

The Ondangwa CID branch investigated cases within the operational area. "Now, the police gave us two Casspirs and a Buffel. Two detectives and a driver had to go out to investigate cases. But the area was hot. At the same time, the army deployed in platoon strength, with Koevoet in fighting teams of 45 men. We had to do it alone. So I made a plan. I 'co-opted' Koevoet and some friends I had there. They would come to Ondangwa to pick me up and drive me to the base where I was to to do my investigation. Later they would come along and pick me up and drop me back off at the station.

"For nearly three years I heard the stories and saw the dead insurgents, but I never experienced a contact. I tried everything I could. Nine attempts to get a transfer. All applications were unsuccessful. Then I realized that my father and the commanding officer in Oshakati were conniving against me. Every time I applied, my father lodged a counter-application to his friend Brigadier Pool, and so I remained a detective. Each time the reason for the rejection was: 'Member has not successfully completed a counter-insurgency course'."

But with three years' exposure to the operational area, Herman was now a well-known personality. The commanding officer of Koevoet, General Hans Dreyer, knew him well. Dreyer had heard about his 'electronics' background and he needed radio technicians. This made the transfer possible.

A new career in the police

General Dreyer encountered Herman on the first day after his transfer to Koevoet. "Get that man a decent uniform," he ordered.

"I was issued with the green combat fatigues worn by Koevoet and ordered to join Fighting Team ZF. Zulu Foxtrot was commanded by Warrant Officer Louis 'Boats' Botha. "I would never come even close to repairing a radio. For the next three years, Fighting Team Zulu Foxtrot would be my home." Zulu was the callsign for the Namibian police counter-insurgency unit; X-ray was the South African counter-insurgency callsign.

The seasons were decisive in fighting the war in Ovamboland. The Ovambos were subsistence farmers and dependent on the rain. Before the rains came, they struggled as their previous harvest petered out. Come the rains, the *mahango*, the staple diet of the Ovambos, grew. Then came the harvest and full circle to the next season. But the SWAPO insurgents were also dependent on the local population for food and water. So, with the coming of the rainy season, came SWAPO. When Herman arrived at Koevoet in September 1986, everything was quiet. The rainy season was three months away. "We spent one week in the bush, then the next week at base repairing and cleaning everything, before leaving for the next week in the bush. For the first three months I camped in the bush every second week. No action. I was beginning to think I was never going to see any action."

As a newcomer, he was posted to car number 4. There was a hierarchy in each team. The hierarchy dictated how you fitted into the *modus operandi*, which comprised the following: the Ovambo trackers picked up spoor and identified it as those of a possible insurgent. Often, the local population informed on the insurgents; sometimes it was picked up at the cut line on the border; often it was 'stolen' from the army. Also, the scenes of landmine blasts or sabotage incidents virtually always provided tracks to pursue.

Then the big follow-up started. The trackers were masters. Among hundreds of other tracks they could identify one specific set. "We once caught an insurgent who proved to be a SWAPO tracking instructor. We 'converted' him to our side, and many a time, if we crossed a track, he would identify it as one of his previous students. We knew exactly whom we were pursuing. Some of these guys were outstanding."

Ops K operated with four armoured personnel carriers, mostly Casspirs and later Namibian-manufactured Wolf armoured assault vehicles. A Blesbok support vehicle accompanied the four vehicles. Some of the cars were equipped with 'five-0' .50-calibre (12.7mm) machine guns or 20mm cannons. The other vehicles were equipped with 'three-0' .30-calibre Browning turret or 7.62mm light machine guns.

A team usually consisted of 40 black Ovambo policemen and four white car commanders. The Blesbok carried a driver and a machine-gun operator. But on the ground the senior warrant officers and sergeants among the trackers retained command. The whites relayed the information over the radio. The trackers, however, had an ability to describe a spoor over the radio for the benefit of their Ovambo colleagues and the whites were often sidelined.

No white member could ever be part of a team unless he had proved himself to his team. Before you had proved yourself to the trackers you remained a nonentity. Many a time a white member was transferred between teams because he could not get along with the black members. Once a white started to shuffle among teams, his days as a unit member were almost surely numbered.

"Car number 1 was the team commander with the best trackers. They always stuck close to the tracks. The Blesbok supported them. Car number 2 was the second best, which usually worked up front, operating 100 to 200 metres ahead of car number 1, searching for the spoor.

Car number 3 operated around 800 metres or so to the front, looking to cross, or cut, the tracks. Lastly, came car number 4, which usually carried the poorer trackers, the lazy ones, those who drank too much and the rookies. Brave men, nonetheless.

Car number 4 operated as far as two kilometres in front of car number 1. Sod's law: they were virtually always the car that ran into an ambush. The more experienced and better you became, the more you moved up in the hierarchy.

Once the spoor had been found up front, the cars at the back were informed. The senior cars would rush up the line and the whole process would start again. This way the insurgents' head-start shrank rapidly.

Terrain also had an influence on tactics. In the mountainous Kaokoland teams mostly used infantry tactics. They would establish observation posts and lay ambushes—a lot of night work. Once a SWAPO presence was identified, the stopper groups would be laid out and the ambush set. Then it became a waiting game. In this kind of terrain vehicles were unable to operate. Mortars had to stand in for the heavy machine guns.

In the sparsely populated Kavango, teams would always attempt to break up the insurgency groups. The insurgents could then be dealt with individually or in twos or threes. "We chased the groups of five or six until we thought we were fairly close. We would then fire a few mortars to about 2,000 metres' range. This made the insurgents think we knew where they were and they would bombshell. If we reached the mortar range and they were still all together as the larger group, we would again fire a few mortars until we achieved our goal. We would then start chasing the individual members of the gang. It reduced the risk considerably. One or two against 40 is a bit better than five or six against forty, especially when they had the luxury of ambush on their side.

"In Ovamboland we could not use the mortar tactic because of the density of the population. We could not simply fire blindly into an area for fear of killing or injuring the local people. At times, when we had helicopter support, we could puruse this option as the helicopter could act as a spotter, but the helicopter had to get out of the way first!"

First blood in the mahango

It was now December 1986. Herman had been with Koevoet for three months and he was still untrained. In an attempt to counter the anti-security force propaganda, the police hierarchy and the South African government decided to place, or embed in today's parlance, an independent American journalist, Jim Hooper, with Koevoet. The journalist would be allowed to mingle freely with the teams when and where he wanted. Totally by chance, Hooper one day decided to get into the Casspirs of Zulu Foxtrot.[1]

"We were busy pursuing information at a kraal," relates Herman. "Car number 4 was still in the process of leaving the kraal. Only the driver, radio operator, the medic and I were in the car, when shots were fired at three other cars, about 100 metres to our front. Boats's car was passing some low bushes next to a *mahango* field when three insurgents fired at them. Our driver instinctively accelerated towards the contact. I was in the turret. Before the other cars could turn around to re-engage the enemy, we confronted them. I spotted one of the insurgents and fired a burst or two from the machine guns. Our car claimed one kill."

Jim Hooper wrote about my first contact in his book, *Koevoet*. He also published a photograph he took through the dust and smoke.

After this contact, the black policemen had a degree of trust in their white counterpart. He was now one of them. He had had his first encounter and had showed his mettle.

But Herman's lack of training eventually caught up with him, as it did with all the other untrained members. In an attempt to bring them up to standard, a selection course was held. Sixty men started the course. "Lots of walking and *opfok*," as Herman would later label it (*opfok*: literally 'fuck up'—military jargon for unnecessary running and getting dirty, i.e. being fucked around—endlessly). For six weeks, they marched 30 kilometres every second day. The sand and heat made carrying a rifle, backpack and other equipment heavygoing. The days in between were covered by firearm, mortar and tactical training (with huge doses of *opfok* thrown in). The last day saw a route march of 100 kilometres. Endurance walking for men with the best counter-insurgency vehicles in the world! Forty-five of the 60 passed.

Thus Herman became a selected, trained and trusted member of the unit. His service with car number 4 taught him much. He was involved in many contacts. Many of the insurgents had been mere schoolchildren when abducted by SWAPO. If caught, it did not take much to turn them against their old masters. They joined the unit.

However, one 'converted' insurgent could not be trusted so easily. He had been a counter-tracking instructor at a SWAPO base. "He is kept in the back of the Casspir until the insurgent we are chasing starts anti-tracking. Then we take him out and let the teacher unravel the riddle before we put him back in the vehicle and then the follow-up continues.

"The uncooperative SWAPOs are given a choice. They are either sent to a farm where they have a degree of freedom, but they may not leave the area. If they do, they are handed over to the courts and are dealt with according to the law. In PLAN, like in any unit, one finds the good and the bad soldiers. The useless ones tried half-heartedly to plant mines or conduct sabotage, and then with great speed made for the border. There were the even more useless: those who crossed the border and cached their weapons, before disappearing into the rural areas or into the soft life of the locations. New PLAN members usually infiltrated in gangs of five or six under the control of a seasoned veteran. Those who survived were promoted and separated from the new recruits."

Then there was the 'Typhoon' detachment. They were the best, trained to wreak deadly havoc. Every now and then, SWAPO would send Typhoon members in groups of 20 to 30 in an attempt to reach the white farming areas to the south. Sometimes up to three groups operated individually. They had to walk 300 kilometres to get to their target. They always tried to avoid the local population and the security forces. Very seldom the remnants of a group would reach the farms. Nearly always they were tracked down and hunted.

"Once we tracked and destroyed 19 out of a 20-member group.

"Yes, we did get paid 'head money', but it was a policy initiated by the government and it was applied to all. Any person handing in weapons, ammunition, landmines or equipment was paid a certain amount. Money was also paid for handing over an insurgent, not just for dead ones. The head money for an insurgent was about R900. If shared, each man would get a mere R20—not much. But it did lead to some scheming. Teams usually worked alone, as far as possible. Getting helped by another team meant that the R20 would be cut to R10 per insurgent. It also led to many a team or a car 'getting lost' and ending up with the team following up spoor. This way the 'lost car' also claimed the head money when running into a contact. When necessary, Zulu Foxtrot would call in the sister team, Zulu Hotel, to come and help."

The kill ratio of the unit was also much higher than that of any other unit in the then South West Africa. This can be ascribed to the effective tactics and the overwhelming firepower of five heavily armed vehicles and the rifles of the 40 occupants. A handful of insurgents never really stood a chance. In a contact with all guns firing, surrendering was not necessarily a logical option. An insurgent was on death's doorstep. In its ten years of existence, the unit killed more than 3,200 insurgents. In a conventional war this is equivalent to the destruction of four combat battalions.[2]

The rest of the world would view Koevoet, through false propaganda, as a band of violent, merciless killers. Herman never experienced this on any scale. In his days as detective, he investigated cases against the security forces, Koevoet included.

"Yes, there was violence against insurgents, and the local population. But seldom very serious. You always worked in an environment where your own or the death of your colleague was imminent. It was not a place for debate. We needed the information and we needed it fast. But I never came across any form of torture, nor am I aware of any such incident. Yes, it did happen that huts and kraals were burned down. We fired tracers, and the huts were made of grass and pole; it was inevitable that a fire would start from time to time. It must always be remembered that our policemen came from the same villages. We needed information and the local population gave it to us, of their own free will. If we had mistreated them in any way, such information would not have been forthcoming.

"As in many other units, like the army, rapes did occur. Yes, after hours, off duty. Never on operations. We acted against such perpetrators and handed them over to the criminal investigators. There was also an incident where a white soldier was prosecuted and found guilty of murdering a local tribesman. There were also a number of cases where white policemen were transferred back to South Africa when they had behaved excessively. As an unwavering rule, the unit was well disciplined. General Hans Dreyer was a man of discipline and there were no short cuts."

Bravery in the smoke and dust

After three years, Herman became commander of fighting team Zulu Foxtrot.

In 1988, Angola, South Africa and Cuba came to an agreement. After 70 years, the communist USSR had run out of steam, as had the Angolans. Of the once-proud Angolan nation nothing was left to pay for the Cuban soldiers, except from Cabinda oil revenues. For Cuba, it had become their Vietnam. And the Angolans were weary of war. The South Africans were willing to implement UN Resolution 435 on condition that the Cubans withdraw their 50,000 soldiers. By now it was possible.[3]

As part of the New York agreement, SWAPO would not have any members south of the 16° latitude. It was also agreed that all SADF fighting units would return to their bases. Unlike the army, the police could continue with patrols, but without heavy machine guns on their Koevoet vehicles.[4]

For the next six months, this most effective counter-insurgency unit became a most successful counter-poaching unit. Poaching around Etosha National Park dropped to zero. The famous green uniforms were exchanged for the grey of the conventional Namibian police.

But Koevoet informers were still on the ground. In October 1988 Zulu 3, the intelligence wing, followed up on information and caught a SWAPO political commissar who had infiltrated Ovamboland. He had information regarding a large operation being planned for 1 April, the day Resolution 435 was to be implemented with the UN taking over the administration of the country. This information was fed through to the appropriate channels, but the South African government rejected it as false. Six months later, after more than 300 men had been killed, South African Minister of Foreign Affairs, Pik Botha, stated on TV that the South African government had known about the insurrection for more than six months beforehand.[5]

Every now and again, more information emerged, clearly not false alarms. It was decided to deploy some of the unit's men and vehicles to the empty army bases around Ovamboland every night in case SWAPO decided to occupy these bases. On 31 March the Casspirs were pulled out from the bases and positioned along the border at specific points. It did not take long before Zulu Quebec, under Constable Danie Fourie, caught an insurgent dressed in civilian clothes crossing the cut line. He was armed with a Makarov pistol. He explained that he was on a reconnaissance mission, and that the large group he was preceding would be coming through the next day. He was to meet them at a spot 80 kilometres south, where they were to establish a base. He also said that four groups of 70 insurgents each would cross the border between beacons 21 and 25. There, just south of the border, they would amalgamate into two groups before moving south. It was all part of a bigger plan. SWAPO would bring along SAM-7s, RPG-7s and RPG-75 rocket-propelled grenades and launchers, 60mm and 82mm mortars and armour-piercing rounds for their rifles. About 1,200 SWAPO insurgents were expected.[6]

The next day, 1 April 1989, the situation exploded. Hundreds of SWAPO soldiers poured across the border, expecting the army to be cowering in their bases and the police to be toothless. Not unreasoanbly, SWAPO also expected the UN to handle them with kid gloves.

Everywhere police units ran into heavily armed SWAPO gangs. They had brought along the heavy stuff: RPGs and thousands of armour-piercing rounds, RPD rounds that could slice through the side armour of a Casspir. And the police in their grey uniforms had had their heavy weapons removed from their vehicles. The air force was not allowed to lend support except to transport wounded.[7] The battles were heavy and bloody. The tactics had changed from one team tracking a few, to a few teams hunting many. There were between 50 and 100 insurgents to a group. However, in an act of foresight the Koevoet operational commander, Colonel Fouché, had removed the machine guns as instructed but had kept them close at hand. The vehicles raced back and forth between base workshops and the combat zone, frantically re-installing their machine guns and 20mm cannons.

On 2 April, Zulu Quebec picked up the spoor of the groups that the talkative insurgent had warned them of two nights before. The groups had already consolidated into two larger groups of about 100 insurgents each. They were moving south in two parallel lines a few hundred metres apart.

"We were busy at Eenhana replacing the 20mms and five-0s when we received a message that Zulu Quebec had found the spoor of the expected group and was calling for reinforcements. Zulu Foxtrot and Zulu Hotel were dispatched, but had to leave some of their cars behind that were still undergoing repair and refitting. With half teams, we arrived at Zulu Quebec near beacon 25. Two more teams also arrived.

"We combined the teams and I took over as commander. We were to follow up in two extended lines, one behind the other, with about 20 cars in total. The line stretched for about two kilometres across, with the second line around 30 metres back. The heavy weapons, the 20mms and five-0s, were in the front and the lighter-armed vehicles with the three-0s, and the Blesboks in the second row. As soon as we made contact, the second row would race forward and plug any gaps in the first line.

"About five kilometres south of beacon 25 we arrived at a kraal in the Opepela ward, but it was virtually empty. Most of the population had fled. Not a good sign. The few people left told us that there were hundreds of SWAPO and they were heavily armed. They were using donkeys to carry the heavy weapons. SWAPO had also left a message for us: 'Tell the police they are too few; they should get reinforcements. Today we will kill them all.'

"We moved out. It was clear that the two SWAPO groups were now using the same track. There was disagreement among the trackers. Some said the spoor was two hours old; others said the urine marks were five minutes old. A few hundred metres farther on the trackers asked me to stop. I got out with a few of the senior black policemen. Again, argument over the age of the tracks began. But the feeling of imminent contact was now almost tangible. And yes, there were donkey tracks. Everyone got back into the vehicles, even the trackers, as the tracks were clearly visible from the vehicles.

"About 500 metres beyond the kraal where we had stopped—the bush was very thick—my Wolf came to a small clearing of about 25 metres in width. Suddenly an insurgent in camouflage uniform rose up right in front of me, the RPG rocket launcher on his shoulder aimed straight at me. As he stood, he fired the RPG-7 rocket-propelled grenade. He was too fast for me to react."

The shot to initiate the ambush was a direct hit. The projectile hit the Wolf right between the two front windows. Herman was hit in the leg where he was standing in the machine-gun hatch. The shrapnel wreaked havoc in the confined space of the interior. Everybody, except the driver, was wounded. Two men with serious head wounds later died, another had his leg shot off at the hip. Most of the others had wounds to their faces and to their eyes.

The Wolf came to a jarring halt. The engine stopped. Inside the driver's cab the wiring was burning. There was blue smoke everywhere. Herman recalls: "I fired a few bursts, not more than 20 rounds in total with the 20mm, and then my radio cord got entangled in the ammunition belt. I struggled to get it loose but to no avail. There was not enough time. I shifted over to the five-0 Browning machine gun. My concern was that our vehicle might be charged and overwhelmed. But I had to be cautious. Our five-0 was all we had left with which to defend ourselves. A few metres behind us, to our right—at a 90-degree angle—stood another damaged car.

"The two of us now fought it out with the insurgents at close range. Somewhere below me I felt the driver, Daniel Uyepa, moving to the back. I thought he was running out on me, but far from it. He was in fighting mood and needed a weapon. He fired until the first R5 assault rifle was empty and then grabbed another. He had ten weapons at his disposal.

"I felt dizzy. When the rocket struck, I'd felt something of a shock in my leg, but did not realize what had happened. When I looked down I saw blood and a gaping wound in my right leg. It was only then that I realized how serious it was. Below my knee about 20 centimetres of bone was missing.

"The fight raged on, but suddenly the mortars that had been pounding us, stopped. When we had left Eenhana, the remaining cars of our two teams, Zulu Foxtrot and Zulu Hotel, were still being repaired and re-fitted. These cars, in an attempt to get to us faster, had taken the Oom Willie se Pad. Then they'd turned off and bundu-bashed in our direction. It was there that they ran into the SWAPO mortar position five kilometres to our south. A heavy firefight erupted and the SWAPO position was overrun. Ten more minutes of the SWAPO 82mm mortar barrage would have signalled the end of us." Warrant Officer Attie Hattingh, one of the unit's old hands, was commanding these vehicles.

"I gave the order to debus. We struggled to get out. We began to treat the more seriously wounded. As a tourniquet, I had already applied the radio cord just above my knee. I knew that my leg could not be saved and the flapping, useless lower leg was having a serious impact on my mobility. I asked one of our trackers, Gabriel Moses, to hand me his hunting knife. He put two and two together and refused. After a very serious threat, he unwillingly handed me the knife. I cut through the skin and muscle and removed my leg."

Herman amputated his leg with the knife they had always joked about—the one that "Moses could not open a rat-pack tin with".

"I already had a drip going. I think I used 38 units of blood between being wounded and admitted to 1 Military Hospital in Pretoria. But it was only after I had made the cut, that the most hideous ghost pains hit me. I injected myself with a painkiller and then stuffed a handful of ampoules, injections and syringes into my shirt pocket. The pain abated somewhat.

"As the team commander and a trained medic, I had all the team's medical history with me in a notebook. I asked someone to bring it to me and we wrote down the blood groups of the wounded on their foreheads. We then prepared the casualties for the casevac flight. After two hours a Puma, flown by Major Willie Ras, arrived,[8] but 21 were seriously wounded and the Puma could not take them all. So the pilot ignored regulations and loaded all 21 into the aircraft. He took a chance and saved many lives. The overloaded Puma struggled to get airborne. My friend Danie Fourie was lying next to me in the Puma. He had a serious head wound. He would not survive the day.

"We landed at Ondangwa and I lost consciousness. We had to fly to Waterkloof in the Flossie [C-130]. On board the aircraft the shock and hallucinations hit me hard. It felt as if I was in a bath of water. Through a haze I heard the doctor saying to someone, 'He thinks he is lying in his own blood.' I had a bizarre idea that they wanted to implant a pink tooth into my mouth, and I put up a huge struggle.

"At Waterkloof we were placed in ambulances for the short ride to the hospital. I was the last to leave. But the ambulance wouldn't start. Everybody got out to push, but the thing had an automatic transmission. So I stayed put on the tarmac for 30 minutes before another ambulance arrived and transported me to the hospital."

Herman spent two months in 1 Military Hospital. His field evaluation of his wound proved to be 100-percent correct. His right leg was, as he had expected, amputated above the knee.

Life goes on

As a temporary member of the South African Police in 1990, Herman was transferred back to Ovamboland, but this time in the role of game ranger. When the unit was eventually closed down on 12 January 1990, he boarded an aircraft for South Africa. Suddenly life seemed to make no sense any more. For a long time, he had tried to get an official transfer to the South African Police. All that remained now was one month's leave, before undergoing a psychological evaluation, at the same time as another ex-Koevoet member. The other member went overboard the night before and had a hangover when he arrived for the test. Herman was sober and well prepared. Of the two, Herman failed. "You cannot work with people," he was told, and thus received only a temporary appointment.

But then a few things happened that had a serious impact on his future. In 1989 the South African government and the police made various pledges that they would accept any former Namibian policemen who wanted to move to South Africa. An official plan was drawn up with proposed routes to be used, as well as final destinations. They would all eventually be settled at Van Zylsrus in the northern Cape Kalahari.

But the first six members did not know anything of these plans. All they knew was that they should get to Pretoria, and that is what they did. "And here sat these six Ovambos in front of Police Headquarters and the police did not know what to do with them. So they instructed Colonel Fouché, the last operational commander of the unit, to make a plan. Colonel Fouché contacted Temporary Sergeant Herman Grobler. The trickle by now had since developed into a flood. More than 600 men and their families were waiting around at Upington. Men, women and children; more than 2,500 souls. So Herman, the guy who apparently could not work with people, ended up looking after 2,500 people! We moved them to a number of police farms near Rustenburg. To begin with, we housed them in tents."

Later, when the Rooiberg Mine fell into disuse, the police acquired the complex. Everybody was moved to the mine. But what to do with these people still remained a challenge.

"These people all came from the rural areas of Ovamboland. Most of them could not do much more than basic reading and writing. They were people who had been taken out of school after Standard One, to tend cattle. Which is why they became such outstanding trackers."

Then Colonel Fouché came up with the idea of 'police auxiliaries'. These old warriors would be employed as assistants in areas where the police had a personnel shortage or where they were under pressure because of volumes of crime. The first batch of 60 men was sent to Natal where stock theft was a huge problem. Within a few months, the problem was totally eradicated, with the criminals all apprehended and put through the judicial process. Most area commanders saw the benefits of the unit. When in 1992 the first farm murders occurred near Pietersburg, 40 members were sent into the area. In all the cases the murderers were arrested.[9]

But at the Pretoria Police Headquarters were a number of senior officers who had no interest in these people. They openly pressurized the area commanders to force the Ovambos into accepting severance packages. Perhaps they interpreted the politics of the day incorrectly, or perhaps they wanted to impress the new minister and the state president, neither of whom supported the security forces.

So in 1994 the regional head office at Rustenburg 'offered' packages. Virtually all the old members were pressurized into breaking their ties with the police. By the time Herman Grobler and Colonel Fouché became involved, the ship was well below the waterline. In one case, a senior officer said to Herman, "We have paid these people their money. We do not have any contract with them; we owe them nothing." If he had had a fraction of the courage these men had, this officer would have taken a more humane approach. He was a pen pusher, only out to impress his bosses. When they were bleeding and fighting in the bush, he was a staff officer in a cosy office somewhere far away from the war. Such is the way of war.

Except for a small group in Pietersburg and another small group in the Cape, no black Ovambo members stayed on in the police. They were sold out for less than a mess of porridge. Herman took a transfer to the Firearm Tracking Unit in Rustenburg where he met his future wife.

On his wedding day the police eventually decided to appoint him permanently.

Tribute

Herman says, "I am often asked if I would do it all again if given the same choices, even if it meant losing my leg. And I always answer the same. Definitely! I always wanted to be a soldier. I lived my dream. I sleep peacefully every night. For my old enemy, SWAPO, I have the greatest respect. I've always respected them. When we wore our uniforms we were all soldiers, and we recognized one another as being soldiers and opponents. I remember one occasion during a firefight after a follow-up. There was a whole team of us. The insurgent was alone. He took up an ambush position right in front of us. His magazines were laid out in front of him for quick reloading. He never stood a chance, and yet he was prepared to fight to the end. Such a man deserves respect."

Not a single policeman who was involved in stopping the senseless and mindless April 1989 invasion was ever honoured for his bravery. Medals were issued for loyal service and merit, that was all. But between doing what is expected as one's duty and going that extra mile with extreme bravery and leadership is a different matter all together.

Surely, we can then write a tribute of our own:

'On 2 April 1989, near the Odila River in the Opepela ward, north of Eenhana in Ovamboland, Sergeant Herman Grobler distinguished himself as leader of a combined combat team of 20 Casspir and Wolf armoured assault vehicles.

He led his group against a determined and well-established SWAPO force of 200 insurgents. Even when seriously wounded, he continued commanding his men until the SWAPO ambushers were eventually destroyed. As a trained operational medic, and in spite of amputating his own leg, he took charge of the casevac preparation of the 21 seriously wounded men under his command. Sergeant Grobler's gallantry and courage is far above and beyond the normal call of duty.

Conclusion

The tide has turned. How the black policemen from Namibia were treated by both the South African Police Force and the later South African Police Service will forever be an appalling disgrace. These men sacrificed their all. The manner in which the National Party politicians and some senior officers left these people in the lurch, is even worse than the treatment experienced by the brave men of the former 32 Battalion. It will stain their names forever.

Today these same politicians and senior policemen are retired on handsome pensions.

When the black policemen came to South Africa after the war, the South African government asked them to drop their civil claims against SWAPO, 'because it undermined the international relationships between the the Republic of South Africa and the new Namibia'. The aggrieved would be compensated with a once-off payment by the South African government. The result was a payment of less than 2 percent of the initial claim.

Was the evacuation of the Ovambos to Rustenburg tenable? In 2000 the UN Commission for Human Rights and other human rights organizations uncovered five mass graves in northern Namibia, which were identified as the remains of 'Koevoet members' murdered by SWAPO during the run-up to the election in 1990. There are likely more mass graves still undiscovered.[10] At the time of writing, the one co-author tried to attract sponsorship to continue research. There are two companies which made millions of rands out of the the war; one supplied armoured vehicles to the police. This company refused point blank to get involved and refused to take telephone calls or respond to emails. The other is a medical company. They were sympathetic, but apologetic and the request was rejected, kindly.

This is the way times have changed. Some believed in the cause, others saw it as a way to make money without any accompanying responsibility, much like those who left the Ovambos to their fate. The ex-Koevoet members all still live in corrugated-iron shacks at Vingerkraal. The Bela-Bela City Council has recently partnered with a foreign lodge developer, and is currently trying to evict them.

With nowhere else to go.

Notes

[1] Hooper, J. 1988. *Koevoet.* Southern.

[2]. Stiff, P. 2004. *The covert war: Koevoet operations 1979–1989.* Galago.

[3]. Geldenhuys, J. Wenners.

[4]. *Beeld.*

[5] Stiff, P. 1989. *Nine days of war.* Lemur.

[6] Stiff, P. 1989. *Nine days of war*; Stiff, P. 2004. *The covert war.*

[7] Stiff, P. 1989. *Nine days of war.*

[8] Stiff, P. 2004. *The covert war.*

[9] *Beeld,* 27 February 1992.

[10] ICRC document, published in 2000.

Appendix III

'On the spoor with Koevoet: an SADF Ratel 90 gunner's perspective of a follow-up with Koevoet trackers, East Ovamboland, 3 April 1989'

by Jacques Myburgh

Jacques Myburgh was a 19-year-old conscript gunner in one of the Ratel 90s of the newly formed 63 Mechanized Battalion, when he had his first contact, led by Koevoet. The Koevoet trackers made a huge impression on Jacques who wrote this article as part of a series, 20 years after the war, unaware then that it would become part of this book.

For the first time in many weeks we had a prayer parade. It was a senior member of Koevoet who called everybody together and read a few verses from the Bible on that Monday morning, 3 April 1989. What he precisely read I cannot remember, but it was not one of the usual extracts, such as 'O, keep your faith sinner and ye shall overcome', which one would expect to be fitting in view of the unfolding events.

After scripture reading, a black Koevoet stepped forward and said a prayer in the best Afrikaans I have ever heard.

Koevoet was just different. They had courage.

They picked up the crap that was seldom reported and, if reported, then only as a barely passing mention. In the four months before that day, we travelled widely across a fairly large portion of Ovamboland and we only saw Koevoet once. We could all be forgiven for being doubting Thomases about Koevoet and what they purportedly did.

Reputation, however, has a way of being halfway around the planet before the truth gets out of bed and puts its boots on. Having said that, never would we doubt the ability and integrity of these policemen. With them around, we young troepies would, to a degree, feel like were were being shielded by the wings of mother hen. Despite the overwhelming force that we could bring to bear on a target, we were fuck-all. We could not find a 'Swap' in a rat pack if our lives depended on it.

Until a few hours before, none of us had ever had any experience with Koevoet, but even so we felt safe with them. I know it sounds absurd because we had some serious firepower, but Koevoet had the knowledge. What we were about to go out and do would be a life-changing event for all us troepies. For Koevoet, it was just another day. I think subconsciously we recognized it, and it brought about calmness to what—you better believe it—was a very stormy sea. For fucksakes, recruits into SWAPO were probably older than us, and I think the old hands in that Koevoet unit recognized that. From us, there was respect for what they were and what they did; and probably they appreciated that we knew, that without them, we were lambs to the slaughter. Even so, we were now a newly formed force, a force that planned to dish out more pain than what it expected to receive.

Just after prayer parade, a strange thing happened. We were getting ready to report 'march ready' when a Koevoet rocked up at Ratel 52 Charlie with a very strange request. He asked that when we made contact, we keep the empty 90mm copper shells for him. He would exchange them with us for Russian tinned food, an AK or captured uniforms. He made it sound as if he would collect the loot when he passed through our way again. But it was game on, a deal. It was only a minute or so after he had left that we realized he'd said 'when' and not 'if' we made contact.

After the daily drills and battle-readiness checks, we moved out of Oshikango. With our new Koevoet allies, we drove to the scene where one of the Koevoet cars had been shot out during an ambush the previous afternoon.

In the School of Life, you learn in two ways: the hard way, or by watching someone else and learning from them. We watched and learned. It was clear that Koevoet was in charge, and so they went ahead and did what they did best. We came upon the spot where they had recovered the burned-out Casspir earlier that morning. Here we stood down for a few minutes to give the Koevoet trackers time to establish what was going on in the sand. Then we moved off. The follow-up had started in all earnest.

For us young, inexperienced troops, it was a new experience. Traditionally, the army tactics were to move onto a rather static target, with good information and 'eyes-on-the-target' information. We always had to know the 'what, where and how many' to be brutally efficient. This Koevoet thing fucked with everything we'd been taught, and we had to adapt. Quickly. It forced flexibility in tactics that we simply had to grow into.

It was clear from the start that this was a sizeable SWAPO group we were following; they were well equipped and highly mobile. Within the first click from the Casspir ambush spot, we were shown where a medic post had been laid out where injured Swaps were treated after the brief firefight late the previous afternoon. There were clear marks on the ground where patients had been treated, with a plethora of medical equipment and shit, like bandages and stuff, lying around. Even an empty saline drip bag. This find was cause for some concern—it seemed that none of the Koevoet had ever come across anything like this before; it implied that this group had come prepared. It was not your average run-of-the-mill, 'see-the-Boers-fire-one-shot-drop-everything-and-run' group. There was also a spot which was quite obviously a grave. Pulled one back on the scoreboard right there.

We formed up into what can best be described without sketches as an arrowhead formation. Koevoet trackers were in front, then two Koevoet Wolfs formed the tip, right behind the trackers. Three Ratel 90s were deployed on either side of the Wolfs. Then the rest of the Koevoet cars and Ratels with infantry would follow behind the Ratels on the flanks. This meant that only eight vehicles had to bundu-bash. The vehicles behind drove in the tracks of the leading vehicles. In follow-up tracks, it made sense, but what was the plan of action if we made contact? The figure-8 drill we practised so many times at De Brug was out of the question. 52C was on the right-hand flank in front. In the middle, behind the Wolfs, was 52, with 52B on the other flank. No figure 8 possible.

We had not travelled far when two Alouette gunships from Eenhana arrived overhead with 20mm guns pointing out of the left-hand doors. These were things we'd only ever got the chance to look at from a distance; never imagined we would actually get to see them in action. We were busy following spoor and passing to the left of a fairly large wooded area when a streak of smoke made its way from the wooded area toward the choppers. The best way to describe it is a 'Huh?'

And then a large explosion erupted right in front of my Ratel. Having seen the smoke streak to the right-hand side, and deducing that it was therefore 52's gunner who'd taken a shot and shot short right in front of us, I got on the radio and shouted to Gunner Stumpke, "Are you fucking mad to fire so short in front of us?" He could have shot the living daylights out of us!

His reply, short but sobering, was: "I am still aiming to the right, you fucker. I have not fired yet!"

Okay, so it turns out that the Swaps doubled back on their tracks after passing the wooded area, where they were now entrenched, and let rip with an RPG-7 at the choppers. They then opened up on us with 82mm mortars. Right where they knew we'd be. Zeroed in on us. We were right next to them. In their field of fire, their killing zone!

Hollywood conditions one to believe that you can hear an incoming mortar. That's bullshit. There is no whistling sound like in the movies. Trust me. I can tell you—no sound. It's just a special effect created to entertain a viewer seated safely in an air-conditioned theatre with eyes on screen and popcorn and slush puppy in hand. It does not happen like that. You don't get to hear them coming in. They don't ring the bell or knock on your door. They just show up. Like mother-in-law, but with more vengeance.

Now we were on our own. This was where the proverbial paw-paw hit the fan. It was 'fire-belt action' time. (A fire-belt action is when the guns drop as fast as possible with as much ammunition as possible on a target.) Before we started that morning, it was in everybody's mind that we would answer any attack on us with a fire-belt action.

Now it was crunch time.

The drivers did not even have time to turn the cars into the attack. We had already turned the guns to the right and were firing our three 90mm guns from the side into the tree line, and the gunships with their 20mms from above. From the way fire-belts are produced and the amount of shells fired, one can appreciate that it is a rather labour-intensive action. I was the gunner, but with the help of the crew, we fired that 90mm gun at the rate of a slow Browning machine gun. The driver was passing the ammunition and the crew commander and I were alternating with the loading. It must have been a quite impressive sight. Unfortunately, the SADF did not have on-board cameras to film the activity inside that Ratel at that time. These were not protocols or procedures ever practised in training, but at that moment it just seemed like the best thing to do. And it worked. We managed to pump sufficient 90mm HE rounds into that wooded area to spook the Swaps, and the gunships reported that they were bombshelling.

Bombshelling in effect means that you take your tools and fuck off as fast as possible in a direction of your own choice at a speed only adrenalin can make you achieve. Much like the effect of a bomb when it scatters shrapnel in every direction possible.

The ambush had some interesting results. We were working in a controlled manner when we were attacked. However, before we could deploy in a proper armour formation, Koevoet had broken the back of the engagement. In a brilliant move, the Casspirs cut around the edge of the bushed area, with all guns blazing, and drove into the area whence the ambush was staged. A truly inspired flanking manoeuvre. With the immense combined firepower of the 90s, the gunships and the Casspirs, the ambush was neutralized. The Koevoet trackers picked up clear identifiable spoor, and even had the luxury of having time to identify, from evidence on the ground, who the leaders probably were, and in which direction they had fled. We disregarded the spoor of all the others and followed the leaders.

Confucius says: Man on wheel is faster than man on foot. Believe it.

A comparatively sedate chase commenced. I believe the reason was mainly because we suddenly changed from woodland to open grass veld interspersed with occasional bushy patches. During the D-Day landings of 1944, Allied troops, once off the Normandy beachheads, found the going incredibly tough because of the almost impenetrable hedgerows inland, which also provided ideal ambush positions for the Germans. That morning we encountered a couple of places not unlike those French hedgerows.

We maintained a steady pace on the trail of the Swaps, but every now and again we would draw fire from one of the thick, bushy 'hedgerows'. Koevoet would sort that issue out very quickly with their Brownings mounted on top of the Wolfs. That was until fire was directed at us from a large tree. A Koevoet was hit and pulled into a Wolf by his mates. We received a request for something we'd never even considered up to that point: the car with the best bearing on the tree in question would fire one round of 90mm HE up into the branches of said tree. The effect of this is comparable to an airburst from an artillery shell. The first tree yielded nothing. The second tree was different. Knowing what a 90mm HE does when it detonates and the safety limits imposed on that round in practice (1,300 metres), it's really hard to tell exactly how many bodies fell from the tree. It could have been four, maybe more. What's for sure is that an adjustment to the SWAPO *Evade And Avoid Capture* manual was needed from that moment on, as it became standard practice to fire one round of 90mm HE into any tree that might conceivably offer shelter to a human body.

Most trees came up empty. But not all.

The choppers reported bingo fuel and returned to Eenhana. That led to a slowdown in the pace of the chase, but only for as long as it took the choppers to return. In the meantime, it became clear that during the course of the morning, terrs were constantly joining and breaking away from the group we were following.

How these Koevoet trackers applied that dark art of theirs I will not even dare speculate. To read and understand what's written is sometimes not an easy thing to do; for the Koevoet trackers to read and interpret what's *not* written is truly a gift. If I have to venture into conjecture: I would hazard that they identified the tracks of the leaders by their shoe size or gait or whatever, and noted but ignored any other tracks that joined and left the group in flight. This appears the most logical way, considering that I was, and still am, a total ignoramus in that level of fieldcraft.

Shortly after the choppers returned there was a halt in the chase while the trackers convened a short meeting. What intriguing tactical information were they discussing was the question that probably went through most of our minds.

Turned out they were hungry. Everything stopped.

A hungry tracker will stop and eat when he damn well pleases. Nothing can change that. Considering that these were also the very same guys who entered a contact unprotected by the armour of a Wolf and on foot, they get to decide on these kinds of issues. Besides, the Swaps up ahead were not going to grow wings and fly away.

So we had brunch. Or whatever could be opened from a rat pack. (Note to the reader: Never try to use a can opener when charged up on adrenalin; you will just embarrass yourself when you can't get the tin opened due to the shaking hands and fingers. It does have its benefits when you take a pee, though.)

After finishing our brunch, we continued the chase. Not too far from our brunch spot, the trackers informed us that only two terrs remained. They had turned north, toward the Angolan border. One of the terrs was wounded. Here the choppers returned to Eenhana. It would be stupid to risk a chopper to the luck of two terrs.

The chase got hot. As a boy from a farm school, I was intrigued by the way the trackers worked. They worked in groups from the two Wolfs in the middle of the follow-up in 10- to 15-minute shifts. The trackers from the one car would jog on the tracks, to be relieved by the other car's trackers after their time had lapsed. In a quarter of an hour, they would swop again.

A nice afternoon jog—but with a purpose, like a pack of African wild dogs, knowing that they will get their prey—running at a pace the prey can never keep up with. Slowly but surely, we were gaining. Viewers of the Tour de France know that a *peloton* can chase down a breakaway group practically at will because they can cycle and conserve energy more efficiently than the breakaway. There were no cycles in sight that day, but the principle remains the same.

It took 16 kilometres and countless tracker relays before we caught up with the two terrs in a *shona*.

To this day, I prefer to believe that they ran themselves to death and that the Wolfs that went into that *shona* with all Brownings blazing simply delivered the *coup de grâce*.

Standing back and watching this spectacle, I was amazed at how good Koevoet actually was at what they did. You probably won't find it in any manual, but I'm sure they knew that by creating chaos, they confused SWAPO to such a level that SWAPO could not sustain a concentrated point of attack on any one vehicle.

Koevoet burst into that *shona* in what can only be described as an orgy of smoke, dust, sand, shit and hair. A Wolf or two came back with a flat tyre, but no terr could withstand that level of 'surround sound'. Demolition Derby comes to mind; just add machine guns on top of the vehicles and free fire and you'll get the idea of what we saw. It wasn't pretty from a military purist's point of view, but it was brutally effective.

I never saw the two terrs, but that they had no chance was clear.

After the contact we drove back to Oshikango and moved back into the same positions as the previous evening. What happened to the two dead terrs? You won't find that stat in any book. We did not stop to pick them up. Another Koevoet car, however, did briefly stop to collect the weapons.

This time in Oshikango there was time for a shower, and we went crazy in that cold shower.

Koevoet got their man. They had their payback.

After we concocted supper from rats, our visitor from the morning appeared as he'd said he would. We had collected a reasonable amount of empty 90mm shells, but were sceptical about what we would get out of the supposed deal.

He took the shell casings and disappeared in the direction of the Koevoet cars. A few minutes later, he re-emerged with two tins of Russian gammon, a SWAPO cap and a web belt.

The cap had a bullet hole dead centre above the peak and the belt was bloodstained.

And that's how the day ended for us—showered, stuffed on Russian pork and a cap with the blood on it not yet dry.

Tuesday 4 April 1989 was a few hours away.

This day was over.

Postscript

by Leon Bezuidenhout

It is six months since we started to write this book. It's never been a secret. Late one winter afternoon, my mobile phone rings. I see on the screen it is a strange number. A foreign number, but not one of those investment agents from Hong Kong who thinks I have lots of money to invest in their shipping containers, I think.

"Hello, Leon?"

"Yes."

"This is Sam Mohlongo. I phone from Ondangwa in Namibia."

Thankfully it is not someone from Hong Kong.

"Yes, Sam, good to hear from someone from Namibia."

"I saw on the internet you are writing a book with someone on Koevoet."

"Yes, that is true."

"I see that you are also writing a bit about Opepela."

"Yes, that is correct, with a full story about Herman Grobler. He lost his leg there. It was with the first shot of the ambush that he was wounded."

"I was a detachment commander with PLAN. I was there that day. The first shot at the vehicles was fired from an RPG-75. I know who fired that shot."

This much is true. I know it was an RPG-75 and not an RPG-7. Not many people know that. After about 30 minutes of chatting, Sam says he wants to come to South Africa to meet Herman.

Can I organize it?

Yes, I can.

In January 2011 Sam arrived in Pretoria. I took him to the Voortrekker Monument, the SADF Border War memorial. A white car stopped. A man got out of the car. Herman Grobler. With his prostetic limb he walks without any obvious signs of a disabled man. The tall man from Koevoet and the short stocky PLAN commander stood before each other.

"Sam Mohlongo, this is Herman Grobler. Herman, this is Sam," I said.

For a second, they clasped each other's hands and looked each other in the eyes. Then there was an embrace. An embrace not of two schoolboys after a playground fight. No, a sincere, warm embrace. Rather like two friends who have just played a tough rugby match against each other and who feel privileged to have had the other as an opponent.

An honest, warm meeting.

At last, the two men have met to remember a day which had a huge impact on the lives of two young men. I was astonished to see this interaction. It was a celebration of life, a celebration of shared experience. A shared feeling of 'I do not have to tell you how it was; you know yourself ... you were there'. Words are not necessary.

For the next hour or so the two old enemies exchanged life stories, their respect for each other as men and as soldiers, obvious.

Then someone brought forward a wreath. Together the two former adversaries laid a wreath in memory of the fallen of that day, 4 April 1989, and the rest of the war, at a memorial where neither the fallen of Koevoet nor SWAPO are mentioned or honoured, a monument for others who shed blood for the same causes.

But it was good enough.

Then a moment of silence.

Then another embrace.

When Sam had to leave, Herman said to me, "You know, an hour is not enough; we have a lot to talk about. I will have to go to Ondangwa."

I know he will.

During Sam's visit, we also visited Shorty at his new prefabricated house. When we arrived, three men were sitting outside: Shorty, his friend Rustus Mbundu from Zulu-4 Echo and his uncle Daniel Kambungu, the old corporal from 32 Battalion. It was only after the initial hearty welcome that I realized how much respect these old bush fighters have for each other. Forget about the cheap anti-Koevoet propaganda of the war and thereafter.

Interactions like these could never take place if there was any hint of dishonesty.

This came from the heart.

I tell you that I respect you; I respect your tracking abilities; I respect your ability to avoid us; I respect your willingness and courage to stand up against our onslaught. You were good.

We were all good—but very foolish to land ourselves up in a war, a war against our brothers.

A day later, Sam also met up with Francois du Toit. He attended Francois's 50th birthday a day or two later as a guest of honour.

And so this book has brought men together; without this book, these good things would not have happened.

Did I learn?

Yes: no bitterness toward your enemy.

It was war; ugly things were committed by both sides.

It is over.

We survived.

We made peace.

You are my friend, my brother.

For you I have a place of honour.

Glossary of terms, acronyms and abbreviations

32: 32 Battalion, South African combat battalion consisting mainly of black ex-Angolan, Portuguese-speaking soldiers.

101: 101 Battalion of the SWA Territorial Force; an army unit utilizing the same tactics as Koevoet and which also used Casspirs.

202: 202 Battalion of SWA Territorial Force; based at Rundu and consisting, like the Zulu 4 policemen, mostly of Kavango soldiers.

1,000-footer: 300-metre illumination flare.

AK-47: 7.62 x 39mm standard automatic rifle used by SWAPO, FAPLA and Unita; produced by several Eastern Bloc countries, as well as China.

Alouette: French-manufactured helicopter, mostly for air support, equipped with a 20mm cannon; the best-kept 'open secret' of the war.

B10: Soviet-manufactured 82mm recoilless rifle.

Blesbok: armoured support vehicle.

bombshell: sudden deliberate splitting up of a group of insurgents to shake off followers, to regroup later.

Buffel: South African-manufactured mine-resistant troop carrier.

bundu-bash: to drive directly through the bush, mainly to avoid landmines.

car: armoured car, Casspir or Wolf.

car 1, 2, 3, 4: each car in a team had its own number; numbers followed a hierarchy, with car number 1 the command car.

casevac: casualty evacuation, normally by helicopter.

Casspir: mine- and ambush-resistant vehicle (MARV) manufactured in South Africa; could carry ten men, a driver and co-driver; equipped with machine guns and light cannons for the commander and assistant driver.

chana: flat grassland, parts of which become shallow pans in the rainy season; also *shona* and *oshana*; similar to South African *vlei*.

Chandelier Road: the main dirt road between Rundu and Ovamboland; also known as Oom Willie se Pad and the White Road (east of Okongo).

COIN: counter-insurgency.

contact: firefight; to make contact with the enemy.

CSIR: Council for Scientific and Industrial Research; South African strategic research facility.

cuca: rural store, the name derived from the Angolan Cuca beer sold before the war; *cucas* sold everything, but beer was the top seller.

cut line: the border between Ovamboland and Angola, so named because of the bush cut and cleared to demarcate the international border.

DTA: Democratic Turnhalle Alliance.

FAPLA: People's Armed Forces for the Liberation of Angola, the Angolan Defence Force, and the MPLA's military wing.

five-0: .50 calibre (12.7mm) Browning machine gun.

G3: 7.62mm Portuguese-manufactured automatic rifle.

giant: Puma helicopter (Ovambo slang).

Golf Sierra (GS): gunship; South African Air Force Alouette helicopter equipped with a 20mm cannon used as air support for men on the ground.

HE: high explosive.

heat-strim: SKS rifle grenade; *also* strim.

Impala: South African-manufactured jet fighter-bomber.

Jati: 60-metre-wide deforested strip on the border between Angola and SWA during the war (named after Jan and Timo); *also* Yati.

JMC: Joint Monitoring Commission, formed to ensure SWAPO kept to their side of the border in 1984/5.

Koevoet: South West African Police counter-insurgency unit.

komesho: Ovambo word for 'forward'.

kraal: group of traditional huts surrounded by a brush or pole fence.

LMG: 7.62mm light machine gun, usually mounted on a vehicle, but sometimes carried by men on foot patrol.

mahango: pearl millet (*Pennisetum glaucum*); also *manna* or *babala*; staple diet of of northern Namibia; most kraals had their own *mahango* fields, the dense vegetation making them ideal ambush spots.

MARV: mine- and ambush-resistant vehicle

Mike Romeo: reaction force; from the Afrikaans *reaksie mag*.

MPLA: Popular Movement for the Liberation of Angola, FAPLA's political movement.

Okongo: eastern Ovamboland town; the military base here was Nkongo, also spelled Ekongo; for simplicity only the town's name is used.

Oom Willie se pad: *see* Chandelier Road *and* White Road.

Ops K: Operation Koevoet.

oshana: see *chana*.

PKM: 7.62mm communist-manufactured light machine gun.

PLAN: People's Liberation Army of Namibia, SWAPO's military wing.

Puma: South African Air Force transport helicopter; *see also* giant.

R1: 7.62mm automatic rifle. South African-made under licence by FN Herstal.

R4: 5.56mm automatic rifle; standard infantry weapon of the South African Defence Force; copy of the Israeli Galil.

R5: 5.56mm automatic rifle; shorter-barrelled version of the R4; standard Koevoet weapon; made under licence by Israeli Galil.

Ratel 90: SADF armoured attack vehicle equipped with 90mm cannon.

rat pack ('rat'): ration pack; contains food for one soldier for 24 hours.

RDP house: Reconstruction and Development Project—small house to upgrade people from shanties.

Recce: South African Special Forces operator (Reconnaissance Commandos).

RPD: 7.62mm communist-manufactured light machine gun.

RPG-7: communist armour-piercing rocket-propelled grenade; self destructs at 800 metres; *also* RPG-75.

RSA: Republic of South Africa.

SADF: South African Defence Force.

SAP: South African Police.

SAPS: South African Police Service.

shona: see *chana*.

SKS: communist semi-automatic rifle; capable of firing armour-piercing grenades (heat-strims).

Snotneus: 37mm grenade launcher ('snot nose').

strim: SKS rifle grenade; *also* heat-strim.

SWA: South West Africa (Namibia).

SWAPO: South West African People's Organization; Soviet-backed political party which embarked on armed struggle against South Africa in the early 1960s. PLAN was its military wing, but distinction was seldom made between the two, e.g. SWAPO terrorist = PLAN terrorist.

SWAPOLCOIN: South West African Police Counter-Insurgency Unit; a later name for Koevoet.

SWATF: South West African Territorial Force

Takie: member of the elite Special Task Force.

TB (Tango Bravo): temporary base; overnight base in the bush.

team: a Koevoet group consisting of four Casspirs or Wolfs with a Blesbok or Strandwolf vehicle in support; included up to 50 men.

terr: terrorist.

three-0: .303 Browning machine gun.

UN: United Nations.

Unit 19: riot squad; large unit sent in reaction to problem areas.

Unita: Union for the Total Independence of Angola; Jonas Savimbi's pro-Western resistance movement, which controlled southeastern Angola.

UNTAG: United Nations Transitional Assistance Group; military implementation of UN Resolution 435; supposed to take over military and administrative control of SWA/Namibia on 1 April 1989.

USSR: Union of Soviet Socialist Republics.

VY (Victor Yankee): *Vyand*; Afrikaans for 'enemy'.

vlamgat: Jet-engine aircraft (Mirage); Afrikaans for 'flaming arse'.

White Road: the Chandelier Road east of Okongo; *also* Oom Willie se Pad.

WO: warrant officer.

Wolf: Namibian-manufactured MARV armoured vehicle, similar to the Casspir.

ZARP: Zuid-Afrikaansche Republiek Politie.

zero line: most northerly limit of Koevoet operations inside Angola; approximately 100 kilometres into Unita territory and approximately 50 kilometres north of Ovamboland.

Koevoet Roll of Honour
† Lest we forget †

1979

Special Constable	W. Shamoketa	1979-04-05
Special Constable	P. Mabashe	1979-05-20
Sergeant	A.P. van Niewenhuizen	
	Esterhuizen	1979-05-28
Special Warrant Officer	D. Gabriel	1979-05-28

1980

Constable	H.J. van Heerden	1980-09-19

1981

Constable	A. Schreuder	1981-01-04
Special Warrant Officer	A. Chiwale	1981-05-25
Constable	A.C. Bezuidenhout	1981-12-13
Special Constable	J. Shitaleni	1981-12-13

1982

Special Constable	S. Hamukwaya	1982-04-10
Special Constable	P. Sakaria	1982-04-11
Constable	F.A.F. Claassen	1982-04-20
Special Sergeant	N. Tamunila	1982-05-04
Special Constable	P. Venasio	1982-06-02
Special Constable	A. Ndawedapo	1982-06-17
Constable	J.G. Holtshauzen	1982-06-02
Special Constable	P. Antonius	1982-06-21
Special Constable	I. Kavulu	1982-06-21
Special Constable	T. Ndevelo	1982-06-21
Special Sergeant	H. Thomas	1982-07-02
Special Warrant Officer	H. Elangwa	1982-07-14
Special Constable	W. Timotheus	1982-07-14

Special Constable	M. Hakonya	1982-07-14
Special Constable	V. Tsiposa	1982-07-15
Special Constable	T. Nekundi	1982-11-25

1983

Special Constable	T. Matias	1983-01-25
Special Constable	K. Tjiumbua	1983-01-25
Constable	A. Delport	1983-02-18
Special Constable	J. Joseph	1983-02-20
Special Constable	S. Iyambo	1983-03-03
Sergeant	J.A. Nel	1983-03-25
Special Constable	M. Funet	1983-03-27
Special Constable	E. Mutuku	1983-03-27
Special Constable	J. Muyongo	1983-03-27
Special Constable	N. Nghiyayela	1983-03-28
Special Sergeant	T. Maritina	1983-04-18
Sergeant	J.H. Meisenheimer	1983-04-18
Special Sergeant	J. Saulo	1983-04-18
Special Warrant Officer	L. Vilho	1983-05-07
Constable	N.J. Swiegers	1983-05-07
Special Constable	U. Maundu	1983-05-10
Special Constable	T. Mbendura	1983-05-10
Special Constable	J. Musaso	1983-05-10
Sergeant	A. Willem	1983-05-10
Sergeant	A. Costa	1983-05-25
Special Constable	K. Kambirua	1983-06-12
Special Constable	F. Hamutewya	1983-07-20
Special Constable	K. Mpase	1983-07-20
Constable	P.J. Opperman	1983-07-04
Special Constable	U. Ndiaombe	1983-09-19
Lieutenant	F.B.J. Conradie	1983-09-23
Sergeant	H. Hamakali	1983-09-23
Special Warrant Officer	I. Hendjala	1983-10-13

1984

Special Sergeant	B. Markus	1984-01-05
Special Constable	P. Kangombe	1984-01-27
Special Constable	M. Kaibotya	1984-02-06
Special Constable	P. Tobias	1984-02-22
Special Warrant Officer	L. Likuis	1984-02-23
Special Warrant Officer	H. Hosea	1984-02-24
Special Constable	F. Lukas	1984-04-08
Special Warrant Officer	F. Joseph	1984-05-02
Special Sergeant	F. Matheus	1984-05-07
Warrant Officer	J.F. Coetzee	1984-05-18
Special Constable	M. Nghishikushtya	1984-05-19
Special Sergeant	N. Nghifino	1984-06-16
Special Constable	B. Kutenda	1984-06-20
Special Constable	E. Ipinge	1984-10-17
Sergeant	N. Abrahams	1984-11-08

1985

Special Constable	S. Hatutale	1985-01-17
Sergeant	W. van As	1985-01-31
Special Constable	J. Tobias	1985-02-21
Special Constable	M. Oukongo	1985-03-06
Special Constable	J. Andungi	1985-03-14
Special Constable	J. Tjiposa	1985-04-03
Special Sergeant	S. Naholo	1985-04-07
Special Warrant Officer	A. Kumulo	1985-04-19
Special Constable	L. Abraham	1985-04-08
Special Constable	K. Tjindunda	1985-05-15
Special Constable	F. Bajiyu	1985-05-28
Constable	J.J. Vos	1985-05-28
Special Warrant Officer	J.M. Tsitula	1985-06-06
Special Sergeant	L. Valentino	1985-06-06
Special Constable	S. Simson	1985-06-18

Special Constable	U. Ngombe	1985-07-11
Special Warrant Officer	J. Stephanus	1985-09-26
Sergeant	P.R.L. Venter	1985-12-12

1986

Special Constable	A. Kenahama	1986-01-07
Special Constable	S. Fillipus	1986-01-06
Special Constable	A. Utewga	1986-02-16
Special Constable	A. Metiesta	1986-02-23
Special Constable	T. Amunyongi	1986-02-27
Special Constable	E. Hishidivali	1986-03-15
Constable	J.L. Jacobs	1986-03-22
Special Constable	A. Mwaninovanhu	1986-04-01
Special Constable	M. Vilho	1986-04-11
Special Constable	Godfrey	1986-04-11
Special Constable	S. Toivo	1986-04-11
Special Constable	S. Shindele	1984-04-11
Constable	F. van Zyl	1986-05-11
Special Constable	T. Virero	1986-07-10
Special Constable	J. Sam	1986-11-24
Special Constable	S. Daniel	1986-10-18

1987

Special Sergeant	U.P. Kandjii	1987-01-05
Special Constable	M. Fesiango	1987-01-15
Special Constable	S. Dhilimbulukweni	1987-01-15
Special Sergeant	T. Lungameni	1987-01-29
Special Sergeant	P. Pius	1987-01-29
Sergeant	P.J. Collen	1987-01-29
Constable	W.C. Scheepers	1987-01-29
Sergeant	C.L. Fourie	1987-02-14
Constable	R.L. Erasmus	1987-02-14
Lieutenant Colonel	G.J. Steyn	1987-02-14

Special Sergeant	M. Mwanyengange	1987-02-23
Special Sergeant	J. Naffral	1987-02-23
Sergeant	C.P. Momberg	1987-02-25
Special Constable	S. Venusiu	1987-03-12
Special Constable	N. Vilho	1987-03-14
Special Sergeant	M. Lukas	1987-03-28
Special Constable	S.W. Kanghende	1987-04-26
Constable	E.B. Brink	1987-05-01
Special Sergeant	S. Shikulo	1987-09-10

1988

Special Sergeant	S. Kandyongu	1988-02-04
Special Sergeant	V. Noemuweda	1988-02-04
Special Warrant Officer	F. Creneus	1988-02-27
Special Constable	T. Kanitus	1988-03-01
Special Sergeant	D. Mandume	1988-03-02
Special Sergeant	H. Wakumbilwa	1988-03-02
Special Constable	F. Lukas	1988-03-09
Constable	J.I. van Zyl	1988-03-23
Constable	C.W. Pearce	1988-03-28
Special Constable	M. Sevelenu	1988-03-28
Special Sergeant	K. Tenaseu	1988-04-02
Special Sergeant	U. Ndemwimba	1988-04-02
Special Constable	U. Tjiumbu	1988-05-05
Special Warrant Officer	D. Katapotle	1988-06-18
Special Constable	A. Ipinge	1988-08-13
Special Constable	F. Ndevaumba	1988-08-17
Special Constable	T. Mbunguha	1988-08-15
Constable	H.J.C. du Plessis	1988-09-07
Constable	A. Hattingh	1988-09-07
Special Constable	T. Kastodiu	1988-10-03

1989

Special Sergeant	S. David	1989-04-01
Special Constable	M. Lukas	1989-04-01
Special Constable	U. Rjiposa	1989-04-01
Special Constable	D. Sakaria	1989-04-01
Special Sergeant	Z. Uaapulatena	1989-04-01
Special Constable	N. Abiatal	1989-04-02
Special Constable	J. Andreas	1989-04-02
Special Warrant Officer	L. Benjamin	1989-04-02
Special Constable	T. Johannes	1989-04-02
Special Constable	F. Joseph	1989-04-02
Special Constable	M. Kakonyi	1989-04-02
Special Sergeant	D. Teteoko	1989-04-02
Special Constable	F. Tyipoya	1989-04-02
Special Constable	A. Siivanus	1989-04-02
Sergeant	S.H. van Tonder	1989-04-02
Constable	L. Thorne	1989-04-02
Constable	J.J. Badenhorst	1989-04-02
Constable	D.J.J. Fourie	1989-04-03
Corporal	H. Carstens	1989-04-04
	(SADF Special Forces)	

★

At the going down of the sun, and in the morning, we will remember them

★

Sources: Koevoet Bond; Stiff, P. 2004. *The covert war: Koevoet operations 1979–1989*. Galago.

Index